dahlia 'Arabian Night'

ranunculus asiaticus

chasmanthe floribunda

ornithogalum dubium

sinningia 'Hollywood'

pleione formosana

bulbs for all seasons

photography by Jonathan Buckley and Michelle Garrett

Kathy Brown

CADCC

First published in 2000 by Aquamarine

© Anness Publishing Limited 2000

Aquamarine is an imprint of
Anness Publishing Limited
Hermes House
88–89 Blackfriars Road
London SE1 8HA

Published in the USA by Aquamarine
Anness Publishing Inc., 27 West 20th Street
New York, NY10011
(800) 354-9657

A CIP catalogue record for this book is available
from the British Library

Publisher Joanna Lorenz
Executive Editor Caroline Davison
Designer Ruth Hope
Production Controller Claire Rae
Reader Richard McGinlay
Photographers Jonathan Buckley and Michelle Garrett
Stylist Michelle Garrett

Printed and bound in Singapore

10 9 8 7 6 5 4 3 2 1

Page 1 *Narcissus poeticus* var. *recurvus* with *Camassia leichtlinii*.
Page 2 Blue *Agapanthus* with *Hemerocallis* (day lily) and pink alliums.
Page 4 *Narcissus* 'Actaea'.

Note to reader:
The inspirational projects in this book include lists of decorative
elements, such as the choice of bulbs and other plants as well as
the type of container required. These lists do not include less visible
but nonetheless essential items such as compost (soil mix).
Always read the project carefully first before embarking upon it.

contents

introduction

This book is bursting with ideas on how to use bulbs in your garden. It describes how to grow them in borders, grassland and woodland as well as in containers outside, and it combines practical advice with inspirational planting ideas. It also has a section on the use of bulbs as houseplants, showing how they can be displayed in a conservatory or on a windowsill.

The word "bulbs" is used in this book as an umbrella for all those plants that have a root system that has been adapted to withstand long periods of drought by storing food reserves beneath ground. It includes true bulbs, corms, tubers and rhizomes, as well as fleshy roots. These plants make leaf and root growth in the moist period, then come into flower and go dormant in the summer drought. They come mainly from those regions of the world where the winters are cool and moist, and the summers are hot and dry, including the typical Mediterranean climates of Europe, California and South Africa as well as a whole swathe of mountainous areas in Central Asia.

Countries such as Spain, France, Italy, Greece and Turkey, which border the Mediterranean Sea, are home to a host of species daffodils, blue and white anemones, tiny scillas and chionodoxas, dainty *Galanthus* (snowdrop) and *Leucojum* (snowflake). California is the source of yellow calochortus, while South Africa is the home of colourful gladioli, stately agapanthus, shapely *Zantedeschia* (arum lily), scented freesias, pretty watsonias and gorgeous gloriosa, to name but a few. Central Asia provides brilliant coloured tulips, tall *Eremurus* (foxtail lily) and scented lilies.

Other more tender plants, such as dahlias and *Tigridia* (tiger flower), come from Mexico and Central America, while many of the begonias come from the Andes of Peru and Bolivia. Hippeastrums, sometimes known as indoor amaryllis, are native to Central and South America.

Bulbs provide wonderful flowers for every season of the year. As soon as midwinter has passed, *Eranthis hyemalis* (winter aconite) begins to thrust up its first shoots, together with snowdrops, early crocuses, anemones and *Iris danfordiae*. Spring welcomes daffodils, hyacinths and tulips, fritillaries and *Hyacinthoides* (bluebell). More irises follow in early summer, along with all the alliums. Then it is time for gladioli, begonias, agapanthus, eremurus, lilies and dahlias. As summer turns to autumn, the dahlias are still in flower, but they are now joined by an array of nerines, crinums, colchicums and cyclamen.

There are bulbs for all places in the garden. Although most prefer a sunny position and well-drained soil – tulips and gladioli are notable examples of such plants – others, such as bluebells and trilliums, will enjoy a shadier home. They also vary widely in height. The short ones, such as anemones and crocuses, are best near the front of a border or in a rock garden, while tall eremurus and lilies are probably better in the middle or back of the border. However, these rules can all be broken. Many bulbs will grow successfully in different garden settings. Lilies are an excellent example. Some of them are so wonderfully flamboyant and beautifully scented that they deserve several homes in the border, next to a path or in pots beside the door. Site them where the intricacies of their petals and stamens can be closely observed.

In 16th-century European gardens, some bulbs were so valuable that they were displayed far apart from each other where they were easy to cultivate and could be appreciated individually. Sometimes a single tulip was the only occupant of an entire bed. Nowadays, commercial propagation allows us to buy most bulbs relatively cheaply, so that ten might be planted in one group or perhaps in a single container. Sometimes double that amount may be planted in a large pot, especially where small bulbs such as crocuses, *Muscari* (grape hyacinth) or anemones, are used to underplant taller ones such as hyacinths, early tulips or early daffodils. There are so many possibilities that you should experiment and really enjoy the glorious results, but, whatever you do, be sure only to buy commercially cultivated bulbs, never those that have been taken from the wild.

Some of our bulbs have strange and wonderful histories, ranging from shipwrecks on the high seas to rock falls in the remote valleys of western China. Others are inextricably bound up with the mighty Ottoman Empire.

the history of bulbs

Plant hunters risked their lives to bring the bulbs that we know today from their native habitats, and sometimes it has taken several attempts to introduce them successfully to the gardens of the West. Fashion has also played a major role in their history. Tulips, for example, became almost beyond price in the heady days of the 1630s, but now they are available in their thousands, and are used in spring bedding schemes around the world.

THE TULIP

Tulips have one of the most colourful histories of all bulbs. Its principal homelands were Persia (now Iran) and Turkey, where even in the 12th and 13th centuries poets sang its praises.

When Süleyman I, the Magnificent, became Sultan in 1520, the Ottoman Empire stretched from the Crimea in the east to Egypt and beyond in the West, and it covered large parts of the Balkans. City gardens were well established, and tulips were one of the most popular flowers. The period even became known as the Tulip Age. Regular tulip festivals were held, and the flower was used to decorate tiles and pottery as well as clothes.

These tulips were introduced to Europe in the middle of the 16th century. Conrad Gesner (1516–65), the Swiss scholar and humanist, recorded how he saw a red tulip growing in a garden in Augsburg, Bavaria, in 1557. The garden belonged to Johannis Heinrich Herwart. Also important in tulip history was the part played by the Flemish ambassador Ghislain de Busbecq (1522–91), who was the representative in Constantinople of the Habsburg Emperor, Ferdinand I. In 1529, Vienna had withstood the Ottoman siege of the city, but the Emperor was keen to maintain trading links with the Ottoman Empire and so continued to send ambassadors to the Sultan. Busbecq, who was sent as Ferdinand's emissary in 1554, admired the tulips growing in the gardens of Constantinople. He was able to obtain seeds and bulbs at a great price, and he eventually sent them back to the Imperial gardens in Vienna, where they were grown under the care of Carolus Clusius (Charles de L'Écluse, 1526–1609).

Clusius was curious to know how the bulbs tasted, and asked an apothecary to preserve them in sugar in the same manner as orchids. He ate them as sweet-meats and said that he preferred them to orchids.

The bulbs travelled with Clusius from Vienna to Frankfurt and eventually to the Netherlands, when in 1593 he was appointed Professor of Botany at Leiden University. There he was given the opportunity of laying out a new botanical garden. As the tulips came into flower, interest in these new bulbs escalated, and people wanted to buy them. Clusius was continually obtaining bulbs from new suppliers, and via his extensive network of contacts throughout Europe he was responsible for tulips reaching many new areas. He demanded very high prices. Such a precious commodity was clearly vulnerable – on many occasions, thieves came and stole the bulbs, which were then grown on and traded. This became the original stock of the Dutch bulb industry.

Below Tulips are now available in a wide selection of colours as well as with an extensive range of flower shapes. Pink tulips are shown to good effect here, underplanted with a sea of silver artemisia.

The tulip retained its value, and soon absurdly high prices were being demanded for a single bulb. To begin with, the tulip was a status symbol among the aristocracy. The length and strength of the stalk, the size and shape of the flower and even the colour of the stamens were remarked upon. A lot of space was regularly given to each tulip, and sometimes a single specimen was given an entire bed in which to be shown off. Soon tulips came to be desired by the wider merchant classes. Prices rose from hundreds of florins (a florin was worth two shillings) for a specific cultivated variety to 3,000 florins in the 1620s. Such was the interest in the trade, rather than necessarily in the actual plant, that a "futures" market developed, by which bulbs were paid for in instalments between the time of lifting in early summer to the time of planting in mid-autumn. During that time the same bulb might be bought and sold several times, as each merchant tried to make a profit on the deal. A dry bulb could not show the colour or quality of the flower it was going to produce, so the whole business depended on trust.

As demand increased, the trade grew and all levels of society were involved, including landowners, farmers, sailors, artists, weavers and servants. Not all the bulbs were expensive: white- and red-flowering tulips could be bought for only twelve florins per pound, compared with the 'Viceroy' tulip, a single bulb of which fetched 4,600 florins at auction in 1637. The 'Viceroy' was a Violette, which had flowers with wonderful, streaked, purple markings on a white background. There is a story that one 'Viceroy' changed hands for 12 fat sheep, 4 fat oxen, 8 fat pigs, 2 loads of wheat, 4 loads of rye, 2 hogsheads of wine, 4 tons of beer, 2 tons of butter, 1,000 pounds of cheese, a silver drinking horn, a suit of clothes and a complete bed! The total value of this single bulb, which was probably recorded by one of the pamphleteers campaigning against the evil and misery caused by gambling, was 3,500 guilders, a fortune in those days, when the average annual income was only 150 florins, and a first-class house was worth 5,000 florins.

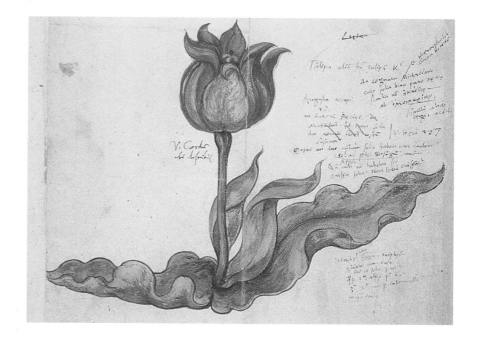

In 1636, tulips were traded on the London Exchange, as well as in Scotland, but there was little interest. In February 1637, the price bubble burst, and when the crash came many people in the Netherlands suffered. Local authorities and growers tried to stabilize the market, but it was many years before people could pay off their debts.

However, Dutch soil was ideal for growing tulips, and, because the flowers were appreciated across Europe, trade continued. In the 1630s and 1640s, at least 650 varieties were still being grown. A list of those cultivated in the gardens of the Margrave of Baden-Durlach in Karlsruhe in 1730 contained almost 2,400 names; three years later he grew nearly 4,000. At the beginning of the World War II, just before the German invasion of the Netherlands, the country was exporting 100 million tulip bulbs to the United States annually. Today, there are about 5,000 cultivars in the trade.

The word "tulip" is thought to have derived from Busbecq's original description of the plant, which he wrote after first seeing it in the gardens near Constantinople around 1554. He recalled the Turkish people called them *tulipam* because of the similarity of the shape of the open flowers to a turban. In fact, the Turkish word for turban is *tulbend*, but, whatever its origin, the name tulip has stuck ever since.

Above *Councillor Herwart's Tulip* was the first painting of a tulip to be published in Europe, as described by Conrad Gesner in 1557 (courtesy of the University Library, Erlangan, Germany). His notes about the foliage and the provenance of the plant are scribbled over the page.

THE NARCISSUS

Most species of *Narcissus* are found in the many countries bordering the Mediterranean, and they have long been appreciated as garden plants. There are many references to them in classical and more recent literature. The popular old names of daffodil, daffodilly and daffadowndilly are thought to be corruptions of the word asphodel or asphodelus, while the old name of Lent lily refers to the season in which they flower – that is, the 40 days leading up to Easter. Another descriptive name, chalice flower, refers to the central cup or corona of the daffodil which resembles the shape of the chalice used to hold the communion wine.

There has long been confusion about the difference between daffodils and narcissi. Nowadays all daffodils fall into the genus *Narcissus*, but in times past, both names have been used in popular poetry and literature. In the early 1800s, the poet William Wordsworth and his sister, Dorothy, were captivated by them. She poignantly described the scene in her diary as they were walking in the woods besides Ullswater in the English Lake District:

> April 15th 1802 *We fancied that the lake had floated seeds ashore, and that the little colony had so sprung up. But as we went along there were more and yet more; and at last, under the boughs of the trees, we saw that there was a long belt of them along the shore, about the breadth of a country turnpike road. I never saw daffodils so beautiful. They grew among the mossy stones about and about them; some rested their heads upon these stones, as on a pillow, for weariness; and the rest tossed and reeled and danced, and seemed as if they verily laughed with the wind that blew upon them over the lake; they looked so gay, ever glancing, ever changing.*

THE DAHLIA

Originating from the mountain ranges of Mexico and south to Colombia, the dahlia was probably used in medicine and as a fodder crop by the Aztecs prior to the Spanish Conquest. In 1789, a handful of seeds was sent by Vincente Cervantes, of the Botanical Gardens in Mexico City, to his friend Abbé Cavanilles, who was in charge of the Botanical Gardens at Madrid. The Abbé later named this Mexican flower after the Swedish botanist Dr Anders Dahl (1751–87). The plant was known, not so much for its single flowers and rather poor stems but for its edible root which was introduced as an alternative to the potato. Dahlia roots came to be eaten a little in France and parts of the Mediterranean coast, but their peculiar, sharp flavour prevented their adoption as a staple food.

One of the keys to its success as a garden plant was the interest taken in it by the Empress Josephine (1763–1814), wife of Napoleon Bonaparte, who kept the garden at Malmaison near Paris, France. She grew dahlias and guarded the roots jealously, refusing to give any away. One of her ladies-in-waiting, Countess de Bougainville, wanted to grow some for herself. She hatched a plan with her lover, a Polish prince, who went to the gardener at Malmaison and offered money to obtain the tubers. The gardener deceived his mistress and apparently sold a hundred plants for one gold louis each. When the Empress found out she was furious. She sacked her gardener, banished both the lady-in-waiting and the prince, and thereafter refused to show any more interest in dahlias.

Left In 1872 a Dutch nurseryman, J.T. van der Berg, was sent some bulbs, roots and tubers from Mexico. Only one root survived, and when it came into flower it was different from any grown before. It became known as the Cactus dahlia because its flowers were bright scarlet, the same as those of *Cereus speciossima*, a popular houseplant of the time. This modern Cactus type, *Dahlia* 'Purple Gem', is widely grown.

Several attempts were made to introduce the tubers to Britain. In 1789, the Marchioness of Bute visited Spain and sent one of the tubers home, but it died. A few years later, Lady Holland, who scandalized polite society by divorcing Sir Godfrey Webster and eloping with the Lord Holland who was ambassador to King Philip of Spain, went to Spain and saw a dahlia in bloom. Captivated by the flower, she too sent plants home. This time they thrived, and so she can be credited with introducing the dahlia to Britain.

Nurserymen began experimenting with its form, and within a short time the single-flowered variety had been dropped in favour of a double "globular" form, which became all the rage and was known as the globe dahlia. These were the precursors of the double "show" and "fancy" types, valued respectively for their single colours and mixed hues. At one time it was recorded that 10,000 varieties were available.

THE NERINE

Nerines also travelled a long way to reach Europe, for these beautiful, flamboyant bulbs are native to South Africa. In 1652, the first 500 colonists arrived at Table Bay to join the new settlement that the Dutch East India Company had established there. Among them were two gardeners whose task was to grow fruit and vegetables for the community and, no doubt, for all the ships that sailed to destinations in the Pacific and those returning to Europe. They were also commissioned to collect any wildflowers that might be valuable to the Dutch at home. They were successful in their work, and seven years later crates of nerines were among a cargo to be shipped to the Netherlands in one of the Dutch East India Company's vessels.

Sadly, the ship was wrecked in the English Channel, off the island of Guernsey. The nerine bulbs were washed ashore and some took root in the sand. Over the years they spread inland, and eventually produced brilliant pink flowers, which locals sent to the London flower market. They became commonly known as the Guernsey lily, and the name has been used ever since.

The islanders assumed that the bulbs were native to Japan because the ship was known to have come originally from the Far East. It was more than a hundred years before the error was realized, when in 1774 Francis Masson, the first ever official to be sent out as a plant hunter by Kew Gardens, England, saw the same flower, *Nerine sarniensis*, growing on the slopes of Table Mountain in South Africa.

Left This beautiful old print of *Nerine sarniensis*, which is commonly known as the Guernsey lily, dates back to 1795, twenty one years after Francis Masson first saw it growing on the slopes of Table Mountain in its native South Africa.

Above E.H. Wilson's epic journey to the Min valley in Western China in 1910 resulted in the successful introduction of *Lilium regale* to Western gardens, but it was at a great personal cost. A rock fall struck his leg and broke it in two places. Eventually, his leg healed, but thereafter Wilson always walked with a limp.

THE EASTER LILY AND THE REGAL LILY

Like other plants, bulbs were sometimes unsuccessful when they were first introduced to the gardens of western Europe. This may have been because the season was inclement, the winter was particularly harsh or the cultural conditions were not right. The lily is one such plant. A German doctor Philipp von Siebold (1796–1866) first sent the lily we now know as the Easter lily from Japan to the Botanical Garden in Ghent in 1830, and it was reintroduced in 1840.

It was, however, a storm in the Atlantic that really changed the course of its history. Sometime in the 1860s, a missionary was returning home to Europe from the coast of China. Among his possessions were a few bulbs of the same lily that von Siebold had tried to introduce earlier. The stormy weather caused his vessel to take refuge in the shelter of St George's harbour on the island of Bermuda. The missionary was looked after there by the Revd Roberts, and, as thanks for the hospitality he had received, he gave

the rector some of his special bulbs, which were planted in the rectory garden. The lilies enjoyed the mild climate and shallow limestone soil, and soon became well established on their new island home. By the end of the 19th century, more than three million bulbs were exported from Bermuda each year, but disease ravaged the stock and ruined it.

The plant hunter E.H. Wilson records that it was Mr Harris, an American nurseryman from Philadelphia, who first brought the bulbs to the trade. Captivated by their elegant, pure white blooms and heavenly scent, which is just like orange blossom, Harris realized that if they could be forced into flower for Easter, he would have a valuable flowering commodity to fill the church vases. He launched his find under the name *Lilium harrisii*, a name by which it is still sometimes known today, although the correct name is now *Lilium longiflorum* var. *eximium*. Its common name is the Easter lily, and it is still used to decorate churches on Easter Day.

Wilson was an expert in lilies from eastern Asia, and he thought he had found one that would surpass the Easter lily. His great quest was the *Lilium regale* which grew in the remote Min valley, where western China borders on Tibet. He had first discovered it in 1903, and the following year had dispatched 300 bulbs to Veitch & Sons, the sponsors of his expedition. He tried again in 1908, but on neither occasion did he succeed in getting them established.

In 1910, Wilson set out yet again, this time working for the Arnold Arboretum in Boston, Massachusetts. His driving ambition was to introduce the lily to the gardens of the West. He recognized its great potential, for it could withstand very cold winters and extremely hot summers, and thrived despite high winds. His journal describing the expedition reveals a story of great courage and determination. He left Boston, Massachusetts, at the end of March 1910 for Europe and from there travelled on the Trans-Siberian Railway, reaching Peking in early May. He had to navigate 2,900km (1,800 miles) up the Yangtze river, northwards up its

tributary, the Min, for another 400km (250 miles) until he at last reached the remote region between China and Tibet which he described as a "no man's land".

He gathered supplies at the town of Sungpang Ting (Songpan) and travelled for seven consecutive days down the endless gorge of the Min river. It was a long route and well trodden by traders, largely coolies and mule trains, exchanging the goods of Tibet with those of wealthy Szechwan (Sichuan). The path was winding and difficult, with few passing places. Wilson walked for most of the day, although he also had a light sedan chair made of rattan which was an outward sign of importance and respectability, crucial in those far-off places where Western travellers were rare and treated with great suspicion. His dog always went with him. Fleas were a nightmare, as were cockroaches and other insects, and one of Wilson's nightly rituals was to place containers filled with insect repellent beneath the four legs of his camp bed. On the eighth day, Wilson decided to make a base camp from which to explore the area and arrange for the autumn collection of bulbs.

Wilson was in the heart of the Min valley and, although the district was barren and desolate, it was here that he found the lilies growing, clinging to the windswept hillsides. His diary records his excitement at the discovery:

Not in twos and threes but in hundreds, in thousands, aye, in tens of thousands. Its slender stems, each from 2 to 4 feet tall, flexible and tense as steel, overtop the coarse grasses and scrub and are crowned with one to several large funnel-shaped flowers, each more or less wine coloured without, pure white and lustrous on the face, clear canary yellow within the tube, and each stamen filament tipped with a golden anther. The air in the cool of the morning and in the evening is laden with delicious perfume exhaled from every blossom. For a brief season this lily transforms a lonely, semidesert region into a veritable fairyland.

The first flowers began to open in late spring, along the banks of the river some 760m (2,500ft) above sea level. As summer advanced, the band of white trumpets rose up the mountain, so that by midsummer the lilies were blooming at 1,830m (6,000ft). From his camp, Wilson arranged for between 6,000 and 7,000 lily bulbs to be lifted in autumn. The bulbs were to be encased in clay, before being packed in charcoal and sent to America.

Although tired after so many months travelling, it was with a "light heart" and "satisfied mind" that he started on his long homeward journey. As before, the road was tortuous, and he was travelling in his sedan chair when disaster struck: a rock fall started down the hillside. One of the stones hit his chair; another struck his right leg and broke it in two places. He eventually managed to get up, and rode in his boy's chair with his leg lashed to the right pole. It was an agonizing three days before they reached the nearest missionary post at Chengdu. In spite of the threat of amputation, three months later Wilson was able to get about slowly on crutches. He hired a boat to take him eastwards to Shanghai and on to America. He was able to walk unaided again, although always with a limp.

Just a few days after his return, the huge shipment of bulbs arrived. He found them in excellent condition, and they were planted the following spring. Some flowered that first year and even set fertile seed. Since then millions of them have been raised and planted, and they have gone on to become one of the most popular lilies in cultivation today.

Above E.H. Wilson recorded in his diary that he found lilies growing "not in twos or threes but in hundreds, in thousands, aye, in tens of thousands."

Several botanical differences occur between true bulbs, corms, rhizomes and tubers, yet they all have one common purpose which is to store food reserves in long periods of drought.

the botany of bulbs

Above In this group of summer- and autumn-flowering true bulbs, the crinum (top) has a long, tapering neck, while the lilies (middle) and smaller tulips (bottom) are more compact.

Right, above *Chasmanthe* (top) has a wide corm, while freesias (below left) are smaller and, for their size, relatively elongated. Those of gladioli (below right) are more rounded.

Right, below Cannas (top) produce many fairly large, elongated rhizomes each season, and these can be severed to produce new plants. Zantedeschia rhizomes (bottom) can be treated in the same way, although the rhizomes are squatter and more rounded.

The word "bulb" is often used to describe true bulbs, corms, rhizomes, tubers and fleshy roots which have a root system that can cope with long periods of drought by storing food reserves beneath ground.

TRUE BULBS

The inside of a true bulb consists of stems and fleshy leaves, which have been modified for storage. In tulip, hyacinth and daffodil bulbs, the modified leaves are layered closely around each other, with the outer leaves, which are often dry and brown, forming a tunic around the bulb. In other bulbs, the leaves are not wrapped around each other but overlap, and they are far more succulent. These bulbs are known as scaly bulbs, and the lily is one of the best examples.

Individual bulbs usually survive for many years, during which time the old ones will produce offsets or "daughter" bulbs and thus create small groupings. Some tulips are unlikely to produce flowers for a second year from the old bulb, but they do form replacement bulbs, which will flower the following year.

CORMS

Inside all corms there is a stem that is swollen and adapted for food storage. It forms the base of the new shoots. Unlike true bulbs, corms appear solid throughout. After flowering, a new corm, formed at the base of the new stem, will grow on top of the old one, and the old corm will die. Each corm, therefore, has only one season in which to produce a flower. Small young corms will also form on the basal plate, which is slightly concave. Crocosmias, gladioli and crocuses are good examples of cormous plants.

RHIZOMES

A rhizome is a swollen underground stem, from the ends of which shoots, then foliage and flowers emerge, while roots grow on the underside. Side branches will form each year, typically after flowering has occurred, enabling the plant to spread. Cannas and the zantedeschias are typical rhizomatous plants.

TUBERS

A tuber is a swollen underground root or stem, but in this case it is not the base of the stem, as in the corm. It is usually fleshy and rounded, and may be covered with scaly leaves or with fibrous roots. Buds usually develop

on top of the tuber, and produce stems. Tubers get larger with age and can live for years. Dahlias, begonias, anemones and cyclamen are all good examples.

FAMILIES, GENERA, SPECIES AND CULTIVARS
True bulbs, corms, tubers and rhizomes are known by hundreds of different names, yet they belong to a relatively small number of plant "families". These are based on similarities in the reproductive organs within the flower rather than on the appearance of the flower or the storage organ itself. Most of the true bulbs and corms only belong to a few families. Amaryllidaceae includes well-known genera such as *Narcissus* (daffodil), *Nerine*, *Sternbergia* and *Galanthus* (snowdrop); Iridaceae embraces *Freesia*, *Schizostylis*, *Tigridia*, *Gladiolus* and *Iris*, while Liliaceae includes *Lilium* (lily), *Fritillaria* and *Tulipa* (tulip). Tuberous and rhizomatous plants have more widespread family connections. *Cyclamen* is part of the family Primulaceae, *Begonia* of Begoniaceae, *Sinningia* of Gesneriaceae and *Dahlia* are included in Compositae.

Genera are distinct plant groups within the wider family, yet some have a strong family resemblance. For example, some bulbs of the Hyacinthaceae family, as well as the flowers, show marked similarities. *Muscari* (grape hyacinth), *Chionodoxa*, *Scilla*, *Hyacinthus* (hyacinth) and *Hyacinthoides* (bluebell) from Europe and the Middle East have a similar appearance to *Camassia* bulbs from North America. This is particularly true of *Camassia* and *Hyacinthus*; both genera belong to the same family, and yet developed an ocean apart.

Within each genus there is usually more than one species. These might be regarded as extremely close relatives with many common characteristics. Within the genus *Narcissus*, for example, there are about fifty species. These have been found growing wild among the hills, mountains and grasslands of Spain, France, Italy, Greece, around the Middle East and in the mountains of North Africa. Sometimes species vary naturally and these are then known as varieties. A well-known example is *N. poeticus* var. *recurvus* which has been grown for centuries and is known as pheasant's eye.

Often nurserymen breed from a species and the results are referred to as cultivars. Hence, the species *Narcissus cyclamineus*, with its distinctive swept-back petals, has been used to produce popular cultivars such as *N.* 'February Gold', 'Jetfire' and 'Peeping Tom'. As a result, we now have thousands of cultivars from around fifty species of *Narcissus*. They flower at different times, vary in height, range widely in colour and have different flower structures. Despite such diversity, they all belong to the same genus.

Top Begonia tubers (top left) are compact, with a hairy, round base and a concave top from which tiny pink shoots appear. Dahlias (top right) have a clutch of large, fat tuberous "legs", while ranunculus (below left) have thin, claw-like legs. If the legs break off they will not produce new plants. Anemones (below right) are hard and knobbly, and it is from these protuberances that the new growth appears.

Middle, top The Hyacinthaceae family is represented here by five genera: *Camassia* (quamash) and *Hyacinthus* (hyacinth) are the larger bulbs at the back, with *Muscari* (grape hyacinth), *Hyacinthoides* (bluebell) and *Scilla* (squill) from left to right at the front.

Middle, bottom This cross-section shows that corms, such as that of the gladiolus (below), have a more solid appearance, while true bulbs, such as those of lilies (above), are made up of stems and fleshy, scaly leaves.

Bottom These are all bulbs of the same genus, *Narcissus*, commonly known as daffodils. Of the four examples, one is a species growing wild in damp meadowland in the mountains of central and southern Europe. The remainder are cultivars that have been bred by nurserymen for the trade. Note the contrast in bulb size and length of neck.

One of the main characteristics of bulbous plants is that they have a dormant period every year, after the growth cycle of producing flowers, leaves and seeds is over. At this stage they are relatively easy to lift, store and transplant.

buying and planting bulbs

Above The rhizomes of summer-flowering *Canna indica* should be planted out in spring under glass in large containers. These can be moved outside from early to midsummer. Cannas can be transplanted to sunny, sheltered borders at the same time.

Right With careful planning, a wealth of glorious bulbs can be planted in containers in order to provide a splash of welcome colour in the spring.

Obtain bulbs from mail-order suppliers or buy them as soon as they become available in the garden centres when the range on offer will be at its maximum. Keep bulbs in cool, dry conditions and plant when weather conditions are favourable.

PLANTING TIMES

There are two main seasons for buying bulbs: autumn and late winter. In autumn, spring-flowering bulbs and corms, such as daffodils, tulips, hyacinths and crocuses, should be planted. These are all hardy and can withstand winter frosts. In late winter, summer-flowering bulbs, corms, tubers and rhizomes of plants such as crinum, gladioli and begonias are available. These are not necessarily hardy and are best planted outside in spring. Indeed, some, such as begonias and dahlias, are particularly tender and thrive only in warm conditions. These have to be brought into growth indoors and moved outside only after all risk of frost has passed.

HOW TO PLANT

Most bulbs, corms, tubers and rhizomes have a rounded bottom or base from which the old roots grow, and these are sometimes still attached to the bulb. They may also have a pointed or tapering nose at the top, from which the first shoots emerge. The general rule for planting is that the rounded base sits on the soil while the nose points upwards.

The planting depth is normally determined by the size of the bulb, and the general rule is that they should be planted at a depth of three times their own size. Thus, if a bulb measures 5cm (2in) from nose to base, there should be 15cm (6in) of soil on top of it. This means that the hole required for planting is actually 20cm (8in) deep. There are a few exceptions to this rule – nerines and crinums, for example, should be planted close to the surface of the soil, as should *Lilium candidum* (Madonna lily), which should be planted at a depth of about 2.5cm (1in).

Left Most spring-flowering bulbs, tubers, corms and rhizomes should be planted as dry bulbs in autumn. There is a wonderful choice, including these *Hyacinthus* (hyacinth), *Muscari* (grape hyacinth) and anemones.

The size of the bulb also usually determines the tool used for planting. A dibber or trowel may be used for small bulbs, such as crocuses and anemones, but larger ones, such as *Lilium* (lily) and *Narcissus* (daffodils), need a sharp-edged spade to make a deep hole.

SNOWDROPS "IN THE GREEN"
Some bulbs, such as *Galanthus* (snowdrop), do not like being out of the ground too long in late summer before autumn planting. They are among the first to flower in the new year and like to make their root growth early. Many do not adapt well to the drying-out process to which most bulbs are subjected. An alternative method, therefore, is to buy snowdrops "in the green", which are available in late winter either in pots or as a loose clump of plants with the leaves still attached to the bulbs. Plant them in border soil, where they will spread quickly, or in turf where they will spread more slowly but will still naturalize well. Plant in groups of between eight and ten, spacing the individual plants about 7.5cm (3in) apart.

Left The general rule is that bulbs should be planted at a depth of three times their own size. Use a spade, a trowel or a special bulb dibber, depending on the depth required. Check before planting, however, because there are a few exceptions, including nerines, crinums and some lilies, which prefer to be planted with the top of the bulb at soil level.

Bulbs are perfect for borders all year round, beginning with snowdrops and winter aconites in late winter; hyacinths, daffodils and tulips in spring; galtonia, gladioli and lilies in summer; and crinums and nerines in autumn.

planting in borders

Below left This formal spring border contains alternate red *Tulipa* 'Apeldoorn' and white *T*. 'White Dream' underplanted with *Anemone blanda* 'White Splendour'. Tulips can easily be planted in formal lines by holding string taut on pegs or stakes at either end of the border, and then simply planting along the line.

Below right In the same border as the one below left, allium seedheads remain as a testament to their moment of glory. Beside them are *Lilium regale* (regal lily), roses and lavender.

Planting techniques vary according to the style of garden and the effect you want to create. These are just a few of the possibilities.

INFORMAL GROUPS
Planting informal groups of the same bulb can be highly effective and, depending on the size of the border, the groups may be repeated a number of times, with bedding plants or other herbaceous material between them. Groups of tulips may be surrounded by *Myosotis* (forget-me-not) or *Viola* (pansy). Groups of alliums may be grown through nearby *Erysimum cheiri* (wallflower), while groups of gladioli might appear behind penstemons or earlier flowering poppies.

EXTRA DRAINAGE
Lilies are extremely hardy bulbs and can be planted in autumn or in late winter, whenever they become available to buy. However, they strongly dislike sitting in wet ground, much preferring well-drained soil. So, if your soil is naturally very heavy, it is advisable to add a generous layer of grit underneath lilies before planting. This provides good growing conditions, so they can remain in the soil for many years. *Fritillaria imperialis* (crown imperial) is another large bulb that dislikes too much moisture at its base. Use extra grit here, too, and also plant the bulbs so that they are slightly tilted to ensure that moisture does not drain into the open, funnelled tops from where the shoots emerge.

PRE-PLANTING IN POTS

It is possible to lift spring-flowering bulbs in summer, after flowering is over, and replace them with other seasonal bulbs or bedding. Simply dig them up with a spade. Alternatively, plant them in a perforated plastic pot which can be buried in the border. This makes them easier to lift and allows the bulbs to complete their cycle of growth without any root disturbance.

Pre-planting in pots is also a useful technique for dealing with tender summer-flowering bulbs that cannot survive frosty, damp conditions and which are best planted in the garden only after all risk of frost has passed. Bulbs planted in containers the previous autumn, such as *Ornithogalum dubium*, or earlier in spring, such as freesias, can be transferred to the garden in early summer, when they are already well into growth. Similarly, they can be lifted in autumn before the onset of wintry weather.

PLANTING FOR A SUCCESSION OF SPRING COLOUR

Although an individual group of bulbs will enhance any border, it is possible to plant several varieties together at the same time in the autumn. This will create an enormous impact and give colour for many weeks. Choose from any of the dwarf early daffodils, such as *Narcissus* 'February Gold', 'Tête-à-tête', 'Topolino', 'Jumblie' or 'Jetfire', for example, and any of the early tulips, including *Tulipa* 'Shakespeare', 'Heart's Delight' or 'Stresa'. You can then interplant with crocus, chionodoxa or *Muscari* (grape hyacinth). These can be followed by another grouping nearby of midseason daffodils, such as *N.* 'Pipit' or 'Thalia', and tulips, such as *T.* 'White Dream' and 'Attila'. For late spring blooms choose tulips such as *T.* 'Queen of Night' and 'Blue Heron' and late daffodils such as *N. poeticus* var. *recurvus* (pheasant's eye). Choosing bulbs from within these three seasonal groups will give great pleasure throughout early, mid-, and late spring. Plant pansies, violas, polyanthus, primroses, forget-me-nots or wallflowers on top to add extra colour.

PLANTING FOR SPRING AND SUMMER

A bulb border can have summer as well as spring interest, and one autumn planting session can give six months of delightful colour. In a formal box-hedged border, for example, a spring planting of tulips, anemones and fritillaries might give way in summer to groups of *Allium hollandicum* 'Purple Sensation' and white *Lilium regale* (regal lily). All these bulbs can be left in the ground year after year, but it would be possible to lift the tulips and plant summer bedding (annuals) to enhance the alliums and lilies.

Planting in Buried Pots

1 Dig a hole deep enough to contain a large, black, plastic pot. Fill the pot with a 2.5cm (1in) layer of drainage material, such as broken pieces of polystyrene.

2 Add loamy compost (soil mix), and sit the bulbs 15cm (6in) below the rim of the pot.

3 Bury the pot in the hole and cover the top with a thin mulch to keep weeds at bay.

4 Enjoy the flowers, then remove the pot. Dry off the bulbs and fill the space with summer plants.

Drainage for Lilies

Dig a hole 20–30cm (8–12in) deep, depending on size of the bulbs. Add a layer of grit about 2.5cm (1in) thick at the base of the hole. Plant the bulbs with about 15–25cm (6–10in) between each lily, depending on size. Fill in the hole with soil, taking care not to damage any shoots that are showing. Lilies produce only one stem, so if it is damaged they will not flower.

Planting in Informal Groups

Dig a large hole, approximately 40 x 30 x 10cm (16 x 12 x 4in), according to the requirements of the individual bulbs or corms. These gladioli corms are placed, base down and nose up, about 10cm (4in) apart. The packet contained 10 corms, and these were all planted in one large group. Gladioli corms need to be lifted in autumn.

A surprisingly wide range of bulbs can be grown successfully in grass where they will naturalize and produce a beautiful tapestry of colour. This effect is perfect for a natural-looking garden or if there is a wild corner in your garden.

planting in grass

Planting Bulbs Individually

1 Throw the bulbs on to the turf in a random fashion and plant accordingly, but try to allow a distance of about 7.5–20cm (3–8in) between each one.

2 Dig a deep, square hole, of about a spade's width and about 25cm (10in) deep, depending on the size of the bulb. You may need to go deeper than one spade's depth.

3 Plant the bulb, base down and the neck or nose pointing upwards. Cover the bulb with loose soil and replace the top divot. Firm down gently.

Right *Crocus vernus* naturalized in grass.

Using a Metal Bulb Dibber
A bulb dibber for small bulbs makes planting in grass easy. Crocus corms are planted rounded base down and shoot tip upwards, spacing individual bulbs about 7.5cm (3in) apart in random or formal patterns. Cover with loose soil and replace the divot before firming down.

Many of the bulbs that flower in late winter, early spring and mid-spring, such as *Galanthus* (snowdrop), *Eranthis hyemalis* (winter aconite), crocuses, anemones, daffodils and some *Erythronium* (dog's tooth violet), thrive well in grass, coming up year after year and self-seeding where they are particularly happy. However, it is worth pointing out that the more robust bulbs which can withstand competition from grass roots are much more suitable for this type of planting. Early in the year, when the grass is short and competition for light is not a problem, the pointed shoots cut through the turf quite easily.

Some of the late spring bulbs can also be grown successfully in this way. Both *Hyacinthoides non-scripta* (English bluebell) and *H. hispanica* (Spanish bluebell), as well as *Ornithogalum nutans*, *Narcissus poeticus* var. *recurvus* (pheasant's eye) and the camassias, such as *Camassia leichtlinii*, make attractive additions to grassy areas in meadow gardens or between orchard trees. Late-flowering tulips can also be used in these situations, but they will need to be replanted every second or third year.

By mid- to late summer the choice is more restricted because by this time the grass presents too much competition for most bulbs, and most gardeners are, in any case, anxious to cut the grass and keep it neatly mown. It is better to rely on the earlier periods of the year for the extra colour that naturalized bulbs bring.

To ensure that there will be successful displays in future years, any bulbs that are planted in grass need to complete their growing cycle before the grass can be mown and the bulbs' leaves cut off. This generally takes about six weeks after flowering.

PLANTING INDIVIDUALLY

When you are planting small bulbs, a special metal bulb dibber is ideal. Because you should be planting the bulbs to a depth three times their own height, check to see if there are any markings up the side

of the dibber to indicate how far down to press. Choose the spot, push the dibber into the turf, twist slightly and pull it out. This action will remove a small clod of earth. Drop the little bulb or corm into the hole, nose upwards, and break off a little of the base soil from the clod so that it gently covers the bulb or corm before replacing the divot of earth.

Larger bulbs, such as daffodils, are better planted with a spade. Throw the bulbs down at random and plant them where they fall, although you should try to allow a distance of at least 15–20cm (6–8in) between each one. The space allows the bulbs to multiply below ground and over the years to create a much greater display. Some daffodil bulbs are large, more than 6cm (2⅓in) high, and so need more than one spade's depth. In fact, the hole may need to be nearly 25cm (10in) deep. Plant a group of 10 to 20 bulbs or even more in this way so that you create a good show for spring.

PLANTING LARGER GROUPS

Where larger planting areas are planned, it can be easier to remove a whole section of turf with a spade and plant several bulbs in one group. The step-by-step sequence above shows the planting of late-flowering *Narcissus poeticus* var. *recurvus* (pheasant's eye) with *Camassia leichtlinii* in a trench. They were planted to create an outer row of bulbs that would flower in late spring and early summer, flanking an area of earlier flowering daffodils which were planted formally in rows between cherry trees.

Planting Bulbs in Large Groups

1 Dig a trench a spade's width and fold the turf backwards on itself. Use a trowel or dig down deeper so that you reach the required depth, in this case about 25cm (10in), and put the soil on one side.

2 Plant *Narcissus poeticus* var. *recurvus* with *Camassia leichtlinii*, placing them alternately about 20cm (8in) apart.

3 Fill in with loose soil so that the tops of the bulbs are covered. Replace the turf and firm down well with the heel of your boot.

4 The daffodils and camassias look attractive growing among the grass and wild flowers in late spring and early summer.

Left Drifts of daffodils look wonderful in spring grassland where they will multiply generously over the years.

Planting spring bulbs, corms, tubers and rhizomes in a small border beneath ornamental trees is both practical and pleasing, as long as the trees are deciduous and not too shallow rooting.

planting in the eye of a tree

Above An eye-shaped border, 90cm (3ft) long and 60cm (2ft) in width from the centre of a deciduous tree, is ideal for a lawn mower to get around. It can look splendid planted with early, mid- or even late spring bulbs.

Left *Narcissus* 'February Gold' is one of the best of all the early dwarf daffodils. Lustrous in colour, it is early to flower, sturdy, long lasting and elegant in shape. Planted en masse, it creates a generous splash of yellow beneath an old cherry tree.

The soil around the trunks of most evergreen trees is too dry for the planting of bulbs to be successful, while many conifers have comparatively shallow roots. Fruit trees, ornamental crab apples or cherry trees and magnolias, on the other hand, are ideal. The borders can be any shape you choose, but an "eye" that is about 90cm (3ft) long and 60cm (2ft) from the centre of the tree trunk is easiest for a lawn mower to get around.

Choose bulbs that will flower before the trees come into leaf and block out all the sunlight. All the early spring-flowering dwarf daffodils are perfect, and if you combine them with *Anemone blanda*, *Muscari armeniacum* (grape hyacinth), scillas and tulips, as well as earlier flowering *Galanthus* (snowdrop), cyclamen and *Eranthis hyemalis* (winter aconite), you can have a succession of flowering that will be a delight year after year. Herbaceous plants can be used as well. Hellebores, *Tanacetum parthenium* 'Aureum' (golden feverfew), *Lunaria annua* (honesty), *Myosotis* (forget-me-not) and *Galium odoratum* (sweet woodruff) all make excellent bedfellows.

The tubers of *Anemone blanda* are relatively inexpensive to buy and can be planted liberally and allowed to self-seed. This is an ideal choice for this position. Available in many shades of blue, mauve or white, the anemones will eventually form a sea of colour beneath the tree, completely covering the eye border and even expanding into the grass beyond if allowed to do so.

The lumpy tubers should be soaked in water overnight to rehydrate them before they are planted, about 5cm (2in) deep and 5cm (2in) apart. It is difficult to tell which is the top and which is the bottom, but if you can detect any hairy roots you will know they are growing from the bottom. Plant them to accompany wild primroses, golden feverfew and clumps of dwarf daffodils such as *Narcissus* 'February Gold' or 'Tête-à-tête'. The colourings will be exquisite.

If you plan carefully, you can enjoy having flowers in the eye at the same time as the blossom on the tree. Pink midseason tulips, for example, look

lovely flowering with purple-flowering honesty beneath an old apple tree in full spring array.

Allow the bulbs and corms to complete their cycle of growth before clearing away the old leaves in midsummer. By then these borders will be in heavy shade, and little else will grow successfully, except perhaps a few *Digitalis* (foxglove) and a rambling rose. Just as the fruit is turning ripe, however, a range of late summer- to early autumn-flowering bulbs will come into flower. One lovely example is *Colchicum speciosum* 'Album' (autumn crocus), whose white, goblet-shaped flowers open before the foliage appears, giving rise to the common name, naked ladies. The leaves may, in fact, dwarf any spring-flowering bulbs that are planted close by, so take care with the position. *Cyclamen hederifolium* is another autumn and winter subject for this position. It, too, flowers before producing its leaves, but these are low growing and most welcome for their intricate markings.

Above Plant a large group of blue *Muscari armeniacum* (grape hyacinth) about 5cm (2in) apart with their tips about 5cm (2in) below soil level.

Right *Muscari armeniacum* (grape hyacinth) will start into flower in late winter or very early spring and continue to flower for many weeks, producing a gorgeous blue haze. It looks perfect beneath this wonderful magnolia.

The moment you plant a container with bulbs, you have created a focal point
for the future. The choice of colour is personal, of course, but experimenting
is great fun, and a large container offers endless scope.

large containers

A Daffodil Half-barrel

1 large wooden half-barrel (60cm/
   24in across and 40cm/16in deep)
1 *Cornus alba* 'Sibirica'
   (red-stemmed dogwood)
10 pink Trumpet daffodils, such
   as *Narcissus* 'Rose Caprice'
2 *Skimmia japonica* 'Rubella'
2 purple-leaved *Heuchera*
   micrantha var. *diversifolia*
   'Palace Purple'
4 bronze winter-flowering pansies

1 If necesssary, drill six drainage
holes in the base of the half-barrel.
Line the base and sides with a bin
liner or black plastic. Cut slits in
the base of the liner to coincide
with the drainage holes. Add a
7.5cm (3in) layer of drainage
material, such as pieces of polystyrene. If you are using a peat-
based compost (soil-less mix), add
extra grit (in the ratio of about
three parts compost to one part
grit). Fill to about two-thirds full.

2 Position the central shrub (the
cornus) so that it sits just below
the rim. Plant the daffodil bulbs,
base down, nose up, close to
the edge of the barrel, so that
the tips of the bulbs will be at an
eventual depth below soil level
of three times their own height,
allowing for a 5cm (2in) gap at
the top of the container.

3 Add more compost, then
plant the skimmias and
heucheras on opposite sides.

4 Fill in the gaps with more
compost to within 2.5cm (1in)
of the rim. Plant the pansies
around the edge. Water well.

5 Enjoy the daffodils in spring
with their rosy salmon-pink cups.

If you are planting a large container in autumn for a
spring display, choose from among white, yellow
and salmon-pink daffodils, tulips and hyacinths, and
underplant with more white, salmon-pink or yellow
bulbs or add polyanthus, violas, pansies, forget-me-
nots or wallflowers. Combine this with bronze or
bright golden foliage, and you will have a masterpiece.
A completely different effect can be achieved with
combinations of strong blues, reds and pinks, also
available from bulbs, corms, tubers and rhizomes.
Wonderful summer combinations can be achieved by
using lilies, begonias, cannas and dahlias.

It is important to plan before you plant. Think
of the overall shape you want to achieve, and consider
the height and spread of the plants in relation to the
depth of the container. Dwarf daffodils or tulips are
best for a hanging basket, but a large half-barrel will
happily accommodate taller plants, including the midseason tulips and daffodils, which grow to 30–40cm
(12–16in). If there is room, include a shrub or conifer
in the centre to give added structure, or use *Hedera*
(ivy) or *Vinca* (periwinkle) to soften the edge of the
container and make a pleasing shape as they trail.

Consider also when you would like the container
to look its best. If you want an explosion of colour in
mid-spring, use daffodils or tulips with pansies. For a
late splash of colour, use late-flowering tulips with
pansies, forget-me-nots or wallflowers. Wallflowers
are available in a wide range of colours which will
complement almost any choice of tulip. Although
they will not start flowering until mid-spring, they will
provide greenery, and once they start to flower the
show will last for many weeks. The great bonus is that
they are scented, and a fragrant barrel or large
container by the kitchen door is a real spring treat.

If you want colour and interest from the time of
autumn planting right through to mid- or late spring,
however, you will have to choose a variety of plant
material. Winter-flowering pansies and violas will
flower on and off from the time of planting right
through to early summer, depending on the
temperature and how much sun the container
receives. The sunnier the spot, the better the display.

Coloured bark on shrubs will add drama to the
arrangement, particularly as the winter progresses
and the colours deepen. *Cornus alba* 'Sibirica'
(red-stemmed dogwood), which has rich red stems,
is an excellent choice. Evergreen shrubs will provide

coloured berries, buds or flowers. *Viburnum tinus* (laurustinus) is a great favourite, or choose *Skimmia japonica* 'Rubella', which has dark red flower buds throughout the winter months, opening to white flowers in spring. It makes a dramatic association with red-stemmed dogwoods. Add a purple-leaved heuchera, and mahogany-red pansies, and you will have provided a wonderful backdrop for the spring bulbs.

Cyclamen would extend the display in spring, together with crocuses, irises or *Anemone blanda*, which could be followed by later-flowering daffodils or tulips. Any bulb with a coppery or pink colour variation will look stunning with this red and bronze foliage. *Narcissus* 'Rose Caprice' has rosy salmon-pink cups, and 'Salome', with pinkish-orange cups, or 'Rainbow', with coppery pink cups, would also be a lovely combination. The coppery pink tones of lilies, such as *Lilium* 'Pink Tiger', would look good for midsummer.

All containers need to be given adequate drainage, but you must take extra care with winter containers or the bulbs may be damaged. Choose either a soil-based compost (potting mix), or use a peat-based compost (soil-less mix) and add extra grit, in the ratio of approximately three parts compost to one part grit. Before planting, place a generous layer of broken crocks or polystyrene (plastic foam) at the base of the container, which will help to give extra drainage in periods of continued wet weather. The drainage layer will also help to prevent the roots of the plants from blocking up the drainage holes, which are sometimes too small in relation to the size of the pot. Wooden half-barrels sometimes have no holes at all in the base, so drill about six large holes before planting.

Wooden containers will rot eventually. To slow down the process, add a lining of black plastic or plastic sheeting before planting. The plastic retains the moisture in the compost and keeps the wood dry, on the inside at least. Make extra holes in the base of the plastic, coinciding, if possible, with the holes in the container base. The lining also helps to minimize moisture loss through evaporation in mid- to late spring when the container may be in danger of drying out.

A Tulip and Wallflower Terracotta Pot
1 large terracotta pot (48cm/19in deep and 8cm/19in across)
10 midseason or late tulips, such as *Tulipa* 'Apeldoorn' (red), 'Blue Heron' (violet-purple) or 'Queen of Night' (dark purple)
1 bunch of dwarf *Erysimum cheiri* 'Orange Bedder' (wallflower)

1 Loosely cover the drainage hole in the bottom of the pot with broken crocks or large pieces of polystyrene (plastic foam). The drainage layer should be 5–7.5cm (2–3in) deep. Use a soil-based compost (potting mix) or a peat-based compost (soil-less mix), with extra grit mixed in (in the ratio of about three parts compost to one part grit), and begin to fill the pot.

2 Add sufficient compost so that when the tulip bulbs are planted, base down, nose up, they will be at a depth below soil level of three times their own height, allowing for a 5cm (2in) gap at the top of the container. Cover with more compost, bringing the level to just below the rim of the container. It will sink as it settles.

3 Wallflowers are often sold in bunches of ten. Separate them, choosing those with the best root systems.

4 Plant seven or eight of the wallflowers around the top of the container. Firm them down into the soil. Water well.

5 *Tulipa* 'Blue Heron' and these orange wallflowers make a vibrant combination. The perfume from the wallflowers is wonderful.

Small containers offer just as much scope for creativity as large pots and half-barrels, and they can be used to create wonderful spring and summer bulb displays. The only difference is that of scale.

small containers and window boxes

Right *Hyacinthus orientalis* 'Amethyst' is planted in a small container with a pink primrose. Hyacinths and primroses are both sweetly scented and make a good planting combination.

Hyacinths and Primroses

1 shallow terracotta pot (30cm/12in across and 15cm/6in deep)

5 hyacinths such as *Hyacinthus orientalis* 'Amethyst' (lilac) or 'City of Haarlem' (yellow)

4 *Primula vulgaris* (primrose) in colours to match the hyacinths

1 Cover the base of the pot with a 2.5cm (1in) layer of drainage material and cover with about 5cm (2in) of a soil-based compost (potting mix).

2 Add four handfuls of grit to give extra drainage. This is important because hyacinths do not like to be too wet in winter.

3 Plant the bulbs so that their bases sit firmly on the grit, spacing them so that they do not touch each other or the sides of the container.

4 Cover with more compost until their tips are just showing. Plant the primroses in a circle between the outer bulbs. Top up with more compost, bringing the level to within 2.5cm (1in) of the rim of the container. Water well and add more compost if necessary.

Shorter flowering bulbs, tubers and corms are obviously more suitable for small containers and window boxes than for medium to tall containers. There are many to choose from including all the dwarf daffodils, such as *Narcissus* 'February Gold', 'Jack Snipe', 'Jetfire', 'Jumblie', 'Topolino', 'Tête-à-tête' and 'Peeping Tom', and the later flowering 'Hawera.' Dwarf tulips also look wonderful in pots. All the early flowering singles, such as *Tulipa* 'Heart's Delight', 'Shakespeare' and 'Stresa', and the doubles, such as 'Peach Blossom' and 'Willemsoord', can be used. Hyacinths also make excellent container subjects and are available in a wide range of colours including blue (*Hyacinthus orientalis* 'Delft Blue' and 'Blue Magic'), white ('L'Innocence'), yellow ('City of Haarlem'), pink ('Lady Derby') and salmon-pink ('Gipsy Queen'). This is just a small selection, and there are many others.

These main three types of spring bulb – daffodils, tulips and hyacinths – can be treated in four ways. First, plant them on their own, in generous numbers and wait for them to flower. Second, add some bedding plants – pansies, violas, primroses or polyanthus, for example – to extend the season of colour so that there is interest before the main bulb display. Third, adopt a two-tier planting scheme and add another type of lower growing corm, bulb or tuber, which will flower at the same time. The white or blue star-shaped flowers of *Anemone blanda* make a lovely carpet of colour, as do late Dutch crocuses (forms of *Crocus vernus*), *Muscari armeniacum* (grape hyacinth), chionodoxa and, to a lesser extent, scillas. These all have the advantage of being relatively inexpensive and are often sold in packets of ten or twenty. You might also like to combine *Narcissus* 'February Gold' and large Dutch crocus, or yellow hyacinths with white *Anemone blanda*.

The fourth approach is to adopt the two-tier planting scheme and then to add a few violas or primroses. Avoid planting the bedding plants directly above the bulbs because the shoots of the bulbs are sharp and will prise their way between the roots of the bedding plants, lifting them out of the compost.

For summer colour, try Non-Stop and trailing begonias or *Anemone coronaria* De Caen hybrids, which are available in a range of vibrant colours.

Planting depths in containers are sometimes less than in the ground, especially where small pots or shallow containers are used, and this is usually perfectly acceptable as long as the bulbs are not expected to remain as a long-term planting scheme and the pots are put in a sheltered spot during the worst of the winter weather. One of the major problems for bulbs that are overwintered outdoors is inadequate drainage. If possible, use a soil-based compost (potting mix) that has plenty of grit mixed in with it. If you prefer to use a peat-based compost (soil-less mix), add extra grit in the ratio of three parts compost to one part grit. When you are planting more sensitive bulbs, such as hyacinths, dwarf daffodils or lilies, add an extra layer of grit beneath the bulbs. This will improve the drainage still further and avoid their roots sitting in cold, soggy soil.

Daffodils and Violas

1 window box (45 x 20 x 15cm (18 x 8 x 6in); the same plants would adapt easily to a wall pot or trough)
10 *Narcissus* 'Hawera'
2 *Senecio cineraria* (silver-leaved cineraria)
3 *Viola* 'Sunbeam' (yellow)
3 *Viola* 'White Perfection'

1 Cover the base of the window box with a 2.5cm (1in) layer of drainage material, such as small pieces of polystyrene (plastic foam) or broken crocks.

2 Add about 5cm (2in) of soil-based compost (potting mix), or a peat-based compost (soil-less mix) with extra grit (in the ratio of three parts compost to one part grit).

3 Plant the daffodil bulbs in two rows, spacing them so that they do not touch each other or the sides of the container. Cover with more soil so that just the tips of the bulbs show.

4 Bring the level of the soil to within 2.5cm (1in) of the rim of the container and add the bedding plants. Here, two cinerarias are planted in the middle of the window box, with three yellow and three white violas alternating on either side.

5 The window box looks as pretty as a picture with the yellow and white spring flowers set off by the silver-grey foliage of *Senecio cineraria*.

Whether you choose the sophistication of a white and gold colour scheme or opt for a daring riot of bright colours, you will find that spring and summer hanging baskets make a delightful addition to a house wall or patio.

hanging baskets

For spring colour, hanging baskets can be planted with a wide variety of bulbs, including all the dwarf daffodils, dwarf tulips and hyacinths, together with an underplanting of crocus, *Anemone blanda*, *Muscari armeniacum* (grape hyacinth), chionodoxa, scillas and so on. Give structure to autumn and winter schemes by adding *Hedera* (ivy) around the edges or include a small shrub, such as the tree heath, *Erica arborea* 'Albert's Gold', or the Japanese spindle, *Euonymus japonicus* 'Aureopictus'. White or pink winter-flowering heathers can be planted at the sides to soften the edges. Devise your own colour scheme by introducing pansies, violas, primroses and daisies as well. Create summer baskets that are vibrant with colour, too, by filling them with sumptuous begonias.

USING IVY

Ivy is a simple but effective edging plant to clothe the sides of a spring bulb hanging basket. The main problem comes in mid- to late winter, when cold winds dry out the leaves, turning them brown and ragged. Take a tip from Victorian gardeners and use small wires to fix the ivy trails to the moss lining. The effect is to create a ball of ivy, where the trails stay close to the sides of the basket and do not get spoilt in the wintry winds. By spring the daffodils, tulips or grape hyacinths, for example, will be in full flower. Meanwhile, the ivy will have started to root in the moss and within a season you will have an ivy ball, which will make summer and next winter's planting easy.

WEATHER WARNING

Severe winter weather can spoil autumn-planted, spring-flowering baskets because the mossy lining provides little insulation. In extremely cold or windy conditions, take the basket off its bracket and place it in a porch or garage. Never water in frosty conditions. It is better to keep all containers on the dry side in freezing weather as long as you keep the compost (soil mix) just moist. This is important in spring, when growth is taking place. If you have used bedding plants, such as pansies, apply a liquid feed in early spring to encourage a good display to coincide with the bulbs.

A Colourful Hanging Basket

1 wire hanging basket, 35cm (14in) in diameter
9 *Viola* 'Bowles Black' and 'Johnny Jump Up'
9 *Viola* × *wittrockiana* (pansy) from the Universal, Joker or Senator Series
10 mixed Double Early tulips
20 *Muscari armeniacum* (grape hyacinth)

1 Cover the base of the basket with a generous amount of moss. Bring the moss one-third of the way up the sides. Cover the moss base with a piece of plastic sheeting about the size of a dinner plate, and cut three or four 2.5cm (1in) slits in the bottom. Add a layer of compost (soil mix) to a depth of about 5cm (2in). Plant three violas, spacing them widely, on top of the moss wall with their roots firmly in the compost.

2 Plant three of the pansies between them.

3 Tuck a large handful of moss around the shoulders of each plant so that no gaps remain. Bring the moss wall two-thirds up the sides of the basket.

4 Plant the top tier so that a viola sits above a pansy and vice versa. Add more moss around each plant, bringing the wall 2.5cm (1in) above the rim.

5 Plant the tulip bulbs in outer and inner circles.

6 Cover with more soil until just the tips of the bulbs show, and add the *Muscari armeniacum*.

7 Add more soil to cover all the bulbs. Plant the remaining violas and pansies on opposite sides on the top. Fill in the gaps with soil. Water well, and add more moss and soil if needed. Hang the basket in a sunny sheltered spot.

8 The bulbs are long lasting and make a wonderful contrast among the violas and pansies.

Opposite Blue *Muscari* (grape hyacinth) and red tulips.

In gardening terms, bulbs do not demand a great deal of lavish care or attention, particularly if they are growing in the right conditions and are not too overcrowded. This must surely be one of their great attractions.

care and maintenance

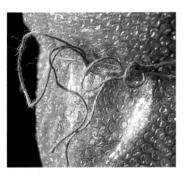

Top If possible, move containers close to a south-facing house or garage wall where they will have extra protection from extreme temperatures. In severely cold weather it may be better to move them inside the garage or porch.

Above If pots are too heavy to move, use bubble wrap as a protective coat and tie it securely in place.

Right Metal ring supports should be placed around dahlias as soon as growth begins to get above about 30cm (12in). Otherwise, use wooden stakes and string.

The common spring-flowering bulbs, including daffodils, tulips and hyacinths, are fully hardy and will cope with frosty weather, but some summer- and autumn-flowering plants, such as crinums and nerines, are only borderline hardy. In extreme winter weather they will benefit from a protective mulch of dry peat, bracken or sacking.

Some sites may be too windy for certain bulbs. If shelter is not available, it is best to choose plants that can cope best with the conditions in your garden. For example, large-flowering, midseason daffodils are often planted in grassland. Some will be fine planted in this way, but those with weak stems are best avoided. Instead, choose shorter, earlier flowering daffodils with small flowers which will stand up well to the buffeting of spring winds.

WINTER PROTECTION FOR CONTAINERS

Hardy spring-flowering bulbs are more sensitive to the cold if they are planted in exposed containers. Normal frosty weather will not be a problem, especially if sensible procedures are followed. You should, for example, always use plenty of drainage material, such as broken pieces of polystyrene (plastic foam), at the base of pots and then be sure to provide a well-drained soil

for all autumn and winter planting schemes. This means planting in either a soil-based compost (potting mix) or a peat-based compost (soil-less mix) with added grit. Avoid placing pots in exposed sites, such as sunless house walls or on a windy corner. Although the compost needs to be kept moist, never water in frosty conditions, and beware of watering on a sunny winter day – clear night skies cause the temperature to plummet. In extreme conditions, when temperatures threaten to fall below freezing for several days on end, all containers will benefit from some form of protection.

STAKING

Some plants – cannas, large dahlias, some gladioli and most lilies, for example – grow tall in summer and will benefit from being grown in sheltered positions where wind will not be a major problem. Summer storms can harm these plants, and dahlias in particular, whose growth is bushy as well as high, must be staked. Anticipate the problem, rather than wait for it to happen, by using metal plant supports or wooden stakes with string to contain the growth in early to midsummer. This might look unsightly at first, but dahlias grow quickly and the supports will soon be hidden by the foliage.

Lilies with large trumpet-shaped flowers also need extra support. When they are in full bloom, the heads are heavy. The stems are often strong and wiry and will remain intact, but the weight of the flowers will pull the heads downwards and the display will be less impressive. They are such brilliant flowers that they should be enjoyed to the full, and a single metal stake and ring support is ideal, as it allows movement but is discreet. Otherwise, use a bamboo cane and string. Tall gladioli are best supported in the same way.

DRAINAGE

Some plants, notably lilies, hate having their roots constantly in wet soil, and it is always a good idea to plant lily bulbs on a layer of extra grit to aid drainage, whether they are grown in pots or in garden soil.

Far left It is important to add a layer of grit when planting lilies in the garden or in containers.

Left *Allium hollandicum* 'Purple Sensation' produces beautiful seedheads which may be dried in a well-ventilated spot and used later in an indoor flower arrangement.

WATERING

Watering is important throughout the year, not just in summer, and all newly planted bulbs need adequate moisture to allow their roots to grow in autumn. When bulbs are planted in garden soil this is not normally a problem, but it is important that the compost (soil mix) in containers, such as hanging baskets and window boxes, is kept moist. This is even more important in spring, when rainfall may miss hanging baskets and window boxes that are in the rain shadow cast by the house.

In summer, extra moisture is vital, particularly in dry spells. With begonias, in particular, however, it is easy to cause damage by splashing water on to leaves where it may remain when the sun is shining. The scorch marks that result are not only unattractive but may harm the plant itself. Always water at soil level, not above the plant.

FEEDING

Providing additional nutrients is helpful to most bulbs, especially those with long displays, such as cannas and dahlias, which may be described as gross feeders. They respond well to a liberal dressing of well-rotted manure or a granular fertilizer when they are planted out in spring. It is less important to feed the flowers of bulbs such as daffodils, tulips and hyacinths, but it is crucial that all the foliage is left intact until it has died down naturally, thus allowing all the goodness from the foliage to be used in forming the basis of the following year's display. Avoid pulling the leaves off tulips in the herbaceous border, for example, until they have really withered and come away easily in the hand.

If several different types of bulbs have been growing in a grassy area, leave the mowing until at least six weeks after the last bulb has flowered. Where camassias have followed snowdrops and daffodils, this may mean that the mowing is delayed until midsummer. The grass will look untidy in the meantime, but it will soon recover and you may even enjoy a display of buttercups and other wild flowers while you wait.

DEADHEADING AND SEEDHEADS

Many bulbs, including fritillaries, *Eranthis hyemalis* (winter aconite), *Hyacinthoides* (bluebell), lilies, *Anemone blanda* and alliums, can be propagated by seed if it is gathered before nature disperses it. Some of these bulbs have attractive seedheads – the rosette that appears on the winter aconite is most endearing.

Much larger seedheads appear after the alliums have flowered. The seedheads of *Allium hollandicum* 'Purple Sensation' are lovely in dried flower displays. Gather the seedheads while they still have purple colouring and hang them upside down to dry. Those left in the border can be enjoyed there for many weeks.

Some flowers are, however, best deadheaded long before seed production is allowed to take place, especially to encourage further flowers. Dahlias, cannas and begonias all benefit from thorough, regular deadheading, resulting in an abundance of flowers until autumn. This also applies to daffodils, tulips and lilies, for example, where it is best to remove the flowers and so avoid the plant wasting energy in seed production. There is another group where too much self-seeding might take place – bluebells are notoriously difficult to control, so deadhead immediately after flowering.

Left Remove the flowerheads of daffodils before the seed has time to develop, so that the energy needed for rebuilding the original bulb is not wasted.

Autumn is always a period of great activity in the garden. As well as planting the spring-flowering bulbs, all the tender summer-flowering bulbs – dahlias, begonias, cannas and gladioli, for example – must be lifted, dried and stored.

dormancy and winter treatment

Lifting and Replanting Dahlias

1 Remove the foliage, leaving about 20cm (8in) of each stem.

2 Fork gently around the plant, leaving a radius of 25–40cm (10–16in) from the main stem, depending on the amount of growth it has made. Pompon dahlias might be small, but the large Decorative hybrids will be bigger. Gently lift the root, taking care not to damage the tubers.

3 Place the plant upside down in a box so that any moisture can drain down the hollow stems. Store in a dry, frost-free place and remove the soil from the tubers once it has dried off. Dust any damaged tubers with a fungicide such as yellow or green sulphate of ammonia and then place in boxes of barely moist peat. Overwinter in a dry, well-ventilated, cool, frost-free place.

4 When green shoots begin to emerge in spring, water sparingly to keep the compost moist. In late spring or early summer, after all risk of frost has passed, choose a sunny, sheltered spot and prepare a deep planting hole, approximately a spade's depth, but deeper if the tubers are large. Add a generous quantity of well-rotted manure or a long-term granular feed, and mix well into the soil at the bottom of the hole.

5 Carefully lower the dahlia into the prepared hole and add more compost (soil mix) as necessary to bring to soil level.

6 Gently firm in the plant with your hands or heels. Water well.

Tender summer-flowering plants, such as dahlias, begonias, cannas and gladioli, need to be lifted in autumn and then brought into growth again in spring for flowering in the summer. Their tubers and corms should be dried and stored in dry, cool, frost-free conditions. Begonias, gladioli and chasmanthe are stored dry; dahlias and cannas should be stored in barely moist peat or coarse vermiculite.

In most cases, lifting must be done before the first frosts of the autumn. Only dahlias will benefit if their foliage is actually killed off by frost. When this happens, the leaves become blackened. If the dahlias have stopped flowering, but there have still been no autumn frosts, then lift them anyway. In some mild areas it is possible simply to cut off the foliage from dahlias and leave the tubers in the ground, with a

Left In early spring, plant begonia tubers, hollow side up, on barely moist compost (soil mix). Keep them in a warm environment until the growth buds begin to expand. Increase the frequency of watering as the leaves emerge, but do not plant out until all risk of frost has passed.

Left Damaged bulbs should be dusted with a fungicide, such as yellow or green sulphate of ammonia.

Lifting and Replanting Cannas

Cannas are treated in much the same way as dahlias, except that the stalks of cannas are not hollow and it is not, therefore, necessary to hang them upside down to drain, as with dahlias. Moreover, cannas produce rhizomes, not tubers, and these are easily separated to produce new plants.

1 Lift the entire clump in the autumn, before any hard frosts, and place it in a large box.

2 Remove all the foliage to about 7.5cm (3in).

3 Allow the soil to dry off around the rhizomes, before cleaning them and storing in barely moist peat or vermiculite. Treat any damaged rhizomes with a fungicide, such as yellow or green sulphate of ammonia.

4 In spring, when the new shoots start to emerge, the clumps can be divided. Each rhizome will make a substantial show of colour in one summer, so it is a great opportunity to propagate. Where the rhizome is severed, dust with the same fungicide as before. Pot up into moist compost (soil mix).

5 In late spring or early summer, after all risk of frost has passed, choose a sunny, sheltered spot and prepare a large planting hole. Mix in a long-term granular feed or some well-rotted manure.

6 Plant the canna in a prepared hole and firm in gently. Water in well.

protective mulch over them, in the same way that nerines, crinums and the hardier types of agapanthus are left in the ground. However, with dahlias it is always a risk, especially if the ensuing winter happens to be severe.

Lift begonia plants in autumn and remove all foliage, leaving about 7.5cm (3in) of stem. When the soil has dried, clean the tubers and remove the stems.

Store in a dry, frost-free place at a minimum temperature of 7°C (45°F) throughout winter. In early spring, plant the begonia tubers, hollow side up, on top of barely moist compost (soil mix) and keep them in a warm place until the little pink buds start to expand. Water the tubers more frequently as the leaves emerge. Plant out only after all risk of frost has passed.

One of the wonderful attributes of many bulbs, tubers, corms and rhizomes is that they are successful self-propagators, by creating both new growth below ground and seeds above.

propagation

Propagating Tubers

1 Take a sharp knife and cut the tuber (in this case a begonia tuber) through the middle so that each part has a shoot.

2 Dust the open cuts with a fungicide such as sulphate of ammonia. Prepare two small pots with moist potting compost (soil mix).

3 Plant both halves so that they sit firmly on top of the compost. Keep the compost moist and plant on when new growth is apparent.

Anyone who has planted a canna from what seems like a small rhizome in late winter will be amazed at the sheer quantity of root material that can be dug up the following autumn after just one summer's growth – a mass of rhizomes all waiting to be divided and propagated, if desired. If that was not enough, some cannas are also generous producers of seed.

If you empty a pot of daffodils in summer, you will find that the old bulbs are still intact but have now formed offsets, each one capable of growing on to produce flowering stems and offsets of its own.

Look at the old bulbs of a *Muscari armeniacum* (grape hyacinth). They will have increased in size and produced several tiny ones, each clinging to the parent. In years to come, these will each grow on to become flowering bulbs in their own right. If left, they will form clumps of bulbs and in time produce a beautiful carpet of bright blue flowers. Meanwhile, the flowers will have produced a generous crop of viable seeds. No wonder they naturalize so well. The same is true of alliums, which produce copious quantities of seed. The leaves spring up, looking like chives around the parent plant in spring, each little leaf with a miniature bulb at the base. Grow them on and they will produce flowers within three or four years.

Hyacinthoides (bluebell) are prolific self-seeders. If you wanted to plant a bluebell wood, you would no doubt be impatient for the results, but if you had them growing in your garden borders, you would probably be waging war on the new patches of bulbs before too long. All seedlings, whether they are *Galanthus* (snowdrop), *Eranthis hyemalis* (winter aconite), grape hyacinths or bluebells, seem to do better in border soil than in turf, where there is competition from dense grass, but they will still multiply in grass, albeit more slowly.

Lilies have another way of propagating themselves. In addition to forming offsets and seeds, some lilies will produce bulbils at leaf axils up their stems. These fall off in time and form new plants where they root into the soil at the foot of the parent plant. This type of propagation occurs most commonly on *Lilium*

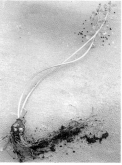

Right This daffodil has produced three excellent offsets in just one season's growth. It is this facility that makes daffodils such good naturalizers in grass or borders.

Far right *Muscari armeniacum*, the common grape hyacinth, is a great self-propagator, both by seed and offsets clustered around the parent.

Taking Begonia and Dahlia Cuttings

1 Gently pull a young begonia stem away from the tuber. A small piece of rooting material may well have come away at the base of the shoot.

2 Plant the new cutting into a prepared pot of moist compost (soil mix) and grow on in warm conditions, out of direct sunlight, until the new plant can be planted out in the garden or in a container.

3 When taking dahlia cuttings, slice through the bottom of the stem with a sharp knife and plant straight into a small pot filled with moist compost. Place on a light, warm windowsill, out of direct sunlight, and cover with a clear plastic bag for several days until the cutting has rooted.

lancifolium (formerly *L. tigrinum*; tiger lily) and many of the Asiatic hybrids. To make sure of collecting the bulbils and making the best use of them, detach them from the stem and plant them into small pots. Grow on for a season before planting out in the garden.

With corms, the story is slightly different. After flowering, the old corm dies and a new one forms on top of the old one, with clusters of cormlets around the sides. In this way some cormous plants, such as crocosmia, are able to form quite large clumps. Cormous plants can also propagate themselves by seed, some more successfully than others – *Crocus tommasinianus* is, for example, very successful in late winter grassland areas where the grass is fine.

Tuberous plants are also great survivors. Individual tubers grow to quite large proportions – surprisingly large compared with the tiny tubers on offer in the shops – and also produce generous quantities of seeds and shoots, which can be propagated. Leave a few *Anemone blanda* tubers planted in the eye of an old apple tree and within a few years it will be a mass of blue flowers as the seeds form new plants and the tubers plump up and grow. Begonia tubers can be successfully propagated in late winter or early spring where two shoots are seen on one tuber.

Begonias can also be propagated from cuttings taken from small shoots that have grown from the tuber in late winter or early spring. Dahlias can be propagated from cuttings taken from new growth during these same periods.

Right Allium seedheads produce a rich harvest. It may be better to collect the seed and grow it on in pots elsewhere if other herbaceous plants compete for space around the parent plants in spring.

Far right *Canna indica* produces a generous quantity of shiny black seeds.

pests and diseases

Above Aphids are most likely to be a problem on plants that are grown or stored in pots indoors or in a greenhouse.

Above Dahlias are often dusted with an insecticide such as derris (rotenone) to control earwigs and a range of other pests. Spray the leaves with water first so that the dust adheres well.

Above The lily beetle is quite attractive, but it can inflict terrible damage.

Earwigs may spoil dahlia flowers, vine weevil might damage begonia tubers, snails might attack lily shoots, and pollen beetles will seek out narcissus. Help is at hand in all these cases.

PESTS

Aphids
How to identify Clusters of tiny greenfly will infest emerging bulb buds and foliage, especially those of tulips and hyacinths. Blackfly are also an occasional problem. Tulip bulb aphids mainly attack stored bulbs.
Damage Unsightly and, in the extreme, deforming.
Control Use a soapy water spray as soon as the aphids appear, or use an appropriate insecticide. Stored tulip bulbs should be dusted with an insecticidal powder.

Earwigs
How to identify Slender, dark, glossy creatures with pincers which feed mainly at night on both leaves and flowers.
Damage Particularly noticeable on dahlias. Both leaves and flowers will show rounded indentations where the earwigs have been at work. On a small scale they can be ignored but where an infestation builds up, the holes can be very disfiguring.
Control Stuff small plant pots with straw or newspaper, then spike them on to canes pushed into the ground very close to the dahlias. Empty out each morning and kill the earwigs trapped within. On the same principle, use an insecticide dust to treat the newspaper to destroy the earwigs automatically.

Lily beetle
How to identify The adult beetle is bright red while the humpbacked, maggot-like larvae are covered with black excrement. Both adults and larvae feed at the same time on the foliage of lilies and fritillaries.
Damage Severe destruction of emerging shoots and flower buds.
Control Pick off adults by hand and wash off larvae with a water spray, but where infestations are heavy, use an appropriate insecticide.

Mice and squirrels
How to identify These furry animals will eat dry stored bulbs and those planted in the ground, especially in winter when food is scarce.
Damage Sometimes part-eaten bulbs remain as evidence, otherwise gaps in the planting displays are the eventual sign. Crocus are particularly susceptible.
Control Keep stored bulbs in rodent-proof containers. Use bait or traps where pets and other wild animals will not be affected. For bulbs in containers, add a top layer of bedding plants, thus avoiding bare soil.

Narcissus fly
How to identify The adult flies resemble bees, but you are more likely to find the larvae, which resemble white maggots and feed on narcissus or hyacinth bulbs.
Damage Total destruction at the centre of the bulb.
Control Destroy all affected bulbs to limit the future spread of the fly. Individual bulbs for new planting can be dusted with an insecticide powder.

Pollen beetles
How to identify Very small, shiny, black insects, also known as rape beetles because they are associated with oil seed rape crops. They are strongly attracted to yellow flowers, especially those of yellow narcissus.
Damage In extreme cases, the flowers will be eaten and disfigured.
Control Difficult, but spraying with water should help. Where the flowers are picked for displaying indoors, shake and then leave them in a darkened place outside, where the beetles will fly off in search of the light.

Slugs and snails
How to identify Slugs will mainly attack underground, while snails will do most of the damage above ground, devouring allium leaves and lily shoots as well as attacking tulips and many other bulbs.
Damage Disfiguration or total destruction.
Control Garden-friendly wildlife should be encouraged while biological controls such as nematodes, traps such as upturned grapefuit, or bait can be used.

Left Bulbs are particularly vulnerable to slug damage when the succulent shoots emerge from the ground. Slugs and snails usually come out to feed at night, like those here feasting on some dahlias. Find them with a torch, and destroy them.

Stem and bulb eelworms

How to identify These are microscopic creatures that weave a wavy translucent path through foliage. Irises, hyacinths, narcissi, snowdrops and tulips are all prone.
Damage The bulbs may be soft and the growth weak with leaves streaked or twisted.
Control Dig up and burn affected plants. Avoid replanting in contaminated soil for at least three years.

DISEASES

Basal rot

How to identify Affected bulbs are soft and there may be mould around the base.
Damage The leaves are usually yellow and tend to wilt. *Narcissus* are the most likely to be affected.
Control Lift and destroy affected plants. Avoid replanting in contaminated soil.

Botrytis (grey mould)

How to identify Fluffy grey mould on the leaves and dying flowers. It can also cause spots on the leaves.
Damage Disfigurement of the foliage and bulb rot.
Control Lift and destroy if the bulb is affected, otherwise remove affected parts and spray with systemic fungicide. Prevention is possible through dry storage conditions, removal of soil and decayed outer bulb parts, and a dusting with a fungicidal powder prior to storing.

Bulb and other corm rots

How to identify Many different rots can affect bulbs, but it is difficult to identify specific organisms without expert knowledge. Never plant soft or diseased bulbs.
Damage Patches of bare earth where bulbs have been planted or plants with stunted growth.
Control Do not plant suspect bulbs. Dig up and burn bulbs which have not emerged as planned. Do not replant in contaminated soil.

Tulip fire

How to identify The leaves are distorted and the shoots and flowers are stunted. In moist conditions, the leaves are covered with a grey mould with black fruiting bodies. Small, black scales develop on the outer scales of the bulbs which sometimes rot.
Damage Devastating distortion and poor display.
Control Dig up and burn affected plants. Do not replant in contaminated soil.

Vine weevil

How to identify The adults are black and glossy with a hard, defensive back. Each female lays up to 1,000 eggs in the soil which hatch into creamy maggot-like larvae in two to three weeks. Larvae are destroyed in temperatures below -6°C (21°F) which means that they are far more widespread in areas with milder winters. They are primarily a foe of the container gardener but, in some regions, they will overwinter in garden soil.
Damage The adults feed mainly at night on foliage, causing small notches on the edges of leaves. The larvae are the most destructive, particularly in spring and autumn, although they may attack at any time in a conservatory or greenhouse. They wreak havoc with cyclamen, gloxinia and begonia tubers.
Control Be constantly vigilant and destroy any adults on sight. They are mainly night-time movers (they cannot fly, but will climb). During the day they take refuge in dark places, so check under pots and leaf debris. Special traps can be laid, such as a roll of dark corrugated paper. Use beneficial nematodes in spring and late summer to destroy the larvae or plant all susceptible plants in a special compost (soil mix) containing imidacloprid which acts as a systemic insecticide.

Viruses

How to identify Although viruses themselves are invisible, the symptoms include streaked flowers, streaked or mottled foliage, stunted growth and distorted leaves. Sap-sucking aphids transfer viruses from one plant to another. Bought bulbs might already be infected.
Damage Not necessarily serious, although it can be. In general, leads to a weakening of the stock.
Control Dig up and destroy seriously affected plants. Spray against aphids.

Above A bulb with basal rot. Always check suspect bulbs by pressing the base, and do not plant any that are soft.

Above This "broken" tulip among unaffected plants is probably caused by a virus.

Above Tulip fire is caused by a fungus. Destroy affected plants and do not replant tulips in the same ground.

calendar of care

winter

Above Start dahlias into growth in pots in late winter, under the protection of glass, ready to plant out in early summer.

Right *Eranthis hyemalis* (winter aconite) makes a welcome splash of yellow in late winter.

Choosing Plants Many of the summer- and autumn-flowering bulbs are available to buy at this time of year, including low-growing to medium begonias, *Anemone coronaria*, freesias and taller dahlias, lilies, crinums, nerines, chasmanthe and gladioli. Of these, lilies can be purchased in both autumn and late winter. They are perfectly hardy, and as long as soil conditions allow deep digging to take place, they can be planted at either time.

Most of the bulbs, corms, tubers and rhizomes that are offered for sale in late winter are tender plants, which come from warmer climates where there are no winter frosts. They should be planted in spring, so that when the foliage emerges, all risk of frost has passed. It is possible, however, to cheat the season, because some tubers and corms, such as begonias and dahlias, can be started into growth in pots in late winter, under the protection of glass, so they are ready to plant out in early summer. This method leads to earlier blooms and therefore a long flowering season.

Galanthus (snowdrop) can be bought in late winter in pots or as loose clumps of plants with the leaves still attached to the bulbs. These are known as snowdrops "in the green". Plant them directly into borders or grassland, where they will establish and flower for years to come.

Bringing On Cannas, begonias and dahlias are available in a wonderful array of colours and can be started into growth in late winter or early spring so that they produce a mass of flowers throughout summer. Cannas and dahlias should be planted into, and begonias should be placed on top of, barely moist compost (soil mix) and kept in a light, cool to warm place until growth begins at the roots. Increase the available moisture once leaves begin to emerge.

Planting in Borders or Containers In mild spells, when the ground can be well dug, plant lilies in the border, either singly or in groups of three or more. Alternatively, plant them in deep containers. They thrive on well-drained soil, so add a layer of grit beneath the bulbs in both borders and containers.

Watering This is a time when attention to watering is crucial, especially with container-grown plants. Moisture is necessary to bulbs at all stages of growth, and it is important to check that the compost (soil mix) is moist in all pots, troughs, window boxes and hanging baskets from autumn right through to spring. Pots and troughs will probably fare best, but window boxes and hanging baskets tend to dry out quickly. Lack of moisture in late autumn and early winter will inhibit root growth, and lack of water in late winter, when the leaves and buds are emerging, is also detrimental. Keep an eye on the compost and water as necessary. Do not, however, be tempted to water if frost threatens, as bulbs will not appreciate having their roots in wet, frozen conditions. It is much better to ignore any bright sunny days when nights are likely to be frosty, and water only on overcast days when the nights will be milder.

Feeding This is not a major task at this time of year, although care should be given to any bulbs, tubers, rhizomes and corms in pots if you want to keep the plants for another display next season. Feed at flowering time or once thereafter, so that the foliage is kept healthy and the goodness can go back into the

bulbs as the leaves die down. Border bulbs benefit from a general-purpose feed, which should be applied to the border in late winter or early spring. Container-grown specimens benefit from a liquid feed.

Protection Against Frost All the hardy, autumn-planted bulbs that have been given homes in grassland or borders should not come to any harm in frosty weather. Those such as nerines and crinums, which may be considered borderline in colder areas, will benefit from a mulch of dry leaves. Bulbs and other plants that are in containers are at far greater risk. Hanging baskets should be taken off their brackets if temperatures drop below freezing for any prolonged length of time. A degree or two of frost overnight will not do any harm, but two or three nights and days of continued frost will pose greater problems. Place the baskets in the protection of a porch, garage or greenhouse. Pots and troughs should be given the protection of a house wall, where the temperatures will be less extreme, or put in a garage, porch or greenhouse. Sometimes they are too large and heavy to move easily, in which case they should be wrapped in a cloak of bubble wrap before the temperature drops to freezing. This will at least provide a little protection. Never water in frosty weather, when it is better to keep the compost (soil mix) on the dry side.

Deadheading Removing dead flowerheads means that a plant's energy is not wasted on the production of seed at the expense of increasing the size of the bulb. However, if you want to increase from seed, you should allow the full cycle of growth to continue unabated. Many of the late winter bulbs and corms, including snowdrops, *Eranthis hyemalis* (winter aconite), *Crocus tommasinianus*, cyclamen and *Anemone blanda*, naturalize well by seed propagation.

Propagation Collect seeds from winter aconites in late winter and early spring, and sprinkle them where you want them to flower, either in special propagation boxes or direct on border soil or grass. Divide clumps of snowdrops and *Leucojum vernum* (spring snowflake) and replant.

Pest Watch Squirrels and mice might dig up newly planted bulbs. Snails might attack early daffodils, while birds might eat crocus flowers.

Enjoy Now is the time to enjoy the flowers on many winter bulbs such as *Galanthus nivalis* (common snowdrop), spring snowflakes, early daffodils such as *Narcissus* 'January Gold' and 'February Gold', the early tulips, as well as corms such as the dwarf *Iris danfordiae*, crocus, and also on tubers such as those of the winter aconites, *Anemone blanda* and *Cyclamen coum*.

Above *Galanthus* (snowdrop) multiply quickly where they are growing in damp woodland, and will eventually spread to carpet vast areas. Plant them under shrubs and enjoy a similar, if scaled-down, effect.

Above left *Iris* 'Pauline' has dark violet flowers with distinctive white markings on the falls. This Reticulata iris is sweetly scented. Plant in an individual pot or with winter greenery in a hanging basket.

spring

Choosing Plants Some of the summer-flowering bulbs that were available in late winter will still be on sale, although you should take great care to choose those that are still plump and firm and have not been dried out by over-exposure on the garden-centre shelves. As spring progresses, cannas, begonias and dahlias that are in growth will go on sale. Although these will become excellent garden plants, you will find that the choice of colour and size will be more restricted than if dormant tubers and rhizomes had been purchased.

Bringing On Cannas and dahlias should be planted into, and begonias placed on top of, barely moist compost (soil mix) and kept in a light, cool to warm place until growth begins at the roots. Increase moisture once leaves begin to emerge. Plant outside only when all risk of frost has passed.

Planting in Borders, Grass or Containers Gladioli, *Anemone coronaria* (single De Caen hybrids and semi-double St Brigid varieties), *Zantedeschia* (arum lily), tigridia, sparaxias, crinums and lilies should be planted now. You might like to try a succession of anemones which flower about three months after planting.

Transplanting Transplant dichelostemmas, lilies and ornithogalums that were potted earlier and now have good root formation. Either transfer from the pot or simply bury the pot in the garden borders.

    Galanthus (snowdrop) and *Eranthis hyemalis* (winter aconite) can be purchased in spring as growing plants with their leaves intact. They might be sold in pots or in loose groups after flowering, but whichever kind you obtain, they will successfully transplant and flower well the following season.

Lifting The life-cycle of a bulb normally continues for at least six weeks after flowering has finished, so do not be tempted to lift and dry off bulbs, rhizomes and so on until well after this date. Do not mow grassy areas until six weeks after snowdrops, crocuses or daffodils have finished flowering, or the following year's blooms will be greatly inhibited.

Watering This is essential for container-grown specimens, especially if other bedding plants have been added to the scheme. Take special care with hanging baskets, which tend to dry out quickly, and with window boxes, which often receive little rainfall. Border bulbs, corms and so forth will normally receive adequate natural rainfall, although in exceptionally dry seasons they may benefit from some additional moisture.

Feeding Feed at flowering time or once thereafter so that the foliage is kept healthy and the goodness can go back into the bulbs as the leaves die down. Grassland and border bulbs will benefit from a general-purpose feed applied in late winter or early spring. Container-grown specimens will benefit from a liquid feed.

Above Dahlia tubers are now showing sustained new growth. New shoots can be used for propagation material.

Right *Tulipa* 'Blue Parrot' looks striking in association with this pansy from the Turbo Series, *Viola* × *wittrockiana* 'Light Rose with Blotch'.

Protection Against Frost Hardy bulbs are unlikely to suffer in frosty spring weather, but keep an eye on the temperature in your greenhouse where you might be bringing on cannas, begonias and dahlias. Keep the plants away from the glass, where temperatures drop fastest, and maintain the temperature above freezing. Keep the compost (soil mix) on the dry side.

Deadheading Hyacinths, daffodils and tulips should be deadheaded to avoid energy being wasted on seed production, but if you want to propagate bulbs such as scillas and chionodoxas, allow the seedheads to develop. Collect the seed and sow in propagation boxes or allow them to self-seed in situ.

Propagation Collect ripe seed from winter aconites and, in due course, from *Muscari armeniacum* (grape hyacinth), chionodoxas and scillas. Sow in propagation boxes or simply allow them to self-seed in situ.

Pest Watch Slugs and snails adore succulent growth and will attack the young foliage on tulips and alliums, lilies and daffodil flowers. General garden cleanliness is important in keeping the slug and snail population at bay, and some gardeners use chemicals against certain pests with varying degrees of success.

Rabbits, mice and birds are a nightmare as far as many bulbous plants are concerned, greedily eating off all the new shoots or flowers. Rabbits, fortunately, won't touch daffodils. Buried wire fences can stop rabbits, but there is little to frighten off birds, mice and squirrels.

Enjoy This is a wonderful season for bulbs and corms of all kinds, and there is a multitude of daffodils, tulips, hyacinths, *Erythronium* (dog's tooth violet), fritillaries, irises, *Leucojum* (snowflake), grape hyacinths and trilliums, coming into flower in grasslands, borders and containers. Now is the time to search out your favourite colours for planting next autumn.

Above Enjoy spring colours, such as these striking *Tulipa* 'Striped Bellona' with the red wallflowers.

Above left The sumptuous blue of *Muscari* (grape hyacinth) is set off perfectly by an underplanting of silver foliage.

Left Do not worry about hardy spring-flowering bulbs such as tulips, hyacinths and daffodils being harmed by late spring frosts.

summer

Right Tall-growing lilies can be supported with a special metal stake and detachable hoop.

Choosing Plants Gladioli might still be on sale, and late plantings now will give colour in autumn. Purchases of growing dahlias and begonias, cannas and *Zantedeschia* (arum lily) will allow you to obtain lots of colour this summer, although the range of colours will be more restricted than with dry tubers, rhizomes and so forth purchased in late winter.

Bringing On Late plantings of dahlias and begonias are still possible, and, given warmth and moisture, they will soon grow on and produce good plants for planting out once the roots are well developed.

Planting in Borders, Grass or Containers
Gladioli and anemones (single De Caen hybrids and semi-double St Brigid varieties) can still be planted, although they will be later to flower than if they were planted in spring. Anemones will flower about three months after planting, while gladioli might take up to four months.

Below Allium seedheads are just one of the many delights of summer. They can be enjoyed in the garden or used in dried flower arrangements.

Transplanting This is a major task now. Once all risk of frost has passed, the dahlias, cannas and begonias that were started into growth earlier can be planted out in the garden. They will be suitable for sunny borders or containers. Add slow-release food granules or well-rotted manure to the prepared holes before planting.

Lifting If you want to remove tulips and daffodil bulbs from the borders, now is the time to lift them carefully so that they can be dried off, cleaned, sorted, labelled and stored for use again in the autumn. The best time is when the leaves have withered but are still visible.

Watering Depending on the weather, be prepared to water. Dahlias are thirsty plants, especially in the early stages of growth.

Feeding Once the buds have formed on dahlias, begonias and cannas, they will benefit from a regular liquid feed.

Protection Against Frost This should no longer be necessary.

Left You will need to deadhead begonia blooms regularly to encourage the further production of flowers.

Deadheading Regular deadheading of begonias, dahlias and cannas will ensure longer flower production and bigger blooms. It will also make the plants look much tidier. Gladioli and lilies should be deadheaded to conserve energy for next year's display.

Propagation In midsummer, seeds of *Fritillaria meleagris* (snake's head fritillary) should be collected when ripe and sown in a propagating box. In late summer, small black bulbils will form up the stems of some types of lily, including those derived from *Lilium lancifolium* (formerly *L. tigrinum*; tiger lily). These will eventually fall off and propagate themselves at the foot of the parent plant, or they can be collected and planted in a propagating box.

Mowing Grasslands Where Bulbs Have Flowered Earlier Normally it is best to leave growth intact for at least six weeks before mowing, or the lifecycle of the bulbs will not be completed and next year's flowering will be seriously impaired. Grassed areas with late-flowering daffodils and camassias should not be mown until midsummer.

Staking All tall-growing lilies, gladioli and dahlias will need support. Single canes or special metal hooped supports are adequate for lilies and gladioli, but dahlias, which grow much wider and have many strong branches, will need greater support, either from a metal stake and wider circle, substantial peasticks or from three or four stakes surrounding the plant and linked by string.

Pest Watch Slugs, snails and earwigs think dahlias are wonderful fodder. Look out for vine weevil damage to begonia tubers. The grubs can be killed by beneficial nematodes, which are watered on in late summer or by using a systemic insecticide.

Enjoy In early summer, rich purple is still present in the flowerheads of alliums, while gorgeous blue is possible with tall camassias, which emerge from the borders and grasslands. Later blues are rarer, but they are still possible with freesias, anemones and triteleia. The mid- to late-summer range of tubers, rhizomes, bulbs and corms is dazzling. Dahlias and gladioli are available in dozens of brilliant hues, ranging from red, yellow, orange, pink and purple to white, while begonias and cannas light up the border with fiery yellows, oranges and reds.

Below The seeds of *Fritillaria meleagris* (snake's head fritillary) will be ready for collection in midsummer. They should be sown in a propagating box.

autumn

Choosing Plants The autumn months bring a deluge of dry bulbs into garden centres and shops, some pre-packaged in groups of three, five and sometimes ten at a time, while others, such as the common types of daffodil, tulip and hyacinth, are sold loose so that they can be picked up in any quantity. The pre-packs can be more expensive, but the range is usually far greater. Buy early if you want to obtain special named varieties. Look out for some of your favourite colours in tulips, pick out dwarf daffodils for pots and baskets, and buy hyacinths for scent.

Bringing On Some genera, such as calochortus and dichelostemma, are best planted in pots and kept in a frost-free potting shed, ready for transplanting or plunging into the garden the following summer.

Planting Direct in Borders, Grass or Containers
Autumn-flowering colchicums and *Lilium candidum* (Madonna lily) should be planted as soon as they are available. All the late winter- and spring-flowering varieties, including daffodils, tulips and hyacinths, should be planted direct into borders, grasslands or containers as soon as convenient, so that they can form good roots in autumn and early winter. Summer-flowering lilies should also be planted now, although some will also be available in late winter.

Right Bulbs, such as these tulips, can be planted in formal lines using taught lengths of string as a guide. Attach a long piece of string to two small stakes or supports and position the string over the border where you want to plant the bulbs. Space the tulip bulbs at 15–20cm (6–8in) intervals underneath.

Below So many different varieties of bulb are available for buying and planting now, it is really difficult to know where to begin.

Lifting Tender specimens, such as begonias, dahlias, cannas and gladioli, should be lifted, dried, cleaned, labelled and stored for the winter in frost-free conditions, ready for planting the following year.

Watering This will not be necessary for border or grass-grown plants, but take care with containers, such as hanging baskets and window boxes, which are apt to dry out quickly and may receive little rainfall.

Protection Against Frost Dahlias can be left outside until blackened by the first frost, but gladioli, begonias and cannas should be lifted before any frosts occur.

Deadheading Continue to deadhead cannas, begonias and dahlias until it is time to lift them.

Propagation On replanting daffodils and tulips lifted in early summer, the main large bulb can be replanted to create a flowering clump, while smaller bulbs and corms can be planted out in rows, ready to bulk up in size for flowering in two or three years' time.

Pest Watch Earwigs, slugs and snails will still take their toll on growing plants. Look out for vine weevil damage to begonia tubers. The grubs can be killed by beneficial nematodes or by using a systemic insecticide, which is watered on in late summer. Mice and squirrels might try to dig up newly planted bulbs and corms.

Enjoy Enjoy the last of the dahlia, begonia, gladioli and canna flowers as well as the glorious funnel-shaped blooms of pink amaryllis, crinums and nerines, the broad cups of white and lilac colchicums and yellow sternbergias, the delicate flowers of the little autumn-flowering cyclamen and the taller sprays of schizostylis.

bulbs in the garden

crocus

The bulb garden changes constantly with the seasons. Galanthus *(snowdrop)* and Eranthis hyemalis *(winter aconite)* are the outward signs of late winter, with the first daffodils just beginning to show themselves like daggers through the ground. Soon the garden will be filled with their golden heads waving in spring sunshine. Colourful tulips and stately Fritillaria imperialis *(crown imperial)* will take centre stage, while in woodland areas the little Anemone nemorosa *(wood anemone)* and swaths of Hyacinthoides *(bluebell)* will have their moment of glory. Grasslands will be filled with camassias, and in the borders, the elegant Dutch irises and rounded alliums add an air of exuberance. Summer borders are filled with lilies, begonias and gladioli, with dahlias and cannas joining the summer ranks and following on into autumn, when the nerines, colchicums and cyclamen are at their best. There is so much to choose from and to enjoy.

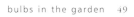

crocosmia 'Lucifer' (front) and *helenium* 'Waldtraut'

mid- to late winter gallery

This is always a quiet period in the garden, with short, cold days and long, frosty nights. However, some plants have adapted well to these cold temperatures and are able to produce exquisite flowers, even in the bleakest of environments. Given the low light levels, cold temperatures and often windy conditions, it is not surprising that most of the winter-flowering bulbs and corms are short in height. Indeed, several of them, such as *Eranthis hyemalis* (winter aconite) and *Galanthus* (snowdrop), actually show their flower buds at ground level, lengthening their stems only gradually as the pale daylight increases.

❮ *Galanthus nivalis* (common snowdrop) is the most familiar of all the snowdrop species grown in gardens. It is found widely throughout Europe, from Spain to western Russia, and also in Britain. It occurs naturally, both with single and double, white flowers, all with a sweet honey scent.

❯ *Narcissus* 'January Gold' is one of only a few daffodils that flower at this time of year. It grows to 30cm (12in) high, with the large, golden flowers borne on relatively short stems which stand up well to buffeting winds.

❯ *Galanthus* 'Atkinsii' grows to 20cm (8in) high and is one of several clones of *Galanthus nivalis* (common snowdrop). This is a tall, early flowerer, highly scented, elegant in its poise, and makes an attractive addition to the winter garden.

❮ *Eranthis hyemalis* (winter aconite) grows to 5–7.5cm (2–3in) high and produces a tightly formed yellow cup. Just as midwinter has passed, each cup will push its shoulder against the cold earth as it struggles to meet the winter air and unfurl its golden petals. As the stems lengthen, a frill of green leafy bracts acts as a ruff beneath each flower. The tubers establish easily and the seeds will spread quickly.

About 15 different snowdrop species are found in Europe, from Spain to western Russia, Crimea and Turkey, with a range of flowering times from early to late winter, many with slightly different markings or variations in flower size. From these species many, many cultivars, each with their own distinctive characteristics, have been developed.

The winter gallery also includes the early crocuses, dwarf irises, tiny cyclamen and low-growing *Anemone blanda*. Only the earliest daffodils, such as *Narcissus* 'January Gold', are significantly taller than the low-growing snowdrops and aconites, and even they still reach only 25–30cm (10–12in) in height.

❮ *Iris danfordiae*, which grows to 10cm (4in) high, is one of several dwarf irises that will flower in late winter. A beautiful shade of yellow, it is often sweetly perfumed and intricately marked. The slightly taller *Iris reticulata*, 10–15cm (4–6in) high, is violet in colour with a yellow ridge to the falls. Narrow, grass-like leaves emerge as the flowers first show colour and then overtake the blooms as the flowers reach maturity.

❮ *Crocus chrysanthus* 'Blue Pearl' is one of the easiest and best of all the early crocuses. It grows to 7.5cm (3in high), and its exquisite pale blue outer colouring, silvery inside and bronze base makes it the perfect choice for many displays, both in borders and in containers.

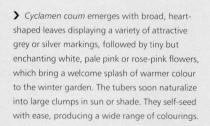

❯ *Cyclamen coum* emerges with broad, heart-shaped leaves displaying a variety of attractive grey or silver markings, followed by tiny but enchanting white, pale pink or rose-pink flowers, which bring a welcome splash of warmer colour to the winter garden. The tubers soon naturalize into large clumps in sun or shade. They self-seed with ease, producing a wide range of colourings.

❮ *Crocus tommasinianus* is a hardy and reliable plant from Hungary, the Balkans and Bulgaria, which grows to 7.5–10cm (3–4in) high and is tolerant of sun or partial shade. It is a prolific self-seeder and, in time, each narrow, pale silvery lilac flower will create a delicate carpet of colour.

❮ *Anemone blanda* grows to a height of 10–15cm (4–6in) and is one of the most rewarding flowers for both the winter and early spring garden, as it blooms for six weeks or more. The blue flowers are shy to begin with, but they gather strength as the sun begins to warm the earth.

Soon after midwinter, tiny white Galanthus (snowdrop) emerge through the frozen ground to greet the winter sunshine. Their flowers are an intricate masterpiece of pure white petals and delicate green markings.

mid- to late winter borders

Right *Eranthis hyemalis* (winter aconite) can be planted to great advantage in front of *Helleborus foetidus* (stinking hellebore).

Right The various shades of pink *Cyclamen coum* make an exquisite combination with pure white snowdrops, the whole enhanced by the silver marking on the cyclamen foliage.

The bulbs that flower in late winter, such as *Galanthus* (snowdrop), cyclamen and early daffodils, can be used alone or in combinations of two or three different types to produce welcome colour in the winter border. Remember to plant them close to a path or within view of your window – it is more comfortable to admire the brave little flowers from inside the home than outside in the cold wintry garden.

Snowdrops look stunning in small individual groups. The commonest ones are *Galanthus nivalis*, in either the single or double form. The single flower is more poised and elegant, particularly in the cultivar *G.* 'S. Arnott', which has long stems and beautifully rounded, drop-like flowers. On warmer days the petals open wide, revealing a labyrinth of green veins. It is worth bending down and looking right into each flower to fully enjoy its intricacies. As an added bonus, you will also discover that it is wonderfully scented.

Snowdrops associate happily with many other bulbs. They make a remarkably warm and welcome grouping with the tiny pink flowers of *Cyclamen coum*, which is further enhanced by the often intricate silver veining on the cyclamen leaves. The fly-away petals of the cyclamen flower are easily recognizable, and there is a darker stain around the nose of each flower. After flowering, the seedhead is pulled down to the ground by the coiled stem so that it comes to rest on the surface of the soil. In early summer the pods burst open, and the sticky seed is ready to be propagated.

In their turn, cyclamen make a pretty partnership with the purple and violet shades of the dwarf Reticulata irises, such as *Iris* 'Pauline', 'Hercules' and 'J.S. Dijt'. Although small, they are packed with colour and vibrancy. *I.* 'George' is a fine example, a gorgeous purple with yellow on its falls, just enough to lift the eye and bring out the lovely pink background of the cyclamen.

Another favourite is the bright yellow *Eranthis hyemalis* (winter aconite) which forms generous groups once it is well established. It is an excellent choice for a damp border beneath deciduous shrubs, where it will have shade in summer but

Left Blue-flowering *Anemone blanda* self-seeds with alacrity over a period of just a few years, so that soon the area beneath a tree, for example, would be completely filled with them. The foliage provides an attractive green carpet above which the pretty daisy-like flowers are poised ready to open in the winter sunshine.

Left *Leucojum vernum* var. *carpathicum* has broad white flowers, each petal tipped with yellow. It creates a stunning picture beside the golden flowers of *Eranthis hyemalis* (winter aconite).

receive more light in winter when it flowers. It associates happily with white snowdrops or the little irises, but also looks lovely with other herbaceous plants, such as dark bronze bugle, *Ajuga reptans* 'Atropurpurea', or lime-green *Helleborus foetidus* (stinking hellebore).

The border "eye" beneath a deciduous tree will usually look bare in the middle of winter, but then the colour will begin to appear. While moisture and light are able to reach the soil, a whole array of plant associations is possible. Late winter- and spring-flowering bulbs, corms and tubers make an excellent choice because they can take advantage of the sparse canopy above to flower and complete their life cycles before the later canopy of leaves excludes moisture and sunlight.

Snowdrops and winter aconites can be planted in separate groups to create a wonderful display, restrained as the first buds begin to appear, but then providing a delightful mass of bloom. Plant several groups of both single and double snowdrops, with a scattering of winter aconites between them. These will soon multiply and give a delightful tapestry of colour. Later groups of bulbs can be planted among them to carry the season forward.

Leucojum vernum (spring snowflake) is similar to the snowdrop, but the flowers are rounder and have six equal petals, unlike those of the snowdrop which have three long and three short petals. They are native to France, central and eastern Europe and are naturalized in parts of Britain, where they are easy to grow in shade or semi-shade in soil that is moist. *L. vernum* var. *carpathicum*, a handsome variant with yellow tips at the ends of the petals, is native to Romania and Poland. The greener, broader leaves are larger than those of snowdrops and make a happy association with the golden, cup-shaped flowers of winter aconites.

The first daffodils are in flower at this time of year. *Narcissus* 'January Gold' is one of the earliest to appear, and the golden cupped flowers last for several weeks, withstanding snow, frost and icy winds.

Above The powerful colouring of *Iris* 'George', a Reticulata iris, looks striking against a background of *Cyclamen coum*.

This is an excellent choice for planting in borders generally or in the eye beneath deciduous trees where later-flowering daffodils can continue the spring display. *N.* 'February Gold' will soon follow, spanning the period between late winter and early spring.

By this time, the first flowers of *Anemone blanda* are beginning to unfurl, opening in the pale sunshine to reveal the bluest of daisy-like flowers. The dainty petals flutter in the winter breeze. White varieties are widely available, although they are more expensive. Also available, and by far the cheapest, are mixtures of mauve, pink, blues and white, with all the shades in between. They soon naturalize in border soil or grass and will escape by self-seeding into the grass around the border "eye". These anemones make a glorious display on their own, but planted in association with a few primroses and early daffodils, the momentum of the display can be carried forward in the most delightful way.

Despite being so low growing, many of the mid- to late winter bulbs,

corms and tubers will happily compete in winter grassland, provided the grass

is short and sparse.

naturalized bulbs for mid- to late winter

Snowdrops, *Leucojum* (snowflake), *Eranthis hyemalis* (winter aconite), *Anemone blanda* and the early daffodils, as well as a wide range of crocuses, create a sparkling display when naturalized and, given time, will multiply successfully. Do not be surprised, however, if the bulbs, corms and tubers in the borders multiply faster than those in grass.

GRASSLAND

Of the many crocus species, *Crocus tommasinianus* and its cultivars are among the most successful in grass, whether they are grown in sun or semi-shade. This crocus will self-seed extensively and, although each flower is narrow and delicate, a well-established group will create a broad sheet of blue when the sun shines and the petals open. *C. flavus* subsp. *flavus*, with its golden petals, will enjoy similar conditions. Although it will not self-seed, it will mass up in clumps as the corms multiply below ground. *C. chrysanthus*, which is native to the Balkans and Turkey, has scented creamy yellow flowers and will compete well in the winter grassland. *C. c.* 'Cream Beauty', with creamy yellow flowers, 'Ladykiller', with blue, white-edged flowers, and 'Zwanenburg Bronze', with pale yellow and bronze flowers, are just three popular cultivars.

Above *Galanthus* 'Magnet' has taller, larger flowers than *Galanthus nivalis* (common snowdrop). Here, it forms a marvellous carpet beneath the witch hazel *Hamamelis* × *intermedia* 'Pallida'.

Left This group of mixed crocuses, which includes *Crocus tommasinianus*, *C. chrysanthus* and *C. vernus*, has formed a natural-looking carpet of colour.

DECIDUOUS SHRUBS AND WOODLAND

Deciduous shrubs and woodland offer a convivial home to early snowdrops, cyclamen, daffodils and winter aconites. The winter tracery of bare branches allows maximum light and moisture to reach early-flowering bulbs, corms and tubers, enabling them to complete most of their life-cycle before the canopy of leaves appears later in spring.

Galanthus nivalis (common snowdrop) will naturalize vast areas of woodland and create a spectacular, virginal sheet of flowers. Single and double varieties will grow in neighbouring groups. Winter aconites colonize with the same effect and, where they are planted with snowdrops, then a wonderful mixture of yellow and white swirls will

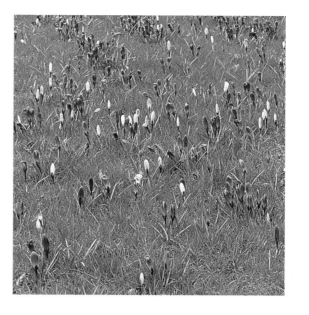

form the woodland floor. Elsewhere, *Cyclamen coum* will naturalize generously, this time creating a broad pink carpet, softened by the silver veining of the rounded leaves. They all enjoy the damp leaf mould of late winter; it does not matter that the summer floor is dry and dark, for by then the bulbs lie dormant.

Below The leaves of *Cyclamen coum* are variably patterned with intricate silver veining or blotches. These create the perfect background for the tiny flowers, which appear in many appealing shades of light and dark pink.

mid- to late winter containers

Right This winter-flowering hanging basket contains lots of different evergreen plants, including variegated ivies and *Euphorbia myrsinites*. The blooms of the winter-flowering heathers and *Viburnum tinus* add extra interest, but the highlight of the basket is the little *Iris* 'Pauline', which combines beautifully with all its bedfellows.

This time of year is often cold and inhospitable for both gardeners and plants, but if you choose carefully, you will find several gems to bring welcome colour even on the dullest days. Plant *Galanthus* (snowdrop), *Leucojum vernum* (spring snowflake), dwarf irises, *Eranthis hyemalis* (winter aconite), *Anemone blanda* and the early daffodils in containers, position them in a sheltered spot outside the house and enjoy them as you enter or leave. Alternatively, simply hang them in a basket close to a window so that you can admire and appreciate them from indoors.

Snowdrop bulbs and the lumpy tubers of winter aconites are sold as small, dry specimens in autumn, and it is a sad fact that, because they are overdried and kept out of the ground too long, only a small number will produce leaf and flower. Once established, however, they will flower and multiply well, massing up underground as well as by self-seeding. Instead of trying to have a lovely container display from new bulbs and tubers bought in autumn, buy them as growing plants at flowering time, pot them on into a larger container and keep for the following year, by which time they should be nicely established. Alternatively, if you already know that you have them growing in the garden but would like to try them nearer the house in small pots, dig them up out of the ground in late autumn and plant them immediately in a well-drained, soil-based compost (potting mix). The advice holds true for snowflakes and *Cyclamen coum* as well. Treat them as single specimens in containers, and they will look simple but charming.

Instead of planting individual pots of bulbs, corms and tubers, try mixing them with winter-flowering shrubs and herbaceous plants. Winter-flowering *Viburnum tinus* (laurustinus) is an excellent centrepiece for a winter pot or hanging basket. It is hardy, evergreen and produces a mass of pink-tinged buds, which open to white any time from late autumn through to spring. White, mauve or purple winter-flowering heathers can be planted around the sides so that when they come into bloom, just after midwinter, they will soften the edge of the basket and give it extra colour. Choose large specimens with plenty of flower buds. Trailing ivies can also be planted around the edge. As they cascade over the sides, peg them into the moss to stop them spoiling in the winter winds. As they touch the moss, they will take root and within a season you will have a well-established ivy ball. Another excellent hardy foliage plant is the evergreen *Euphorbia myrsinites*, with its long, architectural, grey trails, which will flower in early spring.

For the highlight of the winter pot or hanging basket, plant some specimen bulbs, corms or tubers. You might dig up a clump of snowdrops or snowflakes from your own garden, or just a few winter aconites. However, if you want to start with

From the Border to a Pot

1 *Eranthis hyemalis* (winter aconite) may be quite hard to find in border soil because at first they just look like lumps of earth. By late autumn, however, the buds will be showing, and where tubers have grown on and matured they can be 3–4cm (1¼–1½in) across, although younger tubers are tiny.

2 Prepare a small pot with drainage material, such as pieces of polystyrene (plastic foam) or broken crocks, and a soil-based compost (potting mix) and replant one large tuber 5cm (2in) below the surface. Cover with more soil and water well.

3 Place the pot outdoors on your windowsill or in a group with other winter-flowering specimens on a patio table where they will give welcome colour to the winter garden. After blooming, they can be replanted in the garden borders, beneath a deciduous shrub or tree or in short grass.

new bulbs, why not try dwarf irises? For example, *Iris danfordiae*, with its golden-yellow flowers, shows up brilliantly, but there are lots of others to choose from as well, including all the Reticulata irises – *I.* 'Harmony' and 'Joyce' are both sky blue with yellow on their falls, and 'Pauline' is a marvellous dusky violet with flecks of white on the falls. They will flower from late winter to spring, doing best in a sunny position. Planted in a hanging basket, the flowers can be enjoyed at eye level, and at this height they can also be appreciated for their lovely sweet scent. Hang the basket in a sunny, sheltered spot, and, in severe weather, take it off its bracket and keep it in a porch or garage. Keep the soil moist but never water in frosty conditions. To extend the season of interest, you might like to plant early dwarf tulips or daffodils to follow on in early spring.

early spring gallery

As the days begin to lengthen, the garden starts to come alive, and suddenly an array of different bulbs is in flower. This is the main season for all the many types of dwarf daffodil, including old favourites such as *Narcissus* 'February Gold' and 'Tête-à-tête'. Their short, sturdy stems enable them to withstand blustery spring winds.

The little *Anemone blanda* are now in full flower, their starry faces opening to greet the spring sunshine. They are one of the most valuable plants in the garden, lasting for six weeks or more and spreading easily to create a dense carpet of colour. This is also the time for *Crocus* 'Large Dutch Purple', *Scilla sibirica* (Siberian squill),

❮ *Narcissus* 'February Gold' grows to a height of 25cm (10in). It is short, sturdy and one of the longest flowering of all the dwarf daffodils, lasting well over a month. It has a long, golden trumpet with elegant, swept-back petals, so reminiscent of its parent *Narcissus cyclamineus*. It looks magnificent with an underplanting of white or purple large Dutch crocus and also with early Kaufmanniana tulips.

❯ *Muscari armeniacum* (grape hyacinth) will flower for many weeks from early to mid-spring. It grows to 20cm (8in) high and provides a memorable underplanting to many tulips, hyacinths and dwarf daffodils, both in containers and in the border. Grape hyacinths multiply quickly, so allow them to mass up along a path or under a shrub. The only drawback is the straggly leaves, but the gorgeous colour of the flowers makes up for any waywardness.

❯ Double Early *Tulipa* 'Orange Nassau' reaches a height of 20cm (8in) and has a mass of vibrant orange-red petals, a bold combination wherever it grows, whether in borders or containers. Terracotta pots are particularly appropriate. This tulip is excellent with blue or yellow hyacinths, red, orange, yellow or blue primroses or with polyanthus.

❮ *Crocus* 'Large Dutch Purple' reaches a height of 10cm (4in) and is a pivotal player in the spring garden, providing a carpet of bright colour for the early dwarf daffodils. Night-time frosts are to be expected and endured, but as the flowers open in the morning sunshine, they reveal a throng of gorgeous orange stamens. The contrast is brilliant and certainly worth repeating in containers as well as garden borders.

Chionodoxa (glory of the snow) and early single, Kaufmanniana-type tulips, such as *Tulipa* 'Shakespeare', 'Stresa' and 'Heart's Delight'. All of these will happily mix and match to provide endless associations.

As the weeks progress, the first gorgeous blue flowers of *Muscari armeniacum* (grape hyacinth) begin to emerge. These look superb with any of the early double tulips or, indeed, with ordinary bedding hyacinths. The exotic blue of the grape hyacinths looks stunning with yellow *Tulipa* 'Mr Van der Hoef' and with 'Peach Blossom'. Violas, pansies, primroses and polyanthus act as fine bedfellows with any of these bulbs, producing wonderful planting combinations.

❮ *Chionodoxa forbesii* 'Pink Giant' grows to a height of 15cm (6in) and provides racemes of four or more star-shaped flowers, pale pink around the edge, white within. They make a very pretty association with many early spring bulbs, including dwarf daffodils and hyacinths. This is less common than lovely blue *Chionodoxa luciliae*, but it is certainly worth trying in pots and in the garden.

❮ *Narcissus* 'Jetfire', with a height of 25cm (10in), is similar in shape to 'February Gold', having the same fly-away petals. But the trumpet is more orange (rather than yellow), making it a perfect partner for any late purple crocus as well as all the streaked orange Kaufmanniana tulips. It also looks striking planted with orange and purple bicolour pansies.

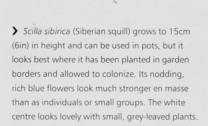

❯ *Scilla sibirica* (Siberian squill) grows to 15cm (6in) in height and can be used in pots, but it looks best where it has been planted in garden borders and allowed to colonize. Its nodding, rich blue flowers look much stronger en masse than as individuals or small groups. The white centre looks lovely with small, grey-leaved plants.

❮ Double Early *Tulipa* 'Kareol' grows to a height of 20cm (8in) and is one of several early double tulips, all of which are lovely in garden borders and containers. Early to flower, sturdy and long lasting, they have wide flowering heads which make them a valuable ingredient where planting space is limited. They are excellent in a range of containers, including hanging baskets, chimney pots, troughs and window boxes.

❮ Double Early *Tulipa* 'Peach Blossom' reaches a height of 20cm (8in) and is one of the most popular of all the early dwarf tulips. It has such a delicate combination of colours in its myriad of petals and looks stunning with blue grape hyacinths. Equally beautiful in a small pot or window box, this is a combination which will last for many happy weeks.

So many different combinations are possible at this time of year that a lifetime of experiments would fail to exhaust the possible permutations. But that is part of the fun of gardening: there is always something new to try.

early spring borders

Above *Tulipa* 'Oranje Nassau' is a fiery mixture of orange and red, which looks extremely vibrant with red polyanthus (primroses). Plant close to *Tanacetum parthenium* 'Aureum' (golden feverfew) or other bright green herbaceous plants.

Right *Narcissus* 'February Gold' and the elegant *Tulipa* 'Stresa', a Kaufmanniana tulip, make a striking combination, both being sturdy and long lasting. This partnership would make an exciting foreground planting to a host of spring-flowering shrubs such as forsythia or *Ribes* (flowering currant).

Plant groups of single types of bulb beside each other or plant more densely, allowing the taller subjects to be underplanted with the shorter ones. In this way, early dwarf daffodils and Kaufmanniana tulips, and slightly later hyacinths and broader Double Early tulips can be associated with or underplanted by purple or white late Dutch crocuses, starry blue, white or mauve *Anemone blanda*, blue or pink chionodoxa, rich blue scillas and bright blue *Muscari armeniacum* (grape hyacinth). Seasons vary and some flowers will last longer than others, depending on the temperature and moisture, but there is usually quite an overlap between all these plants, with the exception only of the late Dutch crocuses. These flower with the early dwarf daffodils and tulips but will not usually last long enough to partner hyacinths and Double Early tulips.

Violets, violas, pansies, double daisies, primroses and polyanthus all play their supportive roles in the early spring border. Among the prettiest sights in the early spring garden are groups of primroses and violets with early dwarf daffodils in small groups among them. There is little to match the sheer delicacy of *Narcissus* 'Topolino', with its white petals and pale yellow cup, seen above a fragrant bed of tiny white violets. A similar effect can be achieved with the other yellow and white bicoloured daffodils, such as dainty *N*. 'Minnow' underplanted with the little white grape hyacinth, *Muscari botryoides* 'Album'. You might also like to try *N*. 'Jack Snipe', or the even smaller 'Canaliculatus' or 'Little Beauty', planted with creamy white violas or *Primula vulgaris* (wild primrose).

For strength and warmth of colour, plant the brighter, richer-coloured tulips and grape hyacinths among vibrant red, orange or blue polyanthus and primroses or amid the blues and purples of violas and pansies. Plan the borders in autumn and reap the rewards in spring. The results will be well worth the care taken over planning.

The early spring season is perfect for the border "eye" around the base of a deciduous tree. Here, the canopy of leaves will not yet have emerged, which means that sunlight and moisture will still be able to reach the ground beneath the crown. The area can then be filled with just one sort of bulb – *Narcissus*

'February Gold', for example – or a massed planting of, say, scillas, chionodoxas or *Anemone blanda*. If you are fortunate enough to have more than one suitable tree, of course, a variety of effects can be created. Given just a few years, all these bulbs will multiply, providing a wealth of colour and interest. Add a few primroses or *Tanacetum parthenium* 'Aureum' (golden feverfew), and you will have a miniature garden that is at its best in spring but that can be allowed to lie dormant for the rest of the year, except for the odd *Digitalis* (foxglove) or rambling rose. In the dry, shady summer months, the bulbs will lie dormant waiting for the cooler autumn rains to bring them into growth once more.

Anemone blanda are wonderful for use in this type of situation where they can be left to colonize undisturbed. Not only will they spread by seed, but their tubers will grow dramatically and provide a wealth of flowers. Plant them beneath an old apple or pear tree and enjoy the sea of blue in the spring sunshine. *Anemone blanda* is sold in autumn as small, hard, knobbly tubers. They can be difficult to establish in the first year, because the tubers can become too dry in the storing process between lifting

and autumn sales. It is a good idea to soak them overnight before planting. They will expand noticeably and then be ready to plant the next day. From their small beginnings in the garden centres in the autumn, the tubers will increase in size over the years to 2.5cm (1in) across, then to as much as 7.5–10cm (3–4in).

Above *Hyacinthus orientalis* 'Pink Pearl' is one of the old favourites, both for its scent and colour. Blues and pinks always look lovely together, but here the combination of the two-tone blue and white pansy, *Viola* 'Universal Marina', with the pink hyacinths is particularly charming. A group of three would work just as well as this mass planting.

Left Within just a few years *Anemone blanda* will have multiplied to create a pool of blue. Plant small pockets of early daffodils, primroses and *Tanacetum parthenium* 'Aureum' (golden feverfew). The anemones will self-seed.

Small groups of dwarf daffodils look very much at home in the damp margins

of a small stream. Narcissus pseudonarcissus and its cultivars will thrive in these

conditions, and may even cross-fertilize, resulting in many delightful variants.

naturalized bulbs for early spring

Above *Narcissus cyclamineus* has distinctive reflexed petals and a long, narrow cup. Although it is difficult to buy as a pure species, it has been used to produce many cultivars, and these are easily obtainable.

Below The little *Narcissus bulbocodium* (hoop-petticoat daffodil) has been allowed to naturalize in the Alpine Meadow at Wisley, in England. It may not prove as prolific in all conditions.

The spring grasslands are transformed by early-flowering daffodils, which are generally quite short by nature, while scillas will create a wonderful woodland display.

GRASSLAND
Generous clumps of daffodils can be planted in grass, but be sure to allow a distance of 7.5–20cm (3–8in) between each one so they have space to multiply around the original planting as well as by self-seeding.

Some species narcissi will spread extremely well if the conditions are favourable. *Narcissus bulbocodium* (hoop-petticoat daffodil), for instance, with its wide-spread cup, which is native to western France, Spain, Portugal and North Africa, seems to prefer peaty, acidic or sandy soils. The sandy conditions of the Alpine Meadow at the Royal Horticultural Society Gardens at Wisley, in England, seem to be ideal – perhaps it is the slope that is vital or the natural spring water that seeps through, or perhaps it is a combination of both factors.

Narcissus pseudonarcissus, often known as the Lent lily, looks delicate with its soft primrose petals and yellow cup. It thrives in various terrains, including meadows, woodland or rocky hillsides.

N. obvallaris, formerly known as *N. pseudonarcissus* subsp. *obvallaris* and commonly known as the Tenby daffodil, is similar in size but has deep yellow petals and cup. Both naturalize well in grass, and the Tenby daffodil will cope particularly well with shadier spots. Of all the miniature Trumpet daffodil cultivars, *N.* 'Topolino' must rank as one of the best for naturalizing in grass. It looks so delicate, with its white petals and pale yellow cup. A clump of primroses or violets close by would be perfect.

Narcissus cyclamineus, which is native to north-western Spain and Portugal, enjoys damp river banks and valley bottoms rather than the higher mountain slopes, as do all its many modern cultivars. With its swept-back petals and long, narrow cup, this is one of the easiest of the species narcissi to identify. Although the species itself is quite difficult to purchase, its progeny is vast, with garden cultivars including *N.* 'February Gold', 'Peeping Tom' and 'Jack Snipe'. Like the parent, these appreciate damp conditions. The species narcissi are sometimes available from garden centres, but you are more likely to find them through specialist bulb companies that deal by mail order.

Low-growing *Anemone blanda* and *Scilla sibirica* (Siberian squill) are better planted where finer grasses are growing, such as between shrubs or beneath deciduous trees. *S. sibirica* will cope with sun or shade, although it prefers a light, sandy soil. *A. blanda*, on the other hand, is at home in full sun or light shade, as long as the soil is well drained. Either looks pretty in a small group beside violets or wild primroses.

As with all spring bulbs grown in grassy areas, it is vital to remember that the grass should not be cut until at least six weeks after the daffodils or other bulbs have finished flowering. Only then will they have had the chance to complete their life-cycle. By this stage, their leaves will have died down and all the nutrients will have gone back into the bulbs ready for new growth in autumn. If the leaves are inadvertently removed, the bulbs may well be blind – that is, without flower – the following year.

Left *Scilla sibirica*, often known as the Siberian squill, is at home in sun or shade but prefers well-drained soils. Here it makes a charming picture in short grass with wild primroses. *S. sibirica* 'Spring Beauty', an improved form, has large, deep blue flowers.

WOODLAND

Some daffodils, such as *Narcissus obvallaris* (Tenby daffodil), and nearly all scillas thrive in the light shade of deciduous woodland, and will therefore adapt well to shady situations in the garden, where they may be grown under deciduous trees or shrubs. When you plant, leave a generous gap between each bulb so that they can multiply readily. Primroses and hellebores are their natural bedfellows, with *Hyacinthoides* (bluebell) following in mid- to late spring.

Below A bank of *Scilla bithynica* looks marvellous in the dappled sunlight beneath a broad deciduous tree.

When planting containers with bulbs, you can create great impact by opting for single-specimen planting schemes, or you can take the opportunity to mix and match for a highly colourful display.

early spring containers

Double Planting Daffodils

1 Double planting in autumn helps to create impact in a relatively small pot. Add drainage material, such as pieces of polystyrene (plastic foam) or brocken crocks, and a small covering of well-draining compost (soil mix). Plant the lower layer of bulbs, close to each other, but not touching. In this case, the bulbs used are *Narcissus* 'February Gold'.

2 Add more soil so that just the noses of the bulbs show, and plant the second layer on the shoulders of the first. Again, they should be close but not touching. Cover with more soil, bringing the level to within 2.5cm (1in) of the rim of the pot.

3 Plant a smaller, similarly coloured pot with crocus bulbs. Add a layer of drainage material and soil before placing the bulbs close together, but not touching. Depending on the number of bulbs in the package, single or double plant them. Here, there were only eight which then fitted in one layer.

4 *Narcissus* 'February Gold' flowers at the same time as these delicate *Crocus sieberi* 'Albus' (formerly known as 'Bowles White') or any of the large white, purple or blue Dutch crocuses. The result is a glorious early spring association.

Nearly all the early spring bulbs are extremely easy to grow in confined conditions and, because many of them are dwarf by nature, they have the perfect proportions for growing in containers of all descriptions.

Growing bulbs in containers offers a wonderful opportunity to show plants off as specimens in their own right. Sitting in a pot or urn on a wall or on the patio table, the plants are slightly divorced from the surrounding garden and become features in their own right, to be admired and enjoyed.

Although the planting space in a small- to medium-sized pot may be limited, it is possible to double plant the bulbs, thereby achieving a much greater impact at flowering time. It is, for example, possible to plant six bulbs of *Narcissus* 'February Gold' in a lower layer in a small glazed ceramic pot, 20cm (8in) across and 18cm (7in) deep, with, after the addition of a little more soil, six more on their shoulders. Although they would be crowded by garden standards, this is not important for container-grown bulbs, which will be grown in these circumstances for only one season. White crocuses, planted in a smaller matching glazed pot, could be planted to flower at the same time, so that their yellow stamens would provide the perfect partnership for the golden-yellow daffodils.

Below The delicate colouring of *Tulipa* 'White Virgin', a Triumph hybrid, is shown to perfection by this underplanting of beautiful, purple-blue, winter-flowering pansies. The colour of the pansies is echoed by the rich blue of the glazed pot. These tulips would look equally delightful against bright green foliage in a border.

Right Crocuses make good container specimens. Instead of allowing them to get spoiled in bad weather, when the flowers remain closed, keep them on a windowsill indoors.

Bottom Dwarf, multi-headed daffodils, such as *Narcissus* 'Tête-à-tête', are excellent in pots.

broad golden cup. All these three are short, sturdy growers, and these qualities make them excellent choices for early spring pots, window boxes and, especially, hanging baskets.

Mix the daffodils with *Anemone blanda*, in shades of blue or white or mixed colours, underplant them with large crocuses, such as *Crocus vernus* 'Remembrance', or with single tulips, such as the Kaufmanniana *Tulipa* 'Shakespeare'. Together these bulbs can create a beautiful early spring picture. Violas, *Bellis perennis* (double daisies) and primroses, combined with winter-flowering heathers and ivies, will make pretty partners.

Evergreen trails of ivy can be used to clothe the outside of a winter basket (see pages 30–31). Use a few wire staples to peg the ivy into the moss sides and so encourage the ivy to make a complete ball of greenery to form the basis of the spring bulb display. This has the added advantage of preventing the ivy from being tossed about in the cold winter winds and damaging the tip ends. Plant the basket in autumn, choosing one with a diameter of 35cm (14in). Use three ivies and a mixture of 15 dwarf multi-headed daffodils, such as dainty *N.* 'Quince', and 15 pretty blue *Anemone blanda*.

All winter hanging baskets should be hung in a sunny, sheltered position. Check that the soil is kept moist, especially in autumn and spring, but never water in frosty conditions. Although all the plants are hardy, play safe and, in severe wintry conditions, take the basket off the bracket and keep in a less exposed position on the ground or in a porch or garage for a day or two, until milder conditions return.

As the days lengthen, the Double Early tulips begin to flower. They have wide heads, full of vibrant petals, and make a wonderful show. Short and sturdy, these tulips also make good subjects for a "ground" container as well as for a hanging basket. They can be purchased as single colours, including red, orange, yellow, white and pink, or in mixed bags or boxes. *Tulipa* 'Peach Blossom' is one of the prettiest hues, starting as a pale pastel pink, sometimes revealing

Dwarf, multi-headed daffodils are an excellent choice if impact is needed but space is limited, which is true of any container. *Narcissus* 'Tête-à-tête' is extremely popular and with good reason, for one bulb will provide two or three flowers on each stem, all of which are well proportioned, with golden heads and cups to match. *N.* 'Jumblie' may be less well known, but it too will provide a mass of flowers. The cups are slightly longer and appear to look in all directions, hence its name. Another great favourite is *N.* 'Quince', which has pale yellow petals and a

streaks of green or red. It is always a winning combination when it is grown with blue *Muscari* (grape hyacinth), but any blue violas and pansies would look equally gorgeous.

For a vibrant hanging basket, try a mixture of Double Early tulips with grape hyacinths, surrounded by a frill of bedding plants such as violas and pansies. The bedding plants will provide a certain amount of colour, even in autumn, but by the time the bulbs flower in early spring they will be in full array, providing a lively and colourful background. Give this basket a sunny, sheltered position.

By now hyacinths are in flower, too. Many beautiful shades – from pink, blue, amethyst and yellow to salmon pink and white – are available, and all the colours seem to have matching or contrasting primroses, with which they associate so well. Strong on impact and excellent on perfume, they associate beautifully with other bulbs, such as the rich blues of *Scilla sibirica* and *Muscari armeniacum* (grape hyacinth), as well as all the Double Early tulips. Violas, pansies and *Tanacetum parthenium* 'Aureum' (golden feverfew) make wonderful bedfellows with them all.

Above These hybrids of *Narcissus cyclamineus*, with their swept-back petals, look beautiful with an underplanting of crocuses. Here, the fiery orange cups of *N*. 'Jetfire' bend as if to caress the bright orange stamens of *Crocus tommasinianus* 'Ruby Giant'.

Far left and left *Narcissus* 'Quince' is an excellent daffodil for inclusion in a hanging basket, because it has a sturdy, short stem and a flowering height of only about 15cm (6in). It produces several flowers on each stem, and each one has delicate pale yellow petals and a miniature broad golden cup. It associates well with blue *Anemone blanda* and the creamy variegations of the ivy leaves.

mid-spring gallery

The spring bulb garden reaches its zenith with midseason tulips and daffodils flowering together, creating one of the most colourful tapestries imaginable. The late winter and early spring bulbs are nearly all of a dwarf stature, but many of the midseason varieties, including *Leucojum aestivum* (summer snowflake), most of the daffodils and almost all tulips are much taller, growing to 35–60cm (14–24in). Meanwhile *Fritillaria imperialis* (crown imperial) rises to a stately height of 70cm (28in), making it one of the most statuesque of all bulbs. The grape hyacinths, including *Muscari armeniacum*, *M. bortryoides* 'Album' and *M. latifolium*, *Anemone nemorosa*

❮ *Leucojum aestivum* (summer snowflake) grows to a height of 45–60cm (18–24in) and likes damp conditions where it soon multiplies to create a large clump of tall, graceful, white flowers, each petal tipped with a distinctive green blotch. It flowers in mid-spring but is known as the summer snowflake to distinguish it from its earlier-flowering relative *L. vernum*, the spring snowflake. It is the perfect plant for a site near water where its swollen seed pod, filled with air, will float away and begin a new colony elsewhere.

❯ *Erythronium dens-canis* (dog's tooth violet) is native to European woodlands, and received its common name because it grows from an elongated bulb rather like a dog's tooth. It adapts well to conditions in a partially shady border or to thin grass or leafy, deciduous woodland soils. The flowers have attractive fly-away petals, while the leaves are sometimes densely mottled.

❯ *Fritillaria meleagris* (snake's head fritillary) is a favourite wild flower of European meadowlands, which adapts well to damp, grassy spots in the garden as well as to border areas. It is a plant with many common names, including the snake's head fritillary and the old-style name of "ginny-hen floure", given because the petals are patterned like feathers of a guinea hen.

❮ With a flowering height of about 30cm (12in), *Narcissus* 'Pipit' is one of the few smaller daffodils to flower in mid-spring. It produces two or three flowers on each stem, each flower being a strong lemon yellow suffused with white streaks. This is one of the most outstanding daffodils for garden and pot culture.

(wood anemone), *Hyacinthoides* (bluebell) and *Erythronium dens-canis* (dog's tooth violet) are shorter, at 15–30cm (6–12in). So are a handful of daffodils, such as *Narcissus* 'Thalia', 'Silver Chimes', 'Pipit' and 'Hawera', and a few of the species tulips, such as lilac *Tulipa saxatilis* and diminutive *T. tarda*.

While tulips and grape hyacinths prefer to bask in spring sunshine, several of the fritillaries, including *Fritillaria meleagris* (snake's head fritillary), and nearly all daffodils are happy in sun or partial shade. Others, such as wood anemones, dog's tooth violets and summer snowflakes enjoy light shade, either in damp grass or woodland.

❮ *Narcissus* 'Salome' reaches a height of about 35cm (14in) which is typical of the mid-season daffodils. It is one of the most beautiful of them all, with milky petals and a coppery pink cup, which darkens with age. It looks lovely in the border near the lime-green foliage of newly emerging herbaceous plants or in grassland beneath the white flowers of a cherry tree.

❮ The Lily-flowered *Tulipa* 'West Point', which grows to 50cm (20in), has exquisite pointed petals. It looks dramatic with strong yellows, red or blues but would also look wonderful with soft grey foliage plants, such as *Senecio cineraria*. Grow it in a sheltered position.

❯ *Muscari latifolium* is an unusual, later flowering form of the ordinary grape hyacinth, *M. armeniacum*, but with urn-shaped flowers in shades of blue, violet and black, and a wider leaf. Growing to 20cm (8in), it is native to the open pine forests of north-western Turkey.

❮ *Tulipa* 'New Design' is a beautiful pink tulip growing to 50cm (20in). It is particularly pretty with the light behind it, when its petals have a translucent appearance. Its leaves are edged with white, making it a favourite with garden designers. Enjoy it simply on its own in a pot or underplanted with variegated *Lamium maculatum* (dead nettle) and white *Bellis perennis* (daisy).

❮ The tall *Fritillaria imperialis* (crown imperial), which can achieve a height of 70cm (28in), has been a favoured bulb of gardens for more than 400 years. Inside the giant cups, large drops of nectar (sometimes called the tears of Mary) collect above the long stamens which glisten in the sunlight. The tufts of leaves at the top of the flowers are distinctive. The whole plant has an unpleasant, foxy smell.

The bulb border, whether formal or informal, is an absolute delight in mid-spring, with an infinite variety of colours. So many of the bulbs are brightly coloured that it is easy to match or clash as personal taste dictates.

mid-spring borders

Right Formal patterns with matching colour schemes can look extremely bright and cheerful. The exquisite Lily-flowered *Tulipa* 'West Point' vies for attention with red and yellow polyanthus, all bordered with the dark blue forget-me-not, *Myosotis sylvatica* 'Music'.

Below right A charming mixed spring border includes bold groups of golden daffodils, red and yellow tulips, *Tulipa* 'Striped Bellona', with large swaths of orange wallflowers, all edged with blue primulas.

Opposite, left The interplanting can be subtle, as here, where the lovely *Tulipa* 'Spring Green' has been underplanted with white bellis daisies. The results are cool and understated.

Opposite, right Quite a different effect can be gained by planting in large groups. The Viridiflora hybrid, *Tulipa* 'Christmas Marvel' is especially successful when it is planted in clumps, repeated along a path among herbaceous plants.

This is one of the most exciting times of year in the bulb garden, and it is rewarding to admire what you planted in the previous autumn, especially if you have introduced some new design ideas. For example, bright yellow *Tulipa* 'Golden Apeldoorn', orange-flecked 'Striped Apeldoorn', scarlet red 'Apeldoorn' and deep purple 'Negrita' each allow strident schemes to be developed with strongly coloured polyanthus, *Myosotis* (forget-me-not), *Bellis perennis* (daisy), pansies and *Erysimum cheiri* (wallflower) in rich shades of deep blue, orange, gold, red, black and purple. You will have wonderfully showy borders, no matter what the weather.

Meanwhile, the pastel-toned tulips, including salmon-pink *Tulipa* 'Apricot Beauty', shell pink 'Esther', 'White Dream' and the lovely cool, creamy white and green 'Spring Green', call for a softer type of colour scheme, involving paler tones of polyanthus, double bellis daisies, pansies and violas, forget-me-nots and wallflowers with combinations of primrose yellows, pale pinks, creams and pale blues. Here the effect is subtle but still beautiful.

So many different styles, both formal and informal, can be adopted. Where there is a strong design with clipped box hedging, formal lines of tulips are most appropriate. The bright green of the new growth on *Buxus* (box) looks good with scarlet tulips, but a different type of formality can be achieved if tulips are interplanted with co-ordinated bedding plants, whether you choose a strident or a subtle approach.

A more informal scheme might use different types of bulb within one large herbaceous border. A few clumps of daffodils, some *Muscari armeniacum* (grape hyacinth), just two or three *Fritillaria imperialis* (crown imperial) and three or four groups of tulips will give a wonderful effect, informal but full and colourful. It might look haphazard, but in reality will have been carefully thought out. Alternatively, you might prefer a minimalist style where bulbs are planted beneath gravel or among different coloured stones or bark, with no other plants around. It is perfectly possible to adopt more than one of these ideas in different parts of the same garden. Experiment and enjoy this wonderful season.

Anemone nemorosa (wood anemone) will naturalize large areas of deciduous woodland, creating a delicate tapestry in the middle of spring, particularly in association with Hyacinthoides (bluebell).

naturalized bulbs for mid-spring

Right *Anemone nemorosa* (wood anemone) and *Erythronium dens-canis* (dog's tooth violet) will grow happily together in leafy soil in the shade beneath trees and shrubs.

Right *Erythronium dens-canis* (dog's tooth violet) will naturalize well among fine, shady grasses.

The fledgling canopy of deciduous trees, as yet immature, still allows shafts of sunlight to reach the ground at this time of year, thus allowing many grassland or woodland bulbs to flourish, including *Erythronium dens-canis* (dog's tooth violet), *Leucojum aestivum* (summer snowflake), *Anemone nemorosa* (wood anemone) and trilliums.

One of the real stars of mid-spring is the delicate *Fritillaria meleagris* (snake's head fritillary). From a distance, their white or lilac heads hang demurely among the short grass, each flower an exquisite checkerboard pattern of intricate veining. Their season overlaps with the early dwarf daffodils and primroses, but the fritillaries will continue to flower with the cowslips and later daffodils. They like sunny, damp conditions and if they are really happy their numbers will multiply quite naturally. Even a handful in a small patch of turf is well worth trying.

Many varieties of daffodil will naturalize in grass, such as the yellow Large-cupped varieties *Narcissus* 'Saint Patrick's Day' and 'Carlton', and the Trumpet variety, *N.* 'King Alfred'. Others have white petals, including the well-known Large-cupped *N.* 'Ice Follies', with its white petals and creamy white cup. Another favourite is *N.* 'Actaea', again with white petals but this time with a distinctive, small, red-tipped cup, rather like *N. poeticus* var. *recurvus* (pheasant's eye), which will flower a few weeks later. Some daffodils have so-called pink cups, which are more a soft salmon pink which darkens with age. *N.* 'Salome', 'Rainbow' and 'Passionale' are all successful in grass.

Several other types of bulb will grow in grassy places. The nodding green and white flowers of *Ornithogalum nutans* will survive well if the soil is well drained; they will also grow among shrubs. *Hyacinthoides* (bluebell), which incidentally can be white or pink as well as blue, are a better example, but they prefer the cool, damp shade near a hedgerow or the leafy soil in a deciduous wood, especially among beech trees. Although they start to flower in mid-spring, their main season is late spring.

Dog's tooth violet prefers sparse grass, although it, too, will grow in the shade of shrubs or deciduous trees. It is one of the prettiest of the spring flowers, with its delicate, swept-back petals in white, pink or lilac. Summer snowflake likes damp soil where it has a good moist root run and will form a lovely graceful clump, whether it is grown in grass or woodland.

Another wonderful naturalizer is the wood anemone which is at its best in a deciduous wood, beneath shrubs or on a shady hillside. It will soon spread to form a dainty white carpet, looking perfect with a clump of dog's tooth violets or a group or two of bluebells. Try it beneath a spring-flowering tree or in the light shade of summer-flowering shrubs.

Above A meadow of *Fritillaria meleagris* (snake's head fritillary) is one of the most pleasing of all spring sights. Even a small patch would be endearing and give pleasure for many, many years.

Left *Leucojum aestivum* (summer snowflake) enjoys the damp, leafy soil beneath a shrub. It will form large groups where it finds moisture-retaining soil.

This is a wonderful time for spring containers, when the choice of both bulbs and bedding plants is tantalizingly generous. Choose from among narcissi, tulips and muscari – to name but a few.

mid-spring containers

Above Both the teapot and teacup are planted with *Narcissus* 'Hawera', which is a neat little daffodil with a multitude of dainty lemon-yellow flowers.

Right The Single Early *Tulipa* 'Christmas Marvel' looks cheerful in its blue pot with the silver-grey foliage of *Senecio cineraria* 'Silver Dust'. It is perfect in a container in its own right or used as an extra in the herbaceous border to add height and focus to the forget-me-nots.

Many of the short daffodils can be used in mid-spring containers. Although they are not all as dwarf as those that flower in early spring, there are several that are suitable for growing in hanging baskets, window boxes and tubs. They are all multi-headed and are valued by gardeners for providing a beautiful display where planting space is at a premium. *Narcissus* 'Hawera' is the most delicate of them all, and the tiny, lemon-yellow flowers seem to last and last. Although dainty in appearance, it has a wiry, sturdy stem and will withstand strong winds. This lovely little daffodil is excellent in hanging baskets, window boxes and small pots. Other daffodils, such as the glistening white *N*. 'Thalia', white 'Silver Chimes' and the fresh-faced, white-streaked, lemon-yellow 'Pipit', are just a little taller. This means that they are less suitable for hanging baskets, although they are perfect for pots, window boxes or troughs. They would look charming with heathers, such as *Erica carnea* 'Springwood White' or *E. arborea* 'Albert's Gold', and winter-flowering pansies.

There are so many midseason tulips at this time that it is very hard to know where to begin. Most of them grow to about 35–50cm (14–20in) in height and are, therefore, best suited to medium or large containers. All the Apeldoorn varieties, for example, with their mainly yellow, orange and scarlet blooms are excellent, being strong in growth, reliable and long lasting. The Fosteriana tulips, such as *Tulipa* 'Orange Emperor', 'Yellow Emperor' and 'Red Emperor', are also firm favourites. They do not grow quite as tall as the Apeldoorns, but are still suitable for medium to large pots. Pansies, chosen from a vast range of rich tones, including deep blue, golden yellow, yellow and red or purple, will make an excellent carpet beneath the strongly coloured blooms. *Tanacetum parthenium* 'Aureum' (golden feverfew), polyanthus and *Erysimum cheiri* (wallflower) will also make good planting partners.

If pink is your preferred colour, consider the pretty *Tulipa* 'Gordon Cooper' or 'Esther', the cherry-pink 'Christmas Marvel' or the glorious,

double, pink 'Angelique'. The soft blues and whites of violas, pansies, polyanthus as well as pale blue *Myosotis* (forget-me-not) will make ideal companions for these tulips. The silver foliage of *Senecio cineraria* 'Silver Dust' will also make an attractive partner.

When they are in the right place, however, you will find that just a few bulbs planted on their own can have a major impact. *Muscari armeniacum* 'Blue Spike', with its double florets of lovely blue flowers, looks stunning in a small pot against a simple background. This does not mean that a carefully co-ordinated scheme, brimming with tulips and underplanted with pansies, would not be equally memorable. A pair of pots planted together and arranged symmetrically could be especially striking.

Tulips and Pansies

1 medium to large blue pot

10 pretty pink, midseason tulips such as *Tulipa* 'Esther'

4 *Viola* × *wittrockiana* (pansy) such as two-toned 'Marina', 'Violet with Blotch', 'Light Blue' or 'True Blue'

1 Cover the base of the pot with a 5cm (2in) layer of drainage material, such as broken pieces of polystyrene (plastic foam) or old crocks. Half-fill the pot with a soil-based compost (potting mix) containing lots of grit, which is vital for good winter drainage.

2 If preferred, use a peat-based compost (soil-less mix) with a layer of grit mixed thoroughly in the bottom half.

3 Plant the ten tulip bulbs in two circles, spacing them so that they are not touching each other or the sides of the pot.

4 Bring the compost level to within 2.5cm (1in) of the top of the pot. Plant four blue winter-flowering pansies.

5 The result is a spring triumph of glorious soft pink tulips and winter-flowering pansies in shades of blue.

Above left *Tulipa* 'Esther' looks delightful among the pale blue forget-me-nots in this old-fashioned orchid pot. The planting scheme is evocative of a cottage garden, but could easily be adapted to a metallic or wooden container.

late spring to early summer gallery

Although most of the daffodils and many of the tulips are now over, there is still a wealth of other bulbs to follow. Late-flowering tulips are among the most exciting, both in colour and shape, and the Parrot tulips produce superb buds, with the petals tightly wrapped around each other, before opening to reveal sumptuous, full-bodied flowers, with streaks of secondary colours. One of the best of all the late tulips is the Fringed *Tulipa* 'Blue Heron', which is not blue at all, but more a warm lilac. The Single Late *T.* 'Queen of Night', a mysterious shade of dark purple, verging on black, is a great performer, whether it is grown in a formal bedding scheme, a cottage border or a container.

❮ *Tulipa* 'Blue Parrot' grows to 55cm (22in) and is a full-bodied, lilac-blue tulip which flowers at the same time as blue forget-me-nots, red or purple aubrieta, and purple- or rose-coloured wallflowers. In maturity, its large flowers are sumptuous.

❯ *Anemone coronaria* De Caen Group 'Die Braut' ('The Bride') is a beautiful, pure white, single-flowered anemone, with a contrasting apple-green centre. Best planted near the front of a sunny border, it grows to 25cm (10in) and associates well with almost any other plant. It does well in containers, too.

❯ *Allium karataviense* grows to 20cm (8in) and has rounded umbels, 5–7.5cm (2–3in) across, of small, pink, star-shaped flowers. Its broad, grey, almost elliptical leaves are a special feature. The flowerheads dry well and look attractive throughout the summer.

❮ *Camassia leichtlinii* subsp. *suksdorfii* Caerulea Group is a good subject for borders or damp grassland, where it will multiply and eventually create large groups of tall blue flower spikes, growing to 75cm (30in) high. Although the flowering period is all too short, the impact is magnificent.

The tall *Camassia* (quamash) from North America, which are also known as Indian lilies or American bluebells, are useful for sunny borders or grassland. They may be blue or white, and both forms associate well with the last of the daffodils, *Narcissus poeticus* var. *recurvus* (pheasant's eye).

For the front of a sunny border *Anemone coronaria* hybrids will make a real splash of colour with their brilliant red, white or blue flowers. Cheap and cheerful, they are also suitable for containers. Meanwhile, alliums and Dutch irises provide rich colours, from white to lilac and purple, and there are also beautiful gold and yellow irises.

❮ *Tulipa* 'Queen of Night', a tall tulip at 60cm (24in), is described as satin black but is really a deep, dark purple. It looks lovely with pale blue forget-me-nots or with tall, purple alliums, with which it overlaps for a fleeting moment. Perhaps the best of all partners, however, are richly scented, orange wallflowers.

❮ *Allium cristophii* grows 60cm (24in) high and has round, open heads, about 20cm (8in) across, with large, star-shaped, amethyst-blue flowers. The leaves are long and strappy and appear early, before beginning to dry off as the flowers open. The huge seedheads are useful in dried flower arrangements.

❯ *Iris* 'Purple Sensation' grows to 45cm (18in) and is one of the many bulbous Dutch irises that are useful for bridging the gap in the sunny border between the late tulips and the taller alliums. They look lovely in small groups beneath wisterias or laburnums and are pretty with pale yellow wallflowers.

❮ Tall *Tulipa* 'Blue Heron' grows to 60cm (24in), and is a strong, elegant tulip, with fringing around its lilac petals. Grow it in the border or in large pots underplanted with orange- or primrose-coloured wallflowers or 'Ivory and Rose Blotch' winter-flowering pansies.

❮ *Allium schubertii* grows to 40cm (16in) and has flowerheads that are about 30cm (12in) across, with an inner compact ball of flowers and an outer sphere shooting off like fireworks. It is certainly a talking point, both when it is in flower and when it is seen as a dried specimen.

Alliums and Dutch irises are perfect for late spring to early summer herbaceous borders, as well as for planting beneath arches of wisteria, laburnum or Robinia hispidia (rose acacia).

late spring to early summer borders

Above *Tulipa* 'Blue Parrot' can be used in a massed bedding display with *Aubrieta* 'Royal Red', which provides a profusion of carmine red flowers beneath the lilac-pink tulip.

Left *Camassia leichtlinii* subsp. *suksdorfii* Caerulea Group is another candidate for mass bedding, here seen with an underplanting of the purple wallflower, *Erysimum cheiri* 'Prince Purple'.

The late tulips are among some of the most sensational of all, particularly the Parrot types, with their full-bodied, curvy petals. *Tulipa* 'Fantasy' is a mixture of salmon pink and reds, with flushes of yellow and green, and it looks wonderful when it is grown with lime-green or deep bronze foliage plants. *T.* 'Blue Parrot' is more lilac than blue, and it looks marvellous with many spring bedding plants, including rose- or purple-coloured wallflowers, rose-pink or pale blue pansies and various shades of aubrieta.

The tall and slender camassias, with their tapering flower spikes, are lovely, whether the white or blue form is grown. They are a versatile bulb and adapt well to the border and to unmown grassy areas as long as the soil is damp and the site is sunny. A spot beside a garden pond would be ideal, but they look just as attractive in a clump in an herbaceous border or in formal bedding patterns with wallflowers as their partner.

Dutch irises can be relied on to provide colour year after year, and each of the beautifully shaped flowers has intricate veining on the petals and falls. They vary in colour from white through to yellow, blue and purple, and sometimes a mixture of more than one colour. For a short period they will be in flower at the same time as the alliums, and together they make an exciting partnership. Indeed, alliums and Dutch irises have a host of suitable homes, including the mixed herbaceous border, the cottage-style garden, or beneath arches of wisteria, laburnum or *Robinia hispidia*.

Most of the alliums are hardy and reliable, unless your garden is one that is visited by rabbits in the early morning. The tallest, at 1.2m (4ft), is the lilac-purple *Allium giganteum*, and the next in stature is the deep purple *A. hollandicum* 'Purple Sensation', which grows to 90cm (3ft). The white *A. nigrum*, which is 70cm (28in) high, is slightly later to flower than the purple and lilac forms, but it looks lovely with silver *Cynara cardunculus* (cardoon) and *Hesperis matronalis* var. *albiflora* (the white form of sweet rocket). Rather shorter is the pale lilac

A. hollandicum (syn. *A. aflatunenese*), which has a flowering height of 60cm (24in); it associates well with the taller *A. hollandicum* 'Purple Sensation' and *A. giganteum*, adding another tier to the picture. Of medium height but larger in flower size and more open in shape is *A. cristophii*, which is followed by *A. schubertii*, which has even larger flowerheads but, at 40cm (16in), is slightly shorter.

All these allium flowers are notable additions to the garden, and their seedheads will last for weeks if not months. The only drawback is the leaves, which appear well before the flower buds emerge, and by the time the flowers open they look very untidy. It is best to grow some other leafy plant nearby to hide the mess, and wallflowers are a perfect foil. In contrast, the foliage of *A. karataviense* is an asset. The broad grey leaves lend themselves to a more minimalist approach, and a carpet of red gravel will provide a sharp, clean background

For a shady spot in the garden, however, *Hyacinthoides* (bluebell) are the answer, providing a generous sea of blue beneath trees and under shrubs. Available in blue, pink or white they will settle down with ease and provide a generous progeny.

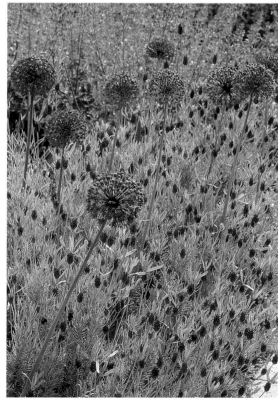

Above *Allium cristophii* creates a striking contrast to the flower spikes of *Saliva sylvestris* 'Lye End'. An underplanting of *Geranium sanguineum* 'Album' lightens the purple palette of this border.

Right The tall and stately *Allium hollandicum* 'Purple Sensation', with its rich purple, star-shaped flowers, towers over a sea of purple *Lavandula stoechas* (French lavender). This allium also looks wonderful beneath long trails of wisteria and laburnum. The seedheads will remain a special feature for many weeks.

In a shady spot in the garden, and most strikingly beneath a collection of trees or shrubs, Hyacinthoides (bluebell) will provide a sea of blue, pink or white, and, once established, will multiply at a good pace.

naturalized bulbs for late spring

Both *Hyacinthoides* (bluebell) and camassias will grow in grass and naturalize well where the conditions suit them, but bluebells prefer a cooler, shadier site while camassias prefer sunny spots. Both plants, however, like moisture-retentive soil. Camassias make an ideal partnership with *Narcissus poeticus* var. *recurvus* (pheasant's eye), which is the last of the daffodils, both flowering in late spring and providing colour long after many of the spring bulbs have finished.

Do not be in a hurry to mow the grass. Leave it for at least six weeks, after the bulbs have finished flowering, before it is cut. By then, the bulbs will have completed their life-cycles and will be resting until root growth starts again in autumn.

Not many gardeners are lucky enough to have an entire woodland to plant with beautiful bluebells, but the blue carpet can still look extremely pretty, even on a relatively modest scale, such as when it is confined to the eye of a single fruit tree or the awkward area beneath spring- or summer-flowering shrubs. Plant bluebells in groups in autumn and allow them to self-seed. Pink and white strains are also available.

Above left Camassias are a major feature of the spring garden. They will naturalize in grass and give years of pleasure. The first buttercups add further colour to the picture.

Left This beautiful white form of *Hyacinthoides non-scripta* (English bluebell) will create a superb carpet of colour from mid- to late spring, transforming deciduous woodlands into one of the best of all spring scenes. Bluebells look lovely in small areas, too, and any shrubby part of the garden is suitable. They will also look attractive beneath fruit trees.

Right The woodland is a wonderful picture now that the *Hyacinthoides non-scripta* (English bluebell) are in full flower, looking like a vast sheet of blue beneath a canopy of emerging oak leaves. They have a sweet, heady perfume, which can be almost over-powering on a large scale. They self-seed freely.

While most of the tulips are over by mid-spring, there are a few noteworthy late flowering specimens, including Tulipa *'Queen of Night' and 'Blue Heron', as well as all the Parrot tulips.*

late spring to early summer containers

With a little careful planning, late-flowering tulips can look sensational in large pots underplanted with old-fashioned red, yellow, orange, purple, rose-pink or white *Erysimum cheiri* (wallflower) or one of the self-coloured or bicoloured winter-flowering pansies. Some brilliant colour schemes can be devised, with both bright, eye-catching plants and gentler, more subtle shades. The Fringed *Tulipa* 'Blue Heron', which has lilac-coloured petals, creates a strong contrast, for example, with rich orange wallflowers, whose scent is welcome on a warm sunny evening. A more restful colour scheme could be achieved by substituting a pale primrose-coloured wallflower or even a rose-pink or purple form.

Wallflowers are usually treated as biennials – that is, they are sown in late spring one year and flower the next. They are normally sold in autumn, either as growing plants in bedding boxes or in bunches of eight or ten with just a little soil attached to their bare roots. They should be thoroughly watered and planted as soon as possible in a sunny position, where they will start to flower the following spring. Once they begin, the show will continue for many weeks, contributing an informal, cottage-garden style to your pots and containers.

For a combination of tulips and wallflowers, prepare the container in the usual way, using drainage material and a soil-based compost (potting mix). Plant ten tulip bulbs so that their eventual depth below soil level is about three times their own height, allowing for a 5cm (2in) gap at the top of the container. Plant seven or eight wallflowers in a wide circle, choosing those plants with the best root systems and discarding the rest. Firm in the plants and water well. Place the container in a sunny sheltered position.

Anemone coronaria hybrids also make excellent container displays, and they can be used to produce many different effects, with colours ranging from brilliant red to rich blue. *A. coronaria* De Caen Group 'The Governor' has bright red flowers, while those of *A. c.* 'Die Braut' ('The Bride') are pure white and the double blooms of *A. c.* St Bridgid Group 'Lord

A Display of Anemones

1 The knobbly tubers of *Anemone coronaria* benefit from being soaked overnight in water to plump them up before planting.

2 Where possible, plant the anemone tubers with their protruding knobs pointing upwards (this is not apparent on all of them), 7.5cm (3in) deep and about 7.5cm (3in) apart.

3 Successive plantings of *Anemone coronaria* tubers provide colour for weeks on end. Enjoy the glorious colours of *Anemone coronaria* De Caen Group 'The Governor'.

Below Some anemones are blue, including the multi-petalled *Anemone coronaria* St Bridgid Group 'Lord Lieutenant'.

Above right *Tulipa* 'Fantasy', a Parrot tulip, has been under-planted with the blue pansy, *Viola × wittrockiana* 'True Blue'.

Opposite Orange-coloured varieties of wallflower are among the most strongly scented. By late spring they will be joined by the *Tulipa* 'Blue Heron' – tall, strong and beautifully shaped, with finely fringed petals.

Lieutenant' are deep blue. In addition, the fern-like foliage is attractive in its own right. Judicious planting at intervals in spring and early summer will give a succession of blooms, while planting two or three pots at the same time will give a sumptuous display. The knobbly tubers are best rehydrated by being soaked overnight before planting. Plant with buds pointing upwards at a depth of about 7.5cm (3in) and 7.5cm (3in) apart, allowing at least three months between planting and early summer flowering, although earlier planting will take longer to produce blooms. Allow the tubers to dry off completely after the life cycle is complete, ready for flowering again the following year.

mid- to late summer gallery

The summer gallery contains many glorious lilies, including familiar border plants like *Lilium regale* (regal lily) as well as a host of others, in all shades of pink, orange, yellow and salmon pink and also in white. Some lilies are now bred without stamens to help those who are allergic to pollen, and these are generally sold as "Kiss" lilies.

Many of the summer bulbs and corms produce tall plants, but exceptional among them all are the cardiocrinums, which can grow to 2–4m (6–12ft) in height. With their long, scented, trumpet-shaped flowers, they are a spectacular choice for a shrubbery or woodland area. Shorter, but still tall, is the creamy white *Galtonia candicans*

❮ *Gladiolus* 'Seraphin', which is a tender, early-flowering, butterfly-type variety, grows to 70cm (28in). It bears ruffled, pink flowers, each with a creamy white throat, and it looks especially good near lime green or yellow. Plant in spring in the herbaceous border to provide colour from mid- to late summer. Lift the corms in autumn.

❯ *Agapanthus praecox* subsp. *maximus* 'Albus' grows to 60–90cm (2–3ft) from thick, fleshy roots, which should be planted in late winter or early spring. They form bold clumps, bearing rounded umbels of large, white, trumpet-shaped flowers. Grow agapanthus in a sunny border beneath a south-facing wall or in pots in a soil-based compost (potting mix), and bring into a dry, frost-free area in winter. They flower best when overcrowded.

❯ *Zantedeschia aethiopica* 'Crowborough', the hardiest of the arum lilies, grows to 90cm (3ft) and is suitable for a damp border or near to a pond. Grow in sun or partial shade. The rhizomes can be treated as an aquatic plant and grown in a planting basket in heavy loam. The large, arrow-shaped leaves are joined in summer by the distinctive funnel-shaped flowers.

❮ Growing to 60–90cm (2–3ft), *Lilium lancifolium* (syn. *L. tigrinum*; tiger lily) has vibrant orange flowers, marked with maroon spots, the same colour as the anthers. Plant the bulbs in autumn or late winter to early spring as soon as they are available. Although it prefers moist, acid conditions, this lily is tolerant of a wide range of soils. Many hybrids have been developed from the species, including *Lilium* 'Enchantment' and 'Pink Tiger'. All associate well with the dark rich colours of hollyhocks or bronze foliage plants, and they are easy to grow in borders or containers.

(Cape hyacinth), as is *Crocosmia* 'Lucifer', whose flowering stems, bearing rich red flowers, might need support. Gladioli are another feature of the summer border, with colourful flowers on long thrusting stems, while elegant white, pink or yellow zantedeschia make a bold statement with their exotic, funnel-shaped, perpendicular flowers.

Begonias also flower throughout summer and well into autumn; they may be upright in habit or trailing, with single or double red, yellow, orange, white or pink flowers, which are sometimes two-toned. Always sumptuous in appearance, they are one of the mainstays of summer containers, although they look lovely in borders too.

❮ *Crocosmia* 'Lucifer' is a graceful plant from South Africa, growing to 90cm (3ft) and bearing exotic sprays of deep orange flowers on tall arching stems. These may need support in a windy spot. Plant the corms in spring, in sun or partial shade, and leave to become established in large clumps. It looks stunning against bronze or light green foliage.

❮ *Gladiolus* 'Charming Beauty' grows to 60cm (24in) and is a hardy variety. The small, rose-coloured, funnel-shaped flowers, with their pointed petals, are delicate to look at and early to appear. Plant the corms when they are available in autumn or spring. An ideal site would be a south-facing border beneath a sunny wall. Leave the corms undisturbed after flowering.

❯ *Galtonia candicans* (Cape hyacinth) grows to 1.1m (3ft 6in) and bears tall spikes of creamy white, pendent flowers. Plant bulbs in early spring in bold groups towards the back of the herbaceous border, where the flowers will add height and grace.

❮ *Lilium regale* (regal lily) does well in containers and grows to 60–180cm (2–6ft). It bears large, white, scented, trumpet-shaped flowers that are streaked with purple on the outside. Plant bulbs in autumn or late winter to early spring as soon as they become available. The regal lily grows well in sun or partial shade and sets seed easily. It is a lime-tolerant, stem-rooting lily which is suitable for a sunny border among spiky lavender or deep purple roses. Do not disturb bulbs once they have been planted.

❮ *Begonia* 'Double Orange' is a vigorous plant, growing to 20cm (8in) and producing large double flowers that are suitable for centre stage in sheltered hanging baskets or in window boxes. The tubers should be planted indoors in late winter or early spring, ready to move outdoors after all risk of frost has passed. Different forms are available in white, pinks, yellows or reds, and are suitable for any colour scheme.

Summer is rich in both colour and variety. Imagine great swaths of crocosmia swaying in the sunshine, forming vibrant patches of oranges, reds and yellows among clumps of gladioli, hemerocallis, tall grasses, veronicas and phlox.

mid- to late summer borders

Above The strappy leaves of agapanthus look good with tall grasses. Blue *Agapanthus* 'Ben Hope' forms a wonderful large grouping in front of the frothy masses of *Chionochloa conspicua* (plumed tussock grass).

Right An all-white section of the border is lovely on hot summer days. White *Agapanthus praecox* subsp. *maximus* 'Albus' contrasts well with the spiky *Veronicastrum virginicum* var. *album*. White dahlias and white gladioli would have a similar effect.

Summer is the season for rich blue or white agapanthus, which crowd together near the front of the border, basking in the heat, while sand-coloured eremurus dominate the back, along with the dainty white spires of galtonias. Groups of yellow, pink, white or orange lilies create more focal points along the way, all planted to provide the magical highlights of this time of year. Apart from the tender gladioli and begonias, all these can be left to mature and multiply for another year.

Agapanthus and eremurus are familiar plants that make a significant contribution to the summer border, but they do not fall into any of the four main categories discussed in this book of bulbs, corms, tubers and rhizomes. Instead these plants have developed thick, fleshy roots to combat the annual droughts they experience in their native habitats. For this reason, they are brought under the wider umbrella of bulbs.

In many gardens, tuberous begonias are planted out in early summer to create brilliant splashes of colour throughout summer and early autumn, a performance that will last for months, not weeks, as is the case with most of the plants described so far. Begonias can be used to create formal patterns of contrasting or matching shades with other summer bedding plants, such as nasurtiums and lobelias, depending on aspect. They will perform well both in full sun and partial shade.

The same formal treatment can also be given to gladioli, whose colour range is as exciting as it is enticing, varying from shades of lilac through pink and salmon pink to cream, yellow and white. Some of the taller types grow to more than 1m (39in) high, but there are also many shorter ones, growing to about 70cm (28in), and a smaller group, known as the Nanus gladioli, which grow to about 60cm (24in). Depending on their height, they can be mixed with other summer annuals, such as crimson, pink or white cosmos, or planted in front of bronze *Atriplex hortensis* (orache). Just be sure to give them a sunny home. Meanwhile, there are lots of herbaceous plants, such as helenium and achillea which would make excellent associations.

Left *Crocosmia* 'Lucifer' produces tall, elegant sprays of rich red flowers, which last for several weeks. They show up well against the bold foliage of the young cannas in the background – this one is *Canna* 'Striata' (syn. *C.* 'Malawiensis Variegata') – and link well with the golden achillea behind.

Far left The luscious white blooms of this tall gladiolus make a winning contribution to this summer scene, cool and elegant, and quite at home among the softer shapes of *Cosmos* 'Sonata Pink' and *Astrantia major* 'Ruby Wedding'.

Left *Eremurus* 'Oase' forms a dense mass of flower spikes, about 90–120cm (3–4ft) high, which are perfect at the back of a sunny herbaceous border, where a dark green background can show them off to full advantage. Dark-leaved cotinus would also make a wonderful planting association.

Right *Cardiocrinum giganteum*
is a giant among lilies with a
height of between 2–4m
(6–12ft). It has enormous,
heart-shaped leaves and an
array of white, pendent,
trumpet-shaped flowers, which
are strongly scented. The
bulb dies after flowering, but
produces lots of offsets, which
will flower in future years. To
have a continuous show of
flowers, you will need to plant
one or two bulbs each year in
autumn for about three years,
which should then establish a
good succession. This is an ideal
plant for a sheltered, shady
border among low shrubs or on
the edge of a woodland garden.

Above right *Lilium regale* (regal
lily) is happy in sun or partial
shade. It is lovely as a single dot
lily in a formal border or in front
of a weeping pink standard rose
such as *Rosa* 'The Fairy'. The
regal lily is also gorgeous as a
bounteous group with other
herbaceous plants. We should
be thankful that E.H. Wilson
successfully introduced it
from China's remote western
mountains in 1910.

Below right *Lilium* Golden
Splendour Group is a special lily
with golden, trumpet-shaped
flowers backed by streaks of
burgundy. It looks good here in
front of the purple stems of
Eupatorium purpureum. It
would look equally sensational
against the bronze foliage of
dark-leaved *Cotinus*, *Foeniculum
vulgare* 'Purpureum' (bronze
fennel) or copper beech.

SHADY BORDERS

Not all garden borders are in a sunny location. Many, indeed most, will receive some shade for at least a few hours of the day, and where this occurs *Zantedeschia* (arum lily) and crocosmias will still flourish, as will many lilies. Most lilies enjoy sunshine on their flowers, but they like to have their roots in shade, and so many are happy to have half the day in sun and half in shade. Some plants, such as *Lilium martagon* (martagon lily) and tall cardiocrinums, will thrive in dappled shade all day long. Cardiocrinums have a sweet scent, as do most lilies, and of all the lilies, *Lilium regale* has one of the best, with a strong, heady perfume that hangs on the evening air.

Tall lilies – and sun-loving gladioli, eremurus and *Crocosmia* 'Lucifer' – will benefit from support, especially when in full flower with heavy heads, or if they are planted in a windy spot.

Staking Lilies

1 First position the metal stake, 15cm (6in) away from the emerging stem. Release one side of the ring and carefully trap the lily stem within.

2 Clip the second end of the ring into the hole provided on the metal support. The lily now has freedom to move but cannot stray too far.

Left *Lilium martagon* (martagon lily) grows 90–180cm (3–6ft) tall and has attractive, but unscented, glossy, pinkish-purple, pendent flowers with darker spots. The flowers are in the shape of a Turk's cap, hence one of its common names, the Turk's cap lily. Plant in autumn or late winter to early spring as soon as the bulbs are available. This is an easy, lime-tolerant, clump-forming lily, which is ideal for planting in partial shade between summer-flowering shrubs.

Beautiful blue triteleias are rarely grown, but they are perfect for borders or containers, where they can follow on from spring-flowering daffodils and hyacinths or provide colour until autumn-flowering bulbs appear.

mid- to late summer containers

Right *Lilium* 'Enchantment' is one of the easiest of all lilies to propagate. Small, black bulbils appear on the stem after flowering, drop off and take root in the compost (potting mix) below. They are best removed in late autumn, every year or second year, during the early winter dormancy period when the main bulbs can be potted on into new compost, and the young plants can be grown on in a separate pot.

Far right Begonias will tolerate sunny conditions and make good planting companions for lampranthus and coleus.

Below right *Triteleia laxa* 'Koningin Fabiola' is a useful summer-flowering corm to add in autumn to a spring-flowering bulb display with daffodils, for example. The narrow, grass-like leaves appear before the flowers, so an evergreen anchor plant, such as *Helleborus foetidus*, is important because it provides background foliage to show off the dainty blue blooms. *Triteleia* also make a delightful display under dwarf yellow lilies.

Many of the hardy summer-flowering bulbs make excellent container plants, and they will perform well year after year. *Zantedeschia* (arum lily), agapanthus, lilies and triteleia can all be grown in containers and are best planted in a gritty, soil-based compost (potting mix). If arum lilies are grown in water, use an aquatic soil and an aquatic planting basket, with perforations around the outside.

Lilies can remain in the same container for many years if they are potted on into new compost occasionally. *Lilium regale* (regal lily) does very well, as do some of the Asiatic hybrids, such as 'Enchantment'. The Oriental lily hybrids derived from *L. speciosum* and *L. auratum* (golden-rayed lily) are later flowering and make brilliant pot plants too. 'Stargazer', which has deep crimson petals, is of special note. Plant three lily bulbs together to create a mass effect and, for extra colour and contrast, underplant with gorgeous blue triteleias. These look particularly attractive with yellow lilies. Always choose a deep pot for lilies, at least 30cm (12in) deep, and use well-drained soil. If you use a peat-based compost (soil-less mix), add extra grit. Apply a low-nitrogen but high-phosphate and high-potash feed for six to eight weeks from the first opening of buds. Deadhead and allow the leaves to die back before removing the stem. Lilies are hardy but need extra protection in hard winters when they are grown in pots, so bring them into a sheltered spot and cover with bubble wrap if necessary.

BEGONIAS

These are probably the most colourful and versatile of all the summer container plants mentioned here. They are ideal for pots, hanging baskets, wall-pots and window boxes, but they will not tolerate frost. They are available as growing plants in early summer, but to make sure of the widest possible choice of colours, choose the tubers in late winter, and plant them in late winter or early spring so that they are ready to plant out after the frosts have finished in early summer.

If you want to save tubers for next year, bring the plants into a frost-free place and withhold water. Allow the foliage to die down. After two or three weeks, remove the tubers and store them in a dry, cool place until the following spring when they can be brought into growth once more.

Begonia tubers suffer badly from being eaten by vine weevil grubs in early autumn. To overcome this, use a natural predator, such as beneficial nematodes, or a specialist compost (potting mix) containing a systemic insecticide, which stops the grubs maturing.

A Begonia Hanging Basket
35cm (14in) wire hanging basket
1 upright orange double begonia
4 trailing begonias, such as 'Giant Flowered Pendula Yellow' or 'Giant Flowered Pendula Orange'
2 trailing yellow-flowered *Bidens*

1 Line the basket with moss, bringing the moss right up the sides. Cut several slits in a circle of black plastic for drainage and then use it to cover the moss. Add 7.5–10cm (3–4in) of compost (potting mix), mixed with water-retaining crystals and a long-term pelleted feed.

2 Plant the upright begonia in the centre of the basket.

3 Plant the trailing begonias and yellow *Bidens* around the edge. Top up with compost and water well. Choose a sheltered site in sun or partial shade.

4 Water every other day, or every day in hot weather, taking care not to splash the leaves, particularly if the sun is shining.

5 Deadhead regularly, removing fading blooms and seedheads.

6 The hanging basket (see also far left) is splendid in its summer glory. Easy to look after and very colourful, all the tubers can be saved for next year without the need for a greenhouse.

autumn gallery

The autumn borders are an absolute delight, with exotic dahlias and cannas vying for attention with strident colours and bold foliage. Both need to be lifted before winter, but several autumn-flowering plants can be left in the ground for many years. Eucomis, for example, have stout spikes surrounded by starry pink or green flowers, with a tuft of leaves at the top that gives rise to the common name, pineapple flower. Autumn is also the time when nerines bear their large heads of frilly, bright pink, trumpet-shaped flowers, which bloom on naked stems, with the leaves appearing later. Dahlias, cannas, nerines and eucomis are all excellent container plants.

❮ *Eucomis bicolor* has a flowering height of up to 60cm (24in) and is commonly known as the pineapple flower because of the tuft of small leaves that grows on top of all the flowers, rather like those on a pineapple fruit. The flower spike is dense, with small, starry, waxy flowers, each tinged with pink. It can be grown singly in a small pot or as a group in a large container. Alternatively, try a clump of three or five at the front of a sheltered, sunny border.

❯ *Canna indica* 'Purpurea' grows to 2m (6ft) and has leaves with bronze edges and veining. The orange-red flowers are less showy but attractive nonetheless. It needs lifting before any severe autumnal frosts.

❯ *Dahlia* 'Clair de Lune' grows to about 1.1m (3ft 6in) high. A Collerette dahlia, the flowers have an open centre, surrounded by a collar of short, flat petals or florets, as they are correctly known, and a single outer row of florets. The light yellow colouring is welcome and shows up well in the border, particularly in the evening light.

❮ *Colchicum autumnale* 'September', which grows to 15cm (6in), is a cultivar of the most commonly grown species. It is happy in full sun or partial shade in well-drained border soil or in rough grass. Each flower is held on a slender, rather weak tube. The leaves follow in spring.

Colchicums are found in various shades of lilac, pink and white and will grow in borders or grass in sun or partial shade. They are often confusingly referred to as autumn crocus because of the shape of their flowers. In fact, several true crocuses flower in autumn; *Crocus sativus* (saffron crocus) is probably the best known.

Other autumn highlights include the sternbergias, with their bright yellow, crocus-like flowers, the crinums which produce a wonderful array of large, pink, funnel-shaped flowers, and the open, cup-shaped flowers of *Schizostylis coccinea* (Kaffir lily), available in shades of pink or red.

❮ *Crinum × powellii* grows to about 1m (39in) and produces a rosette of broad, bright green, fleshy leaves. These are followed by a stout stem with remarkably pretty, funnel-shaped, pink flowers. It is a focal point of the autumn garden but requires thoughtful lower planting companions to hide the untidy leaves.

❮ *Nerine bowdenii* produces its flowers before the leaves. Growing to 45cm (18in), it likes a sunny, sheltered spot – beneath a south-facing wall is ideal or, if it is in a border, make sure it is at or near the front so that other plants do not cast shade.

❯ *Canna* 'Wyoming' is a tall-growing rhizome with broad bronze leaves and large, flamboyant, orange flowers. It must be lifted before any severe autumnal frosts. Plant near other orange flowers, such as dahlias, or in front of silver-leaved plants such as *Eucalyptus gunnii* (cider gum).

❮ *Schizostylis coccinea* 'Sunrise' is a clump-forming, rhizomatous perennial, up to 60cm (24in) tall, bearing spikes of fine, salmon-pink flowers. This is a plant that loves damp soil at the front of a sunny border. It will also grow well in containers.

❮ *Cyclamen hederifolium* is a carpeting plant, growing to only 10cm (4in) tall, which produces its tiny blooms either before or at the same time as the leaves. The flowers have the characteristic nodding heads with fly-away petals of all species of cyclamen and come in various shades of pink or white. The foliage is similar to ivy in shape and has attractive veining. It prefers well-drained soil in light shade beneath a group of trees or shrubs or in the "eye" of a fruit tree.

The autumn border is bursting with fiery gems, evident in both foliage and flowers, and there is a vast selection of orange, gold, red and purple blooms to treasure before the onset of winter.

autumn borders

Autumn gardens are full of contrasting shapes. The tall, slender flower spikes of cannas rise above the large, oval leaves, sometimes with brilliant colouring, which spiral around the stem. In contrast, dahlia flowers are round, ranging from the large, open flowers of the Single forms to the round, tight balls of the Pompon varieties. Some dahlias – *Dahlia* 'Bishop of Llandaff', for example – have bronze leaves.

Begonias of all descriptions will still be looking wonderful, mature now after the long growing season. The long flower spikes of late plantings of gladioli will bring colour, too. All these plants are from hot climates and need to be lifted before winter, but with proper care many will live for years and can be easily propagated.

Hardy plants thrive elsewhere in the borders, often beneath a sunny sheltered wall. Here, nerines, eucomis and sternbergias flourish where the hot sun can bake their bulbs. Colchicums will thrive here, too, although they will also cope with shadier spots beneath shrubs, together with tiny cyclamen and the giant crinums.

Left Dahlias, cannas and grasses make a delightful autumnal picture, graceful and artistic without being overpowering. The border includes *Dahlia* 'Ellen Huston' and *D.* 'David Howard', *Canna* 'Striata' (syn. *C.* 'Malawiensis Variegata') and the ornamental grasses *Calamagrostis* × *acutiflora* 'Karl Foerster' (feather reed grass), *Miscanthus sinensis* and *Cortaderia selloana* 'Pumila' (small pampas grass).

Below left The copper-orange flowers of *Canna* 'Wyoming' set a beautiful autumn scene with *Dahlia* 'David Howard'.

Below right *Dahlia* 'Witteman's Superb' blazes with glorious colour on a foggy autumn morning. It is planted with *Verbena bonariensis*.

Opposite, left By the end of the season, *Canna indica* 'Purpurea' has formed a large clump, growing in the damp margins of a pond, where it enjoys the warmth and moisture.

Opposite, right *Dahlia* 'Tally-ho' has unusual foliage with rich blue tones which makes an exciting association with *Sedum telephium* subsp. *maximum* 'Atropurpureum' (orpine).

Autumn rains and cooler weather mean that the woodland garden or shrubbery can take on a new lease of life when little Cyclamen hederifolium *starts to flower in various shades of pink and white.*

naturalized bulbs for autumn

Both autumn grasslands and woodlands can be rich with flowers. Colchicums, for example, which are happy in sun or partial shade, will grow in grass or lightly shaded woodland areas.

Colchicum autumnale has a rather weak tube to support the flower, and sometimes flops over after a shower. Grow it in grass, where the heads may be supported by the grass itself. *C. bivonae* is a sturdier plant and again easily grown, although it is susceptible to frost in severe winters, so choose a sheltered site. *C. speciosum* is a stronger-growing plant, which will cope with frost and which can be grown in grass in the shade of a shrub or even in a sunny border. However, be aware that the tall strappy colchicum leaves appear after the flowers. They will be very evident in spring and must not be prematurely removed.

Although totally different in scale, cyclamen enjoy the partial shade of a shrubbery or woodland and will spread with ease to create a beautiful autumnal carpet.

Below *Cyclamen hederifolium* creates a carpet of tiny pink and white flowers, self-seeding happily on the woodland floor. A smaller patch would look lovely beneath deciduous shrubs, such as spring-flowering currants (*Ribes*), forsythia or azaleas.

Right *Colchicum bivonae* reaches 10–15cm (4–6in) in height, and its large, funnel-shaped flowers have the advantage of being sturdier than *C. autumnale*.

Opposite, top *Colchicum autumnale*, which is often called meadow saffron, is the commonest of all the species. The pale pink flowers grow about 15cm (6in) high on slender, rather weak tubes. The leaves follow later. It is easily grown in a carpet of rough grass to give it support if the heads flop and to provide a good background colour to show off the pretty flowers.

Opposite, below right *Colchicum speciosm* 'Rosy Dawn' makes a delightful woodland ground cover with *Epimedium rubrum* and periwinkles. It would also look good in the border eye beneath a single tree. It has a stronger flower tube than *Colchicum autumnale*.

Right *Colchicum speciosm* 'Album' flowers in autumn on naked stems with the leaves following in the spring. However, a backdrop of foliage may be supplied in the autumn using a different plant. Here, the foliage is provided by the tiny, grey leaves of *Helichrysum petiolare* 'Variegatum'.

bulbs indoors

The range of bulbs available for growing indoors is extensive, with the opportunity to develop flower displays that are widely spread throughout the year.

Colour in the cooler months is achieved by maintaining frost-free conditions and providing gentle heat for a wonderful range of miniature and fringed cyclamens, as well as gorgeous Hippeastrum *(amaryllis)*. Meanwhile, by growing Narcissus papyraceus *(syn. N. 'Paper White')* and commercially prepared hyacinth bulbs, we can enjoy colour and scent in the middle of winter.

In the hotter, brighter months, indoor planting schemes can produce exotic results with the climbing Gloriosa superba *'Rothschildiana'*, shapely eucomis, colourful achimenes and gloxinias. Yet more plants can be grown either inside or outside in summer, such as freesias, the St Bridgid or De Caen hybrids of anemones, begonias, cannas and Zantedeschia *(arum lily)*.

clockwise from bottom left: hyacinth, hippeastrum and daffodil bulbs

Most bulbs, corms, tubers and rhizomes will tolerate being lifted, cleaned, stored and sold in packets in garden centres and market places. What better way to brighten up the cold winter months than by growing an array of bulbs indoors?

growing techniques

Above Although sturdy in physique, hyacinth bulbs are susceptible to virus diseases and fungus problems. They are, therefore, often treated with a special chemical to maintain their health. Touching the bulbs can produce a mild allergic reaction, so people who have susceptible skins should wear gloves when they handle them.

Above right A plastic pot with drainage holes can be used inside a pretty pot. Place the inner pot on a layer of gravel to the right height. Use more gravel in the inner pot as drainage. Any excess water will drain through to create a moist pool beneath the base, which is helpful in summer when the compost (soil mix) can dry out quickly.

Right Hyacinths cope with a shallow container, only 7.5cm (3in) deep, although they are happy with a deeper root run.

P ackets of commercially prepared hyacinth bulbs, *Hippeastrum* (amaryllis) and *Narcissus papyraceus* (syn. *N.* 'Paper White') are common sights in garden centres during autumn, inviting us to buy the bag to take home and plant. Alternatively, these bulbs can be purchased by mail order and will withstand the rigours of the postal service. This resilience is one of the reasons why they have been so successfully marketed over the centuries.

PROVIDING PROTECTION

Some species of bulb require careful treatment. *Pleione* bulbs, for example, must be handled gently because they can sometimes send up shoots even before planting, and they are, therefore, usually sold individually in packets, surrounded by wood shavings. Completely different to look at are the poisonous tubers of *Gloriosa superba* 'Rothschildiana', which are long and tapering and could be easily damaged in transit. They are often wrapped in tissue. The rhizomes of achimenes are not only brittle but tiny, so they are often sold in a little plastic pot surrounded by peat.

CHOOSING A CONTAINER AND COMPOST

Many indoor containers do not have drainage holes at the base of the pot, which makes it essential that the type of compost (soil mix) and the frequency of watering are watched carefully. With most winter bulb displays it is advisable to use a specially formulated indoor bulb compost, which will help to maintain the balance of the soil and prevent souring. This is particularly true when you use one of the lovely containers that are sold especially for forcing hyacinths and daffodils but that have no drainage holes.

Pots with drainage holes make it possible to grow a wide range of bulbs, corms and so forth and to use different kinds of compost. They are ideal for plants that prefer a well-drained soil, such as freesias and nerines. Use a growing medium such as a soil-based compost (potting mix) with plenty of grit added for good drainage. A glazed tray positioned beneath the pot will save unwanted spoiling of the windowsill or furniture.

To combat summer drought, use a container without drainage holes, and then find a lightweight plastic pot that does have holes to fit inside. Put gravel in the base of the outer container so that the inner pot sits at the right height and add a shallow layer of gravel to the inner one. This way the plant will have its own water reservoir, although care will still be needed not to over- or under-water. A soil-based compost (potting mix) or peat-based compost (soil-less mix), depending on the plant, can be used in these circumstances.

The choice of container gives rise to various further considerations, such as the size of the container. The tall, midwinter-flowering daffodils, such as *Narcissus papyraceus* (syn. *N.* 'Paper White'), make a lot of root growth and need a container that is at least 15cm (6in) deep. However, hyacinths can cope with much shallower containers, needing a minimum of only 7.5cm (3in), although they will also be happy with a deeper root run. Stem-rooting lilies will require a much deeper container, so choose a pot that is at least 20–25cm (8–10in) deep.

GROWING ON WATER

Although compost can always be used, hyacinths, *Narcissus papyraceus* and hippeastrums can be grown on top of water with no compost at all. This is possible only with bulbs that are quick to produce their flowers and only if you do not wish to use the bulbs for a second flowering the following year, because all the food reserves will have been used up and not replenished.

Hyacinths have been grown in this way for many years, and a special glass hyacinth vase has been manufactured, which has an upper cup in which the bulb is held. Charcoal can be added to keep the water fresh and untainted or "sweet". The water level should be kept just beneath the base of the bulb, and

the temperature should be no higher than 7–10°C (45–50°F). After planting, the hyacinths should be kept in a dark, cool place, and within just a matter of weeks the small roots will begin to grow down into the water beneath, soon followed by the thrusting shoot above the neck of the glass. When the shoot is about 5cm (2in) long, move the glass into a light, warm room ready for flowering. Gradually increase the temperature and light as the bud lengthens. To prolong the life of the flowers, avoid direct sunlight and place in a cooler room at night. The bulb is best discarded after flowering.

The addition of stones to the water helps to anchor the roots and stabilize the plants. Good candidates for this treatment are the taller *Narcissus papyraceus* and amaryllis. Many coloured gravels and chippings are available for landscaping and for use in fish tanks, and these are suitable for use with bulbs grown on water.

Growing Bulbs on Water

1 You will need water, charcoal, a bulb (in this case, a hyacinth bulb) and a special glass. You will need a larger container for other bulbs such as hippeastrum.

2 Insert a small piece of charcoal into the glass.

3 Bring the water level just below the neck of the glass. Insert the bulb, ensuring that the base is just above water level. Place the bulb in a cool, dark room, and when the roots are well formed and the shoot is about 5cm (2in) long, bring it out to a light spot, gradually increasing the level of sunlight and temperature. Avoid strong, direct sunlight.

4 Growing hyacinth bulbs in glass vases shows off their beauty to full effect. It is fascinating to see the mass of delicate roots that is produced, an effect rarely seen otherwise.

Moss, coloured stones and gravel, painted nuts, beech twigs, sparkling fleece

and even candles are just some of the many finishing touches that can be

used to decorate planted indoor pots.

finishing touches

Right Subtle tones are reflected in the glittering fleece that surrounds this hyacinth.

Moss or coloured stones can be added at the time of planting or once the bulbs have started to shoot to give the bowl that final finishing touch. Ordinary lawn moss makes a soft, green topping, but, if you want a more vibrant colour, choose some dyed reindeer moss which is obtainable from florists. Gravel or coloured stones, such as those sold for fish tanks, are a good alternative. A thin layer scattered on the surface of the compost (soil mix) will make a neat and colourful addition, especially while you wait for the bulbs to flower. For a natural look, you might like to add nuts or fir cones or, if you are planning to bring bulbs into flower for early winter, you might even make the bowl look more festive by decorating it with silver-painted walnuts or glittery fleece.

Another possible decorative addition are candles, which will add atmosphere to any dark winter's night and can even make the container pretty long before all the flowers open. Fit them into a simple candle holder with a plastic spike on the end – these are readily available from florists – and gently push them into the compost. Never leave lit candles unattended.

USING SUPPORTS
Although it is not always necessary, some bulbs and corms – freesias, for example – will benefit from the support of canes or twigs to prevent the foliage and

flowers from flopping over. Act at the first sign of any waywardness. Cut off pieces of cane or even use long chopsticks tied together with coloured string or raffia. With taller subjects, such as *Narcissus papyraceus* and its relatives, small beech clippings are excellent,

Right Stones of the kind used in fish tanks can be used as a dressing on the surface of the compost (soil mix). Much brighter colours, such as reds and pinks, are also available.

Far right Silver-sprayed walnuts can be used to add a festive air to a bulb display.

as they are sturdy and offer many smaller twigs for support, low down as well as higher up. They can be left uncoloured or sprayed to match the container. Whichever you choose, they will do the job well and look attractive.

Another good support is *Ribes sanguineum* (flowering currant), which has strong, sturdy stems and can easily be sprayed silver or any other colour. Use it where the narcissi are flowering after, rather than before, early winter. *R. sanguineum* is less branching than beech but has the advantage that when it is brought indoors and stuck into moist compost, it continues to live and will produce pretty white flowers. By the time the narcissi have finished blooming, the twigs may well have rooted.

The beautiful *Gloriosa superba* 'Rothschildiana' is a scrambling herbaceous plant, climbing to 1.8m (6ft) in just one summer. Give it the support of a wall frame or a free-standing willow frame, held securely in the pot, to which the tendrils can cling. The flamboyant flowers will be seen to good effect against the background of stems.

Above Reindeer moss is available dyed bright green or red.

Far left Beech twigs make good supports for tall daffodils. You can even spray them to match the colour of the container.

Left Lawn moss gives a natural look to bowls of bulbs.

Cyclamen can be shown off to great advantage simply by placing a single specimen in a small coloured glass vase or pottery dish, which can grace a spare bedroom or cloakroom as well as the more obvious living room.

cyclamen

Above Remove any damaged leaves or fading flowers with a simple sharp tug close to the base of the stem.

Above right Ruffled cyclamen flowers have a distinctive flair, and they are often combined with intricate leaf markings. Always choose a healthy plant. Look for one with stiff foliage, avoiding plants with any limp-looking leaves, and check to see that there are plenty of flower buds emerging from the base.

Right The miniature cyclamen are floriferous, producing a mass of flowers with the fly-away petals that make them so endearing.

Far right Recent breeding developments have resulted in the Miracle Series, which can tolerate cooler conditions outside in the autumn, and then they can be brought indoors for the winter.

Like garden cyclamen, the cyclamen that are sold as indoor houseplants in autumn grow from tubers, which root both from the base and the sides. They are all derived from *Cyclamen persicum*, which is a spring-flowering plant native to the countries of the eastern Mediterranean and Rhodes, Crete and Libya. In the wild the flowers are white, pale mauve, pale pink or deep pink. The leaves are variable but often have intricate silver zoning, spotting or margins.

Many cultivars have been bred from these beautiful plants, which means that the blooms are now available in white, salmon-pink, scarlet and purple as well as pink, and they often have a distinctive darker central spot. In addition, the flowers vary in shape and may be ruffled, double, single or twisted. They are often scented.

In recent decades, attention has been given to breeding miniature flowers, more akin to the species found in the wild, which is a welcome move. The emphasis has been on foliage colour and form, with pride of place being given to intricate markings and contrasting patches of silver and green. In the past few years, there has also been a move to breed plants that will thrive at lower temperatures and serve a dual purpose of flowering in outdoor containers in autumn as well as in indoor containers in winter. The resulting Miracle Series is a great bonus to all

gardeners, both outdoor and indoor. Another positive development has been the increased attention paid to producing highly fragrant flowers. A plant in full flower will quickly fill an entire room with its sweet perfume.

Cyclamen will thrive in light, airy conditions, but they should be kept away from draughts and too much direct sunlight. They abhor both drought and high humidity. Too much or too little water will cause serious damage. Never water over the flowers and foliage, as this will encourage rot. It is far better to water around the plants at soil level, especially where several cyclamen are planted in a single container, or to water into a saucer below the plant if the container has drainage holes. Do not place cyclamen close to a radiator or behind a closed curtain in the evening. A temperature in the range of 18–21°C (64–70°F) is ideal, with a night-time temperature kept above 10°C (50°F). The plants will flower for longer if they are fed every fortnight with a weak liquid fertilizer.

Keep the plants clean and tidy by removing any fading flowers and yellowing leaves. With cyclamen, it is necessary to remove the entire stem, along with either the dying flowers or leaves, because a cut or a broken stem will encourage rot. Take firm hold of the stem near the base of the plant and give a quick tug.

After flowering has finished, the plants should be allowed to go into a state of natural dormancy. Gradually withhold water until all the growth has died down and keep the plant completely dry for two or three months. Modest watering can then start again. The tubers will not need re-potting for a couple of years because they flower best with a restricted root run.

DISPLAYING CYCLAMEN
Cyclamen look charming when they are shown off as a single specimen, and they will suit nearly every room in the house, adding scent and delicacy. The miniature hybrids are often sold in small plastic pots, which can be quickly disguised or easily made to fit into more attractive containers, including coloured flower vases and small china sugar bowls.

A Wired Table Centrepiece
1 Choose a medium-sized container, such as this wire basket, which is 23cm (9in) across and 13cm (5in) deep. Line the basket with moss.

2 Cover the moss with a circle of black plastic cut from a bin liner, and add compost (soil mix).

3 Plant the cyclamen around the edge of the container, taking care to add compost right around the root ball of each plant. Leave a distinct gap in the centre; this will be where you can water with a long-spouted watering can.

4 Add some matching candles as a finishing touch, but take care never to leave the lit candles unattended.

For greater impact, make a massed display by planting three or four plants together in a medium-sized basin, terrine or even a wired table centrepiece. Lighted candles will provide the final touch. Once planted, water only at soil level, remembering never to water directly over the tops of the tubers. It is, in fact, better to wait until the leaves go slightly limp and then to water only moderately. If you want this arrangement for special occasions but your main room is warm, keep it in a cool but well-lit place to prolong the flowering period and only bring it into the higher temperatures when necessary.

Pure white hyacinths look particularly striking grown in a traditional terracotta pot, while pink hyacinths can make a delightful display in a pretty marbled glass container.

indoor winter-flowering hyacinths

The use of commercially prepared bulbs enables us to enjoy hyacinths out of season. Hyacinths normally flower in spring, but by special treatment, such as early lifting and subjection to artificially high and low temperatures, they will flower in early winter. Be sure to buy those that are labelled as having been prepared. A general rule for forced blooms is to allow three months between planting and flowering.

There is a wide range of colours available, including *Hyacinthus orientalis* 'Anne Marie', which is a light rose pink, 'Pink Pearl', which is slightly deeper, 'Bismarck', which is sky blue, 'Delft Blue', which is more of a porcelain-blue shade, 'L'Innocence', which is white, 'Jan Bos', which is a carmine red, and 'City of Haarlem', which is lemon-yellow. Each one is fragrant.

Almost any container can be used for hyacinths, which adapt easily to shallow rooting conditions. For general purposes, however, choose a container that is at least 7.5cm (3in) deep. Terracotta pots, a small galvanized bucket, a china bowl or even a vase are ideal.

Hyacinths can be grown on water or on compost (soil mix). To grow them on compost, use grit at the bottom of the container, topped up with moistened indoor bulb fibre. Plant the bulbs on the top, with just the bottom half of the bulb sitting in the compost (soil mix) and the top half exposed. Plant them so that they are not touching each other or the sides of the

Growing Hyacinths on Compost
1 Place a thin layer of grit at the bottom of the container.

2 If the container has no drainage holes, use a specially prepared indoor bulb fibre, which consists mainly of peat with shell and charcoal added to keep it fresh or "sweet". Use ordinary potting compost (soil mix) if there are adequate drainage holes. Add bulb fibre or compost to within 5cm (2in) of the rim.

3 Plant the hyacinth bulbs with the bottom half of the bulb in compost and the top half exposed. Space the bulbs so that they are touching neither each other nor the container. They should have about half their own width between them. Moisten the compost, but avoid watering the bulbs directly because this can encourage rot.

4 Add grit or moss in order to retain moisture, and then put in a cool, dark place for about 8–10 weeks until the bulbs have made good root growth. The temperature at this stage should not exceed 7–10°C (45–50°F).

5 Return the bulbs to the light when the new shoots are about 5cm (2in) long. Expose them only gradually to increased temperatures and sunlight, as the flower stem emerges. Keep the compost moist; the coloured grit darkens when damp.

Opposite, left *Hyacinthus orientalis* 'L'Innocence' create a beautiful display, but they flower slightly later than the other prepared types of hyacinth.

Opposite, right *Hyacinthus orientalis* 'Pink Pearl' looks striking in a range of containers, including this pretty marbled glass container.

container, and ensure that they have about half their own width between them. Add grit or moss in order to retain moisture, and put the container in a cool, dark place for between eight and ten weeks, until the bulbs have made good root growth. The temperature at this stage should not exceed 7–10°C (45–50°F).

Bring the hyacinths out into the light when the tips of the new shoots are about 5cm (2in) long. The shoots will be bright green in colour but will quickly turn darker when exposed to the light. Expose them only gradually to increased temperatures and levels of sunlight as the flower stem emerges. Too much heat or dryness leads to stunted growth. After flowering, apply a liquid feed and keep the compost moist, thus allowing the bulbs to regenerate for another year; plant them out in the garden in early spring.

This exotic flower, widely but wrongly known as amaryllis, is actually called hippeastrum. The species have been bred to produce many named hybrids, which range in colour from bright red to pink and white.

hippeastrum

The massive bulbs of hippeastrums can be bought in late summer and forced into flower before mid-winter. However, most are available from early autumn until early winter, and will flower after midwinter until spring, depending on the planting time. Commonly available at this stage are the deep red 'Red Velvet' and 'Red Lion', the brilliant red and white 'Christmas Star', the orange 'Florida' and the pink and white 'Flamingo'. Doubles are sometimes to be found as well, including the pink-edged, white 'Mary Lou'.

It might still be possible to buy bulbs in mid-spring, when they will probably be cheaper. If the bulbs are firm, they will still flower. Indeed, the later they are planted, the more quickly they will spring into growth.

The bulbs need warmth to come to life again after their dormant period. Choose a pot that is only about 2.5cm (1in) wider than the bulb itself. Use a soil-based compost (potting mix) if the pot has drainage holes, or an indoor bulb fibre if the pot has no holes. Some heavy grit at the base of the pot will help to stabilize the bulb when it is in flower and also assist with drainage.

Place the potted bulb in a warm spot – an airing cupboard, for example – where the temperature should be 20–25°C (68–77°F). When the shoot has begun to emerge, expose it to moderate warmth and good light. Keep the compost moist during the growing period, and apply a liquid feed, such as tomato fertilizer, every week or ten days once the bud has begun to open.

Remove the first flowering stem and you may find that another one soon emerges. The leaves will begin to grow at this stage. It is important to keep the bulb watered and fed so that it can complete its cycle of growth. Some months later, when the leaves begin to yellow and wither, gradually withhold water and allow the bulb to go into a dormant period. Do not attempt to re-pot, as they resent root disturbance, although they will need re-potting after three or four years, ideally in late summer. Leave the bulb outside in a dry, sheltered spot until autumn when it can be brought indoors again and given moisture and warmth to start the flowering cycle once more.

GROWING ON WATER

Hippeastrum bulbs can be grown on water in a similar way to prepared hyacinths and *Narcissus papyraceus*. Start the bulb into growth as already described, planted on moist compost, and keep in a warm place for a short period. As soon as the bud begins to emerge, carefully wash off the compost. Plant the bulb on top of coloured stones, pebbles, marbles or glass beads, with the water level kept below the base of the bulb.

Left The bulbs of the *Hippeastrum* (amaryllis) are exceptionally large.

Opposite, left These *Hippeastrum* 'Red Velvet' are blooming for a second time in the same container. It is important to feed them after flowering and to continue to water until the leaves show signs of yellowing. Then gradually withhold moisture and allow the leaves to die down, thus allowing the bulbs to complete their life-cycle. Do not disturb the roots; simply begin to water again when the first signs of new growth are seen. The bulbs can be allowed to flower in the same compost (soil mix) for three seasons.

Opposite, right Marbles and other glass beads are available in a variety of colours, and can be used to decorate the container when growing on water. The reflections in the glass are a delightful feature of this dramatic planting scheme, where *Hippeastrum* 'Christmas Star' makes such a marvellous centrepiece.

Left Choose a container that is about 2.5cm (1in) wider than the hippeastrum bulb itself. Two bulbs planted at the same time will give an even more dramatic display.

The diameter of the bulb is huge, so use a wide-necked glass container within which it can sit. Find a small, clean, empty jam (jelly) jar with a light-coloured screw lid to fit inside the container. This allows more light to be reflected and cuts down on the number of marbles or beads that are needed. Place the jar inside the larger container and flood the container with enough green marbles to cover. Include a small piece of charcoal with the marbles to keep the water "sweet". Add a few more marbles and carefully place the bulb so that it rests inside the neck of the container with its roots barely touching the marbles. Add enough water to bring the level just below the base of the bulb. You might like to dress the container with pretty red beads or brightly coloured curly canes, available from florists.

A single bulb will flower beautifully for weeks and may even produce two dramatic flowering spikes, by which time the bulb will have shrunk because it has used up all its food reserves. Bulbs planted in compost can be kept and encouraged to flower again another year, but it is best to discard those grown on water.

Growing narcissi so that they will flower indoors in the middle of winter usually involves Narcissus papyraceus *(syn.* N. *'Paper White') and its forms, which produce stems with eight to ten flowers each.*

indoor winter-flowering narcissi

Far right Once flowering has begun, then the cooler the room temperature the longer the flowers will last, but do not allow the temperature to fall below freezing. If you have a balcony or veranda, you may even wish to place them outside in mild weather. This is also useful if you find the perfume too strong.

The species *Narcissus papyraceus* is native to south-eastern France, south-western Spain and Portugal, where it flowers outdoors in winter, although many of the commercially available bulbs actually come from Israel. It is not surprising, therefore, that when they are given warmth and moisture, the bulbs burst into growth after being planted indoors in autumn. Closely related are *N.* 'Grandiflora Ziva' and N. 'Galilee'. Other candidates are *N.* 'Cragford' and *N.* 'Bridal Crown', both of which are easily available but slightly later flowering. As a rule, the later they flower, the more important it is to give the bulbs a cool period of several weeks after planting.

If you use a container without drainage holes – a painted metal or glazed pot, for instance – it is best to use specially prepared bulb fibre. This will ensure a good growing medium and will avoid the compost (soil mix) becoming sour over the ensuing months. If you use a traditional plant pot with drainage holes, you can use a soil-based compost (potting mix), but place a saucer underneath it in order to protect the furniture.

FORCING NARCISSI

Narcissus papyraceus (syn. *N.* 'Paper White') is the easiest of all the narcissi to bring into flower in the late autumn and winter months. It usually flowers only six weeks after planting and, unlike the later

Right *Narcissus papyraceus* (syn. *N.* 'Paper White') and its forms produce stems with eight or ten flowers each, which means that just two or three bulbs will produce a really worthwhile display. They look equally attractive grown on compost (soil mix) or on water.

flowering and other related daffodils, it requires no special period of cool or darkness to persuade it to grow and flower indoors. Decide when you want the bulbs to bloom and then work backwards. You may wish to try a succession of flowers by planting a number of pots over several weeks in order to have a continual supply.

Each stem produces many flowers, so a display can quite easily include as many as five or six bulbs or as few as two or three. Whatever you choose, the results will be excellent. These bulbs do not tolerate frosty conditions outside, so unless you live in a mild climate, they are best discarded after flowering and new ones purchased for the following season.

PLANTING ON WATER

Narcissus papyraceus and its cultivars grow well on top of water because they are so quick to start into growth and then flower. Other later flowering narcissi need to grow in bulb compost. You can use a pretty bowl filled with gravel to stabilize the roots, or, if you want the fun of watching the roots meandering down through the stones, choose a glass container and fill it with coloured stones. Many coloured gravels and chippings are available for garden landscaping and for indoor fish tanks. A pattern of red and white stones or some seashore stones and shells would look interesting.

A small piece of charcoal can be added among the stones to help keep the water fresh. The bulbs will use all their food reserves by growing on water, and should be discarded after flowering.

Forcing Narcissi

1 Choose firm, plump bulbs, and plant in compost (soil mix), allowing for about six weeks before flowering. Do not worry if the bulbs already have existing shoots, but take care that they are not damaged.

2 Grit at the base of the container is not essential, but it is useful to aid drainage. Fill the container with moistened bulb fibre, bringing the level to within 5cm (2in) of the rim. Plant the bulbs so that they are close together, but away from the sides of the container and not touching each other. A distance apart of about half their width is ideal. Approximately half the top of each bulb should be left exposed.

3 Mulch with moss to retain the moisture as well as to add an attractive finish.

4 You may need to support the leaves and stems with twigs. Only do so if you notice that the stems are beginning to flop, but then act immediately. Natural or painted beech twigs are ideal, as they branch well all the way up the stem and offer support from top to bottom.

Growing bulbs such as dwarf narcissi, grape hyacinths and crocuses indoors is a lovely way to enjoy them at close quarters and really appreciate their colours, shapes and scents.

spring bulbs indoors

Right *Hyacinthus orientalis* 'Amethyst' is a subtle lavender pink, which looks delightful at such close range. Adding a primrose to the planting creates a simple, but charming, picture.

Below Some cultivars of *Crocus vernus* (Dutch crocus) have wonderfully bold purple flowers with strongly contrasting orange stamens. When they are grown outdoors they usually open like a goblet, but in the warmth of a conservatory or on a sunny windowsill they open fully, revealing their thrusting orange centres.

Several bulbs are suitable for planting in small pots before being kept in cool but sheltered conditions outside, such as by a house wall or on a porch, and then brought indoors, when the flowerbuds first show, to flower a week or two earlier than they would otherwise. Crocuses, *Eranthis hyemalis* (winter aconite), *Muscari* (grape hyacinths), dwarf daffodils, dwarf tulips and hyacinths will all bring pleasure if they are treated in this way.

The large *Crocus vernus* (Dutch crocus) are excellent indoor candidates. If the corms are to be planted in containers with no drainage holes, a layer of grit must be added to the base of each pot before special indoor bulb fibre is used to fill the pot. For a maximum show, five crocus corms can be planted in a circle near the bottom of each pot, with another layer of five corms planted in another circle above. Just make sure that the corms are not directly on top of each other. The pots should be kept in a light but covered place, such as a potting shed, in winter and watered occasionally to keep the compost (soil mix) moist. When the shoots just begin to show colour, they can be brought indoors. The display can then be appreciated at close range, with no danger of wind or rain spoiling the delicate petals.

Prepared hyacinths for midwinter flowering are available in a limited range of colours, but bedding hyacinths, which are grown in the garden or in outdoor pots, are available in an enormous number of delicate shades, including apricot as in *Hyacinthus orientalis* 'Gipsy Queen'; violet, lilac, mulberry and burgundy as in 'Violet Pearl', 'Amethyst', 'Mulberry Rose' and 'Woodstock'; blue and white as in 'Blue Jacket'; deep blue as in 'Blue Magic'; and many others. There are also some double-flowering forms, including white 'Ben Nevis', red 'Hollyhock', violet 'King Codro' and pink 'Rosette'. Any of these hyacinths can be grown in groups of three or more or as a single specimen in a simple terracotta pot. Hyacinths, in particular, like good drainage so where they are grown outdoors, open to the winter rain, it is best to choose a pot with drainage holes and use a soil-based compost (potting mix). Remember to use a terracotta or plastic saucer underneath the pot when you bring it inside, to protect your furniture from unsightly watermarks.

USING SPRING BULBS ALREADY IN GROWTH
One of the easiest ways to enjoy bulbs indoors in late winter is to buy small pots of growing bulbs. Use a pretty coloured pot or a plain terracotta pot for display purposes, and place it in a light but cool position to prolong the flowering period. Intense heat or too much direct sunlight will mean that you will enjoy only the briefest of blooms.

Dwarf irises, scillas, *Fritillaria meleagris* (snake's head fritillary), hyacinths and dwarf tulips are among the many plants that are readily available, but of them all, the miniature *Narcissus* 'Tête-à-tête' is probably the most often grown. This is a dwarf, sturdy, multi-headed, hybrid daffodil with rich yellow flowers. After flowering, deadhead each flower and plant them out in the garden in spring so that the bulbs can complete their cycle and flower again year after year.

GROWING NARCISSUS 'TÊTE-À-TÊTE'
An effective method of displaying these little daffodils is to find a simple coloured container that is slightly larger than the pot in which they are already growing. Use grit or stones as necessary in the outer pot to get the level right, insert the pot of daffodils and add a mulch of moss to disguise the inner pots and provide a surface top. Keep the bulbs moist at all times and deadhead the flowers to keep them neat.

Another way of using them is to place the pot-grown plants in a small metal window box, again raising the levels with grit or stones as necessary and topping up with moss between each pot. Reindeer moss provides a lime-green finish. Keep the compost (soil mix) moist and deadhead the daffodils to keep them neat.

A further way to use these daffodils is to incorporate them into a flower and foliage arrangement. Potted bulbs will always last much longer than a bunch of cut flowers, so why not? Mix them with other late winter

foliage and flowers to create a vibrant indoor display. The choice of cut foliage is enormous and will largely depend on what is most widely available. *Euonymus japonicus* 'Aureus', for example, is an excellent choice, as is white *Viburnum tinus* and the long, twisted stems of *Corylus avellana* 'Contorta' (corkscrew hazel). Simple ivy leaves and berries would be equally attractive.

Potted Narcissi

1 You will need secateurs (pruners), a florist's foam ring, a large plate or dish to display the arrangement, three or four pots of dwarf *Narcissus* 'Tête-à-tête', some foliage, such as *Euonymus japonicus* 'Aureus', long twisted stems of *Corylus avellana* 'Contorta' (corkscrew hazel) and a few sprigs of flowering forsythia and viburnums, including white *Viburnum tinus* and pink *V.* × *bodnantense* 'Dawn'.

2 Wet the foam ring thoroughly and give the cut foliage a good long drink in water. Place the ring on a large plate or dish and arrange the pots of bulbs to sit inside. Cut small sprigs of foliage and arrange them in groups, pushing the stems into the foam. Add some flowering forsythia and viburnum in groups and a few single stems of the hazel to give extra height. Bear in mind that within a few days the narcissi will probably grow to about 20cm (8in) or more. If you keep the foam and bulbs moist, the arrangement should stay fresh for ten days or more.

Left A small, metal window box planted with narcissi is perfect for a kitchen windowsill or for the conservatory.

Achimenes (hot water plant) were a favourite conservatory plant in the
Victorian period, and they are now widely available both as dry rhizomes
in late winter and as houseplants in summer.

achimenes

The plants produce long, tubular flowers, ranging in colour from rose, scarlet and blue to violet, and the flowers, which have contrasting throats of gold or white, are sometimes blotched or spotted.

The rhizomes resemble miniature pine cones, are small and easily broken, so they are often sold, four or five at a time, in little plastic tubs surrounded by peat. For all their fragility, however, they are easily grown in shallow containers and the cascading types are delightful in hanging baskets, where they will tumble over the sides. Successive plantings in the winter and spring will produce flowers throughout summer and autumn. Plant the rhizomes about 2.5cm (1in) deep and 5cm (2in) apart. Water sparingly at first, but as shoots appear keep the compost (soil mix) moist at all times. Be warned: a dry period will initiate dormancy and there will be no flowers. Apply a liquid feed every two weeks once they are in full growth. Pinch out shoots to encourage bushiness and provide supports if necessary. Provide bright light, but keep the plants shaded from strong, direct sunlight. In hot weather, spray the foliage with a mister to maintain humidity. Stand pot-grown specimens on a gravel-covered tray and keep the gravel damp.

As the flowering period comes to an end, gradually withhold water until the soil has dried out. Remove the dead foliage and store the rhizomes in dry peat at a minimum temperature of 10°C (50°F). The rhizomes can be propagated when next planted. Do not worry too much if they break; every single scale will produce a new plant.

Planting Achimenes in a Basket
1 Line a wicker basket with black plastic (unless it is already pre-lined), add drainage material, such as small pieces of polystyrene (plastic foam), broken crocks or grit, and cover with a multi-purpose compost (soil mix), bringing the level to within 2.5cm (1in) of the rim.

2 This basket has a 30cm (12in) diameter and contains eight rhizomes, planted about 5cm (2in) apart and 2.5cm (1in) deep. Two different types of achimenes can be alternated, such as *Achimenes* 'Cascade Violet Night' and *A*. 'Violet Charm'.

3 Mist to maintain humidity. Warmth, semi-shade and a damp atmosphere are ideal. The plants will flower for months on end and give endless pleasure.

Freesias are native to South Africa, where they are mainly confined to the Cape Province. Hybridization has resulted in a wide range of colours, including white, yellow, pink, lilac, mauve and blue.

freesia

There are both single- and double-flowered forms of freesia, and the plants vary in height from 10 to 30cm (4 to 12in). Freesias grow from corms, which may be planted indoors to flower in succession from late spring through to early summer, so that their perfume can be enjoyed over many weeks. They can also be purchased as "conditioned" bulbs, and planted in pots indoors, before being moved outdoors, where they can flower in mid- to late summer.

Indoor freesias should be planted in early spring in a moist, soil-based compost (potting mix), about 7.5cm (3in) apart and deep. Maintain moisture throughout the growing period and apply a liquid feed every two weeks as soon as the buds show. Keep in cool to warm conditions but avoid too high a temperature, or the flowering period will be short.

Many freesias are exquisitely fragrant, but some have rather untidy foliage, so a wire ring support can be useful. They are also unpredictable in their willingness to flower. You might be fortunate and have a wonderful pot filled with blooms, or you might have only one or two flowers. The scent will be heavenly, nevertheless.

Left The freesia is one of the most delightfully scented of all corms, and a display will fill a room with its sweet perfume. The metal ring support helps to keep wayward leaves in check.

Far left Freesia corms should be planted in a moist, soil-based compost (potting mix), about 7.5cm (3in) apart and deep.

Left These two pots, decorated with African animal-skin patterns, are an appropriate setting for plants that are native to South Africa. *Freesia* 'Miranda' is pure white, and *F.* 'Beethoven' is light yellow.

For a stylish plant that will bring a touch of the exotic to an indoor display,
try the unusual pineapple lilies, including Eucomis autumnalis, E. bicolor,
E. comosa and E. pallidiflora.

eucomis

Eucomis is commonly called the pineapple lily because it produces a tuft of leafy bracts above the flower spike. It is native to southern Africa, where it grows in grassy, often damp, areas.

This is an easy bulb to grow indoors. In spring, plant individual bulbs in a small pot, 10cm (4in) deep, in a well-drained, soil-based compost (potting mix), or mass the bulbs in groups of three or more in a larger pot. Water sparingly until shoots emerge and, as growth progresses, keep the compost moist at all times. After flowering, allow the plant to complete its lifecycle and gradually withhold water so that it can rest during the dormant period before bringing it into growth again the following spring. In mild areas without frosts, the bulb can be grown outside.

Eucomis autumnalis 'White Dwarf' is a particularly attractive plant with distinctive wavy foliage. It has a column of white flowers with yellow stamens, which open in succession, starting at the base; at the top the leafy hat brings the height to just over 30cm (12in).

Above *Eucomis* flowers last for several weeks, opening at the bottom of the flower spike first and progressively higher up as the weeks pass by. It is an undemanding plant and yet rewarding both in its longevity and its simplicity.

Right *Eucomis autumnalis* 'White Dwarf' has a wonderful silhouette with its wavy foliage, its narrow column of scented flowers and its leafy top. This is an easy bulb to grow indoors.

Sinningia flowers are rich and velvety, and there is often a white edge on the blooms when they first open; the markings on Sinningia 'Hollywood' form an intricate pattern.

sinningia

Although the botanical name for this group of plants is *Sinningia*, the term gloxinia is more well known in the florist trade. The plants are native to tropical areas of Brazil, Argentina and Mexico, where they have adapted to seasonal rainfall and periods of intervening drought, during which the tubers become dormant. The large, velvety flowers grow from tubers that are shaped rather like those of begonias. They should be planted in late winter or early spring on top of moist, multi-purpose compost (soil-less medium). With gentle heat and only moderate moisture at first, they soon start into growth and produce colourful plants, about 20cm (8in) in height and spread. Flowers may be self-coloured or speckled, such as the lovely white with pink S. 'Blanche de Méru', the crimson S. 'Etoile de Feu', the violet S. 'Hollywood,' the red with ivory S. Tigrina Group and the purple and white S. 'Kaiser Wilhelm'.

Pot individual tubers into small containers with drainage holes, using a multi-purpose compost. It is important to use containers with drainage holes because the leaves dislike being splashed with water and will quickly mark, so the plants should be watered from below. Keep the temperature at 21–23°C (70–73°F) until flowering and move to cooler conditions when flowering begins. Provide the plant with well-lit conditions but do not stand them in direct sunlight. Deadhead flowers to prolong flowering, and apply a

dilute liquid feed every two weeks. After flowering is over, gradually withhold water and allow the root ball to go quite dry. Store in a cool, dry place at about 7°C (45°F) until the following season.

A Display of Sinningias

1 Choose a small plastic pot with drainage holes and find a slightly larger, more ornamental pot for display purposes. Grit is useful in the base of the outer pot for raising the inner pot to the right height. It also provides a damp reservoir beneath the base of the plant, enabling the plant to be kept damp, which is particularly important in hot weather.

2 Use a moist, multi-purpose compost (soil-less medium) to fill the pot to within 3cm (1¼in) of the rim. Create a small hollow, and plant the tuber so that it rests on top of the compost. Keep the temperature at 21–23°C (70–73°F) until flowering, and move to cooler conditions when flowering begins. Give the plant well-lit conditions but avoid direct sunlight.

3 Avoid watering directly on top of the leaves. It is much better to water from below, occasionally removing the plant and sitting it in a saucer of water. Alternatively, remove the plant and add water to the base of the outer pot but take care not to leave the roots sitting in a pool of water.

Left *Sinningia* 'Hollywood', with its gorgeous violet blooms, is a real show-stopper, and *S.* 'Etoile de Feu' is a glorious velvety crimson. The two together make a sumptuous display in a simple wicker window box.

The summer bulbs might be flourishing outside in the garden, but indoors a range of tantalizing container displays can be created, using begonias, dahlias, Zantedeschia (arum lily) and lilies.

summer-flowering bulbs and tubers

Right Two or three Non-Stop begonias look marvellous in a pure white window box. Remember to deadhead regularly and apply a liquid feed every week.

Below A highly coloured pot will emphasize the warmth of the colouring of Non-Stop begonias. There are many different colours to choose from, including red, yellow, white, pink, orange and all the shades in between.

Many summer-flowering bulbs and tubers are offered for sale as growing plants, often much earlier in the year than would be possible if they were grown on, at home, from their dry state. Begonias and lilies, therefore, are available from spring onwards, with dahlias following on soon afterwards. They are happy kept inside, in warm, light conditions, but do not place them in full sun, or the flowers will last for only a few days, not weeks.

Terracotta containers always look warm and attractive, but there are many other ways of displaying plants. Silver containers will give a more modern appearance indoors, and can look extremely elegant, especially if the plant is tall and beautifully shaped, such as a *Zantedeschia* (arum lily).

Do not forget to feed the plants every week with a liquid feed and keep them well watered. Frequent deadheading will help to prolong the flowering time of arum lilies, dahlias and begonias. After they have finished flowering, the lilies can be planted out in a sheltered part of the garden, where they will overwinter and come into flower again the following year. The begonia and dahlia tubers can be allowed to go into a dormant state and kept cool and dry until they can be brought into growth again the following spring.

Right *Zantedeschia* (arum lily), with their boldly shaped flowers, look elegant displayed in a series of tall, silver containers. They can also be successfully displayed in a metal window box with just a mulch of white stones.

Above *Zantedeschia* 'Dusky Pink' is one of the many modern cultivars of the arum lily that have these beautifully shaped tubular flowers.

Opposite right Non-Stop begonias are so called because they continue to flower over a long period. They make excellent indoor houseplants, and are available in a wide variety of colours.

Left Dahlias have fantastic flowers, often consisting of many quilled petals, and in the brightest of colours. Choose short-stemmed plants for growing indoors. A wooden window box is an ideal container for several dahlias.

Opposite Lilies make a really wonderful statement with their brilliantly coloured flowers and attractive leaves which catch the light so well. Find an old fruit or vegetable box and lightly colour-wash or spray it with paint to give a warm and interesting texture. Place the pots inside and use a little green or coloured moss to disguise the rims. After flowering, the lilies can be planted out in the garden, where they will overwinter and come into bloom again the following year.

Find brightly coloured pots, window boxes or even an old orange box, which can be given a coat of a light colour wash. You can be as distinctive as you like, especially with dahlias whose flowers are so strongly coloured. Some miniature dahlias, such as the rose pink *D*. 'Sweetheart', are only 30cm (12in) high.

Short-stemmed lilies are ideal for displaying indoors or on a balcony or veranda, and the 'Pixie' types are sometimes only 30–45cm (12–18in) tall. Often lilies have a heady fragrance, and anyone who suffers pollen allergies may be interested to know that some lilies are specially bred to be pollen free. These are known as the "Kiss" lilies and are available in shades of light pink, yellow, orange and white.

Left Here, dahlias are displayed individually in highly coloured containers. Just make sure there are drainage holes in the base of each inner pot.

bulb directory

Exploring the world of bulbs is an exciting journey, and one that will continue to enthral with the more you learn about this fascinating group of plants. Making a selection of bulbs is understandably difficult, but a varied range of bulbs for growing outdoors as well as indoors is presented here to whet your appetite.

These little packages of pent-up beauty, which we call bulbs, show immense diversity. Although they are grown commercially in relatively few countries, such as Holland, England, the United States and South Africa, they are native to many parts of the world, from California to western China. For this reason, there are bulbs to suit many climates and soils, from hot sun to cool woodland.

Each of the plants described in this section is given a hardiness rating, as follows:

Frost tender Plant may be damaged by temperatures below 5°C (41°F).

Frost hardy Plant can withstand temperatures down to -5°C (23°F).

Half hardy Plant can withstand temperatures down to 0°C (32°F).

Fully hardy Plant can withstand temperatures down to -15°C (5°F).

crocus sieberi subsp. *sublimis* 'Tricolor'

achimenes 'Cascade Fairy Pink'

agapanthus 'Ben Hope'

achimenes gesneriaceae

This small but showy plant is often known as the hot water plant because it used to be grown on top of the hot water pipes in Victorian greenhouses, where it would thrive in the warmth and shade before being brought into the main house. It is a genus of about 25 species of winter-dormant, rhizomatous perennials from the subtropical forests of Central America. The many cultivars bear flowers in a wide range of colours, including dark and light pink, blue and primrose-yellow. They may be vigorous upright or trailing perennials. The tiny rhizomes are quite fragile.

Site In frost-prone areas, grow indoors in a conservatory or as houseplants; in frost-free gardens they may be grown in a border. The plants enjoy light shade but not direct sunshine. The trailing forms are well suited to hanging baskets; the others may be grown in shallow pots.

Cultivation In spring, bring into growth at 16–18°C (61–64°F) and water sparingly at first. Plant rhizomes 2.5cm (1in) deep, allowing about one rhizome to 2.5cm (1in) of container (i.e., allow 10 rhizomes to a 25cm/10in pot), in a soil-based compost (potting mix), or a proprietary loamless compost (soil-less mix). Water freely in summer. Apply a weekly liquid fertilizer. In autumn, remove dead top growth and store in containers at 10°C (50°F) in completely dry conditions until spring.

Propagation Divide rhizomes or take stem cuttings in spring.

Pests and disease Aphids, thrips and red spider mites.

Achimenes 'Cascade Fairy Pink'
Solitary light pink flowers, 5cm (2in) across, are borne in generous numbers throughout the summer and autumn. This makes an ideal partner for *A*. 'English Waltz'.
Origins Of garden origin.
Flowering height 20cm (8in) but will trail to 40cm (16in).
Flowering time Summer to autumn.
Hardiness Frost tender.

Achimenes 'Cascade Violet Night'
The purple-blue flowers of this achimenes make a wonderful display from summer to autumn.
Origins Of garden origin.
Flowering height 20cm (8in) but will trail to 40cm (16in).
Flowering time Summer to autumn.
Hardiness Frost tender.

Achimenes 'English Waltz'
The large, funnel-shaped, rose-pink flowers look stunning against the dark green foliage with its bronze-red undertones.
Origins Of garden origin.
Flowering height 20cm (8in).
Flowering time Summer to autumn.
Hardiness Frost tender.

Achimenes 'Violet Charm'
The deep violet-blue flowers create a sumptuous picture either planted on their own or mixed with a trailing variety.
Origins Of garden origin.
Flowering height 20cm (8in).
Flowering time Summer to autumn.
Hardiness Frost tender.

agapanthus alliaceae

This firm favourite is commonly known as the lily of the Nile or the African blue lily. The genus contains about 10 species of vigorous, clump-forming perennials with fleshy roots, and originates in southern Africa. The plants produce strap-shaped, arching leaves and rounded umbels of blue or white flowers, followed by decorative seedheads.

Site Grow in full sun in moist but well-drained soil in borders or in containers.

Cultivation Plant so that the green portion of the stem appears just above soil level. Where grown in borders, mulch in winter as added protection against frost. If grown in containers, use a large, deep pot and plant in a soil-based compost (potting mix), with plenty of drainage at base, and overwinter in a frost-free greenhouse. Apply a liquid feed monthly from spring until flowering.

Propagation Sow seed at 13–15°C (55–59°F) when ripe or in spring. Seedlings take 2 to 3 years to flower. Divide in spring.

Pests and diseases Slugs, snails and viruses.

Agapanthus 'Ben Hope'
The rounded umbels of open, bell-shaped, rich blue flowers make a magnificent display when grown in containers. Plants flower best when overcrowded.
Origins Of garden origin.
Flowering height 1.2m (4ft); Spread 60cm (2ft).
Flowering time Mid- to late summer.
Hardiness Fully hardy.

Agapanthus 'Loch Hope'
The deep blue flowers of this agapanthus, which is one of the tallest in the group, appear in late summer and early autumn above grey-green leaves.
Origins Of garden origin.
Flowering height 1.5m (5ft); Spread 50cm (20in).
Flowering time Late summer to early autumn.
Hardiness Fully hardy.

Agapanthus praecox subsp. *orientalis*
Formerly known as *A. orientalis*, the flowers of this agapanthus are bright blue and supported on sturdy stems. When they appear in late summer, the flowers make a striking contrast with the dark green leaves. This agapanthus is only half hardy and so should be grown in containers, then overwintered in frost-free conditions.
Origins South Africa.
Flowering height 1m (39in); Spread 60cm (2ft).
Flowering time Late summer.
Hardiness Half hardy.

Agapanthus 'Snowy Owl'
The rounded umbels of white flowers appear in late summer. These are set off beautifully by dark green leaves.
Origins South Africa.
Flowering height 1.2m (4ft); Spread 60cm (2ft).
Flowering time Late summer.
Hardiness Fully hardy.

allium caeruleum

allium cristophii

allium sphaerocephalon

amaryllis belladonna

allium alliaceae

This is a large genus of about 700 species of perennial spring-, summer- and autumn-flowering bulbs and rhizomes, which originate in dry and mountainous areas of the northern hemisphere. Alliums are commonly referred to as ornamental onions because of their distinctive smell. In fact, all parts generally smell of onions, including the leaves which often wither by flowering time. They produce short to tall umbels of blue, white or yellow flowers, which are usually followed by decorative seedheads. Contact with bulbs may irritate the skin or aggravate some skin allergies.

Site Grow in full sun in moist but well-drained soil in garden borders. Frost-hardy species such as *A. caeruleum*, *A. cristophii*, *A. nigra* and *A. schubertii* should be mulched in winter to provide extra protection.

Cultivation Plant 15cm (6in) deep in autumn. *A. sphaerocephalon* should be planted 7.5cm (3in) deep in autumn or spring.

Propagation Sow seed at 13–15°C (55–59°F) when ripe or in spring. Divide clumps in autumn.

Pests and diseases White rot, downy mildew and onion fly.

Allium caeruleum

The dense umbels, composed of 30 to 50 bright blue, star-shaped flowers, 3–4cm (1¼–1½in) across, sway on slender stems.
Origins North and Central Asia.
Flowering height 20–80cm (8–32in).
Flowering time Early summer.
Hardiness Frost hardy, so provide a mulch in winter.

Allium cristophii

The umbels, which are 20cm (8in) across, consist of about 50 star-shaped, lilac-purple flowers, which have a lovely rich, metallic sheen in sunlight. It is perfect for planting beneath a laburnum arch or among pale yellow wallflowers.
Origins Of garden origin.
Flowering height 60cm (24in).
Flowering time Early summer.
Hardiness Frost hardy, so provide a mulch in winter.

Allium hollandicum
'Purple Sensation'

The umbels, 7.5cm (3in) across, consist of about 50 star-shaped, rich purple flowers. It is perfect for planting beneath a wisteria arch along with tall Dutch iris.
Origins Of garden origin.
Flowering height 90cm (3ft).
Flowering time Early summer.
Hardiness Fully hardy.

Allium karataviense

The rounded umbels, 5–7.5cm (2–3in) across, consist of 50 or more small, star-shaped, pale pink flowers with purple midribs, borne on stiff stems. The broad, grey, elliptical, almost horizontal, leaves, which are 15–23cm (6–9in) long, are a special feature.
Origins Central Asia.
Flowering height 20cm (8in).
Flowering time Late spring to early summer.
Hardiness Fully hardy.

Allium nigrum

The umbels, 7.5cm (3in) across, consist of about 30 creamy white, cup-shaped flowers, each with a dark green ovary.
Origins Mediterranean.
Flowering height 70cm (28in).
Flowering time Late spring to early summer.
Hardiness Frost hardy, so provide a mulch in winter.

Allium schubertii

The rounded umbels, which are borne on stiff stems, have inner and outer zones of small, star-shaped, mauve-blue flowers.
Origins Eastern Mediterranean to central Asia.
Flowering height 40cm (16in).
Flowering time Early summer.
Hardiness Frost hardy, so provide a mulch in winter.

Allium sphaerocephalon

The ovoid umbels, 2.5cm (1in) across, are formed from densely packed pink to dark red flowers. It looks good with bronze foliage.
Origins Europe, northern Africa and western Asia.
Flowering height 50cm (20in).
Flowering time Early to midsummer.
Hardiness Fully hardy.

amaryllis amaryllidaceae

This is a genus of just one species of autumn-flowering, deciduous, perennial bulbs that originally came from coastal hills and besides streams in the Western Cape, South Africa. The amaryllis is often confused with the tender *Hippeastrum*.

Site Grow in full sun in moist but well-drained soil in garden borders or containers.

Cultivation In late summer, when the large, round bulbs are dormant, plant them so that their necks are just at soil level. If planting in pots, use soil-based compost (potting mix) with additional leaf mould and sand. Protect the foliage from frost when temperatures fall below freezing.

Propagation Sow seed at 16°C (61°F) when ripe. Grow on under glass for 1 to 2 seasons before planting in final position outdoors. Remove offsets in spring.

Pests and diseases Slugs, narcissus bulb fly; under glass, aphids and red spider mite can be a problem.

Amaryllis belladonna

The belladonna lily or Jersey lily, as it is commonly known, bears umbels of 6 or more scented, pink, funnel-shaped flowers, 6–10cm (2–4in) long. The strappy, fleshy leaves are produced after flowering. The belladonna lily looks especially effective planted among low-growing shrubs. In cooler areas, it should be grown against a warm wall. This is a truly glorious bulb, which will add drama to any border scheme.
Origins Western Cape, South Africa.
Flowering height 60cm (24in).
Flowering time Autumn.
Hardiness Frost hardy.

anemone blanda

anemone nemorosa

begonia 'Giant Flowered Pendula Yellow'

begonia 'Double Orange'

anemone ranunculaceae

The Greek word *anemos* means "wind", which helps to explain why the anemone is commonly known as the windflower. The delicate petals quiver in the slightest breeze. This is a genus of about 120 species, some of which have perennial rhizomatous or tuberous rootstocks.

Site Grow in sun or partial shade; plant in garden borders, in the "eye" of a tree or in outdoor containers. *A. nemorosa* prefers light shade.

Cultivation Plant the tubers of *A. blanda* 5cm (2in) deep, as soon as they are available in autumn. Because they do not like to dry out too much, they can be soaked overnight before planting. As the tubers mature, they will grow to about 10cm (4in) across, producing many flowers. These will self-seed to create large colonies. The knobbly, misshapen tubers of *A. coronaria* De Caen Group and St. Bridgid Group are also best soaked overnight before planting and then planted with the buds pointing upwards, 7.5cm (3in) deep, in autumn (with a mulch) or in spring. Allow to dry off after flowering. Plant the rhizomes of *A. nemorosa* 5cm (2in) deep in autumn.

Propagation Separate the tubers when dormant; plants will self-seed.

Pests and diseases Caterpillars, slugs, leaf spot and powdery mildew.

Anemone blanda

The solitary flowers, about 2.5cm (1in) or more across, have 10 to 15 white, pale blue or dark blue, occasionally mauve and pink, petals. The attractive leaves are fern-like. They associate beautifully with primroses and all early dwarf daffodils, and are excellent in garden borders, beneath the eye of a tree or in pots.

Origins Eastern Mediterranean.

Flowering height 10–15cm (4–6in).

Flowering time Late winter to early spring, over 6 to 8 weeks.

Hardiness Fully hardy.

Anemone coronaria De Caen Group and St. Bridgid Group

The De Caen Group has solitary, single, white, red, pink, mauve or blue flowers. These are 3–7.5cm (1–3in) across and have 6 to 8 petals. The St Bridgid Group has double flowers with a multitude of petals. Colours vary from red, pink, violet-blue to white. All these anemones should be grown in a warm sheltered spot near the front of a border or in containers. They make ideal cut flowers.

Origins Both groups derive from the original species, *A. coronaria*, found in the Mediterranean area.

Flowering height 25cm (10in)

Flowering time Late spring to early summer, depending on planting time.

Hardiness Fully hardy.

Anemone nemorosa

Commonly known as the wood anemone, these plants bear dainty, demure, solitary white flowers, sometimes with a pink flush, about 2.5cm (1in) across and with 6 to 8 petals.

Origins Europe.

Flowering height 7.5–15cm (3–6in).

Flowering time Late spring.

Hardiness Fully hardy.

begonia begoniaceae

The genus was named in honour of Michel Bégon (1638–1710), a French botanist and Governor of French Canada. It contains about 900 species, some of which are tuberous rooted. The tuberous begonias, whose tubers are dormant in winter, include the Tuberhybrida, Multiflora and Pendula types, which derive from species growing in the Andes. They may be found under the headings Fimbriata begonias, which bear carnation-type petals, Exotic begonias, which have 2 tones to their colours, the Non-Stop flowering kinds, which are generally compact and good as bedding-out plants, and the Pendulous or Cascading types, which are useful in hanging baskets or raised beds.

Site Grow in sun or partial shade in garden borders or containers.

Cultivation Start the tubers into growth in spring indoors, placing them on the surface of the compost (soil mix), the hollow side upwards, at 16–18°C (61–64°F). Move outside into summer flowering positions after all risk of frost has passed. Allow to dry after flowering. Lift tubers in autumn, dry off and dust with fungicide and store in cool, dry conditions at 5–7°C (41–45°F).

Propagation Sow seed and root basal cuttings in spring.

Pests and diseases Vine weevil is a major problem in late summer.

Begonia 'Billie Langdon'

This very large begonia has pure white flowers, up to 18cm (7in) in diameter. The mid-green leaves can reach 20cm (8in) in length. It is best planted singly in a heavy pot.

Origins Of garden origin.

Flowering height 60cm (24in).

Flowering time Summer.

Hardiness Frost tender.

Begonia 'Champagne'

The double flowers, 5–7.5cm (2–3in) across, with creamy white petals, form generous clusters of cascading colour around the plant. This begonia is ideal for planting in wall pots, window boxes or hanging baskets.

Origins Of garden origin.

Flowering height Trails to 20cm (8in).

Flowering time Summer.

Hardiness Frost tender.

Begonia 'Double Orange'

This upright begonia has double orange flowers which are up to 10cm (4in) across, and look wonderful in pots. There are also double yellow, pink, red and white begonias.

Origins Of garden origin.

Flowering height 20cm (8in).

Flowering time Summer.

Hardiness Frost tender.

Begonia 'Giant Flowered Pendula Yellow'

The large double and single yellow flowers are 5cm (2in) across. This pendulous begonia is ideal for hanging baskets. There is also an attractive 'Giant Flowered Pendula Orange' as well as pink, white and red varieties.

Origins Of garden origin.

Flowering height Trails to 20cm (8in).

Flowering time Summer.

Hardiness Frost tender.

calochortus luteus 'Golden Orb'

camassia leichtlinii subsp. *leichtlinii*

camassia quamash

Begonia grandis subsp. *evansiana*

A tuberous begonia with notched, olive-green leaves, 10cm (4in) long, which are pale green, sometimes red, on the underside. The pink or white flowers are fragrant.
Origins China to Malaysia, Japan.
Flowering height 50cm (20in); **Spread** 30cm (12in).
Flowering time Summer.
Hardiness Half hardy.

Begonia 'Helene Harms'

An upright begonia with many semi-double, bronze-yellow flowers, 5–7.5cm (2–3in) across. The mid-green leaves are 20cm (8in) long.

Origins Of garden origin.
Flowering height 13cm (5in); **Spread** 15cm (6in).
Flowering time Summer.
Hardiness Frost tender.

Begonia 'Pendula Orange'

The flowers of this trailing begonia are finer than those of the Giant Flowered varieties. They reach 5cm (2in) in diameter, but are held on slender stems.
Origins Of garden origin.
Flowering height Spreads and trails to 20cm (8in).
Flowering time Summer.
Hardiness Frost tender.

calochortus lilaceae

The name originated from the Greek words *kalós*, "beautiful", and *chortos*, "grass". The flowers are, indeed, beautiful, and the leaves are grass-like. This is a genus of about 60 species of bulbs from grasslands and open woodland of western North America and Mexico. Common names range from fairy lanterns, cat's ears and butterfly tulip to globe lily.
Site Grow in full sun.
Cultivation Plant the bulbs 7.5cm (3in) deep and 7.5cm (3in) apart in pots containing soil-based compost (potting mix). Then they are best overwintered under cover to guard against rain. In late spring, the pots can be buried in garden soil where they can be allowed to flower. In mild, sunny areas, plant direct into well-drained soil in sheltered borders in autumn. After flowering, the bulbs divide and do not flower again the following year but miss 1 to 2 seasons.
Propagation Sow seed in pots in a cold frame as soon as ripe or remove offsets in late summer.
Pests and diseases None.

Calochortus luteus 'Golden Orb'

Thin but sturdy branched stems bear 1 to 7 deep yellow, open bell-shaped flowers, 4–6cm (1½–2½in) across, each with reddish-brown marks towards the base of the petals. *C. luteus* is commonly known as yellow mariposa. Its yellow flowers with brown blotches appear in spring.
Origins Of garden origin; derived from species growing in California, USA.
Flowering height 50–60cm (20–24in).
Flowering time Summer.
Hardiness Frost hardy.

camassia hyacinthaceae

These plants are commonly known as quamash, the name given by the Native Americans of the Pacific North-west, where they originate. This is a genus of about 5 species, which thrive in damp meadowland. They are also known as wild hyacinths, which they resemble.
Site Grow in sun or partial shade.
Cultivation In autumn, plant the bulbs in borders or grassland at a depth of 10cm (4in) and 10cm (4in) apart and allow to naturalize. They will form good groups.
Propagation Sow seed in pots in a cold frame as soon as ripe or remove offsets in late summer.
Pests and diseases No special problems.

Camassia leichtlinii subsp. *leichtlinii*

Tall racemes, 10–30cm (4–12in) long, produce star-shaped, creamy white flowers, each 5–7.5cm (2–3in) across. Blue forms are also available. This camassia is also known as the Indian lily. It associates well with *Narcissus poeticus* var. *recurvus* (pheasant's eye narcissus).
Origins Western North America, from California to British Columbia.
Flowering height 75cm (30in).
Flowering time Late spring to early summer.
Hardiness Frost hardy.

Camassia quamash

Known as the common camassia or quamash, this summer-flowering bulb bears a spike of star-shaped, white, violet or blue flowers, 7cm (3in) across. The bulbs were once an important source of food for Native Americans.
Origins Canada, USA.
Flowering height 20–80cm (8–32in).
Flowering time Summer.
Hardiness Frost hardy.

canna 'Roi Humbert'

cardiocrinum giganteum

chionodoxa forbesii 'Pink Giant'

canna cannaceae

Commonly known as the Indian shot plant, this is a genus of 50 species of rhizomatous herbaceous perennials from moist open areas of forest in Asia and the tropical parts of North and South America. The genus name comes from the Greek *kanna*, "reed".

Site Grow outdoors in full sun or indoors with some shade from hot sun; can be grown in water.

Cultivation In spring, plant the rhizomes under glass in large containers, 5cm (2in) deep and 60cm (24in) apart; if required, move outside from early to midsummer. At the same time, if wished, transplant from containers into sunny, sheltered borders. Deadhead to promote continuity of flowering. Apply a liquid feed every month. Before the foliage turns black with frost in autumn, remove the stems, dig up roots and store in barely moist peat or leaf mould in frost-free conditions. In just one season a single rhizome will produce a root system up to 50cm (20in) across.

Propagation Sow seed at 21°C (70°F) in spring or autumn. Chip seed or soak for 24 hours in warm water before sowing. In early spring, divide rhizomes into short sections, each with a prominent eye. Pot on and start into growth at 16°C (61°F), watering sparingly at first.

Pests and diseases Outdoors, slugs and caterpillars; indoors, red spider mite.

Canna 'Roi Humbert'

Formerly known as *C.* 'Red King Humbert', this canna bears large racemes, 20–30cm (8–12in) long, of orange-scarlet flowers. These show up well against the striking reddish bronze, paddle-shaped leaves. The colour associates well with other bronze foliage plants such as grasses or *Foeniculum vulgare* 'Purpureum' (bronze fennel).
Origins Of garden origin.
Flowering height 2.1m (7ft).
Flowering time Mid- to late summer.
Hardiness Half hardy.

Canna 'Lucifer'

Long racemes of red flowers, each edged with yellow and 5cm (2in) wide, accompany the mid-green foliage. This short variety is free flowering.
Origins Of garden origin.
Flowering height 60cm (24in).
Flowering time Mid- to late summer.
Hardiness Half hardy.

Canna 'Orange Perfection'

As its name implies, the flowers of this canna are a beautiful soft orange. This is also a short variety.
Origins Of garden origin.
Flowering height 60–80cm (24–32in).
Flowering time Summer.
Hardiness Half hardy.

cardiocrinum lilaceae

A genus of three species of summer-flowering bulbous perennials, the most commonly grown of which is *Cardiocrinum giganteum* (giant lily). These bulbs are grown for their lily-like flowers and attractive, heart-shaped leaves.

Site Requires partial shade and moist, humus-rich soil. Avoid excessive dryness. Ideal for growing in a woodland garden.

Cultivation In autumn, plant bulbs just below the soil surface. Protect emerging growth in spring with a dry mulch. Water well in summer and provide a mulch of organic matter to prevent water evaporating.

Propagation The bulbs die after flowering, but offsets or "daughter" bulbs are produced which will flower in three to five years. Ripe seed may take seven years to flower.

Pests and diseases Lily viruses and slug damage.

Cardiocrinum giganteum

The racemes bear up to 20 fragrant, trumpet-shaped, cream flowers, streaked with purplish red inside, which grow up to 15cm (6in) long, followed by decorative seedheads.
Origins Himalayas, north-west Burma, south-west China.
Flowering height 2m (6½ft).
Flowering time Mid- to late summer.
Hardiness Fully hardy.

chionodoxa hyacinthaceae

Commonly known as the glory of the snow, this is a genus of 6 species of bulbs found on open mountain sides and forests in Crete, western Turkey and Cyprus. They are closely related to scillas.

Site Grow in full sun.

Cultivation In autumn, plant the bulbs 5cm (2in) deep and 5cm (2in) apart.

Propagation Sow seed in pots in a cold frame as soon as ripe. Remove offsets in summer.

Pests and diseases No special problems.

Chionodoxa forbesii 'Pink Giant'

This bulb produces racemes of 4 to 12 star-shaped, pale pink flowers, 1–2cm (½–¾in) wide, which have white centres. Plant several in a pot with violas and dwarf daffodils.
Origins Of garden origin; derived from species in western Turkey.
Flowering height 15cm (6in).
Flowering time Early to mid-spring.
Hardiness Fully hardy.

Chionodoxa luciliae

Up to 3 star-shaped, blue flowers, 1–2cm (½–¾in) wide and with white centres, are borne in racemes. *C. luciliae* will naturalize in borders or beneath trees, where it produces several flower spikes per bulb.
Origins Western Turkey.
Flowering height 15cm (6in).
Flowering time Early to mid-spring.
Hardiness Fully hardy.

colchicum autumnale

corydalis solida

colchicum colchicaceae

Colchicums are commonly known as autumn crocus (because of their resemblance to the better-known spring-flowering crocus) or as naked ladies (because they flower before the leaves emerge). In the United States they are known as naked boys. The genus contains about 45 species of corms from alpine and sub-alpine meadows and stony slopes of Europe, northern Africa, western and central Asia, northern India and western China.

Site Grow in full sun.

Cultivation In summer or early autumn, plant corms 10cm (4in) deep in open ground in borders or grassland.

Propagation Sow seed in pots in a cold frame as soon as ripe, or separate corms when dormant in summer. Increases freely.

Pests and diseases Grey mould and slugs.

Colchicum autumnale 'September'

Each corm produces 1 to 6 goblet-shaped, lavender-pink flowers, with petals 4–6cm (1½–2½in) long. The flowers soon flop over. The broad leaves, 25cm (10in) long, appear after flowering, growing most in spring. The leaves might dwarf other neighbouring spring-flowering bulbs, so take care with the position. This is a good plant for grass. The species, *C. autumnale*, is sometimes known as meadow saffron.
Origins Europe.
Flowering height 15cm (6in).
Flowering time Early autumn.
Hardiness Fully hardy.

Colchicum bivonae

Large, funnel-shaped, pinkish purple flowers, checkered with dark purple, appear in autumn. The leaves are produced in spring.

Origins Italy to west Turkey.
Flowering height 10–15cm (4–6in).
Flowering time Early autumn.
Hardiness Fully hardy.

Colchicum speciosum 'Album'

From 1 to 3 goblet-shaped, weather-resistant, white flowers, with petals 5–7.5cm (2–3in) long, appear before the glossy leaves. This is an excellent plant in open ground in borders or grassland in summer or early autumn. Left undisturbed, these corms will produce large clumps.
Origins Caucasus, north-eastern Turkey, Iran.
Flowering height 18cm (7in).
Flowering time Autumn.
Hardiness Fully hardy.

corydalis papaveraceae

The flowers are an unusual shape. Each one bears a long spur on the upper petal, and this gave rise to the name of the genus, for the Greek word *korydalis* means "lark", and the spur on the flowers was thought to resemble the spur of the lark. This is a genus of about 300 species of fleshy or fibrous-rooted annuals and biennials and tuberous or rhizomatous perennials. Most are herbaceous, although a few are evergreen. Many are from wooded or rocky mountain sites in northern temperate regions.

Site Grow *C. solida* in full sun (although it will tolerate partial shade) and *C. cava* and *C. fumariifolia* in partial shade.

Cultivation In autumn, plant tubers 7.5cm (3in) deep in borders or beneath trees and shrubs, where they will quickly colonize.

Propagation Sow seed in pots in a cold frame as soon as ripe. Divide spring-flowering species in autumn. Plants increase freely.

Pests and diseases Snails and slugs.

Corydalis cava

Formerly known as *C. bulbosa*, this corydalis has dense spikes of dark purple or white flowers, each up to 2.5cm (1in) long with downward curving spurs.
Origins Europe.
Flowering height 10–20cm (4–8in).
Flowering time Spring.
Hardiness Fully hardy.

Corydalis fumariifolia

Formerly known as *C. ambigua*, the bright blue or purplish blue flowers, about 2.5cm (1in) long, have flattened, triangular spurs.
Origins Russia, China, Japan.
Flowering height 10–15cm (4–6in).
Flowering time Spring to summer.
Hardiness Fully hardy.

Corydalis solida

Commonly known as fumewort (and formerly known as *C. transsylvanica*), this plant bears dense racemes of pale mauve-pink to red-purple or white flowers, each to 2cm (¾in) long, with downward-curving spurs, held above grey foliage. *C.* 'George Baker' has deep reddish salmon flowers. They look wonderful with daffodils, which make ideal spring bedfellows, while taller *Lilium martagon* (martagon lilies) can be planted to follow on later.
Origins Northern Europe and Asia.
Flowering height 18cm (7in).
Flowering time Spring.
Hardiness Fully hardy.

crinum × powellii 'Album'

crocosmia 'Lucifer'

crocus chrysanthus 'Blue Pearl'

crinum amaryllidaceae

The genus is named after the Greek word *krinon*, "lily". It includes about 130 species of deciduous or evergreen bulbs which are found near streams and lakes throughout tropical regions and South Africa. Note that contact with the sap may irritate the skin.

Site Grow in full sun outdoors in a sheltered border or in pots under glass.

Cultivation The bulbs are extremely large and can measure up to 20cm (8in) across. In spring, plant so that the neck of the bulb is just above soil level. In a conservatory plant in soil-based compost (potting mix) with added sand and fertilizer, and grow in full or bright but filtered light. Water freely when in growth, keep moist after flowering. Provide a deep mulch in winter.

Propagation Sow seed at 21°C (70°F) as soon as ripe. Remove offsets in spring.

Pests and diseases None.

Crinum × *powellii* 'Album'

Umbels of up to 10 widely flared, fragrant, white flowers, up to 10cm (4in) long, are borne above broad leaves, which may reach up to 1.5m (5ft). *C.* × *powellii* is pink.

Origins Of garden origin; a hybrid of 2 South African species.
Flowering height 1.5m (5ft).
Flowering time Late summer to autumn.
Hardiness Borderline to fully hardy.

crocosmia iridaceae

The name of the genus derives from *krokos*, the Greek name for the saffron crocus, and *osme*, meaning smell, because the dried flowers smell of saffron when immersed in warm water. This is a small genus of only 7 species of clump-forming corms from grassland in South Africa. The name montbretia is generally applied to all crocosmias although, strictly speaking, montbretia is the hybrid *C.* × *crocosmiiflora*.

Site Grow in sun or partial shade.

Cultivation In spring, plant corms 7.5–10cm (3–4in) deep among shrubs or in a herbaceous border, but mulch during the first winter and in subsequent severe prolonged frosty spells. In marginal areas, plant beneath a sheltered south-facing wall. Tall growth will benefit from support in early summer. Lift and divide clumps in spring to retain vigour.

Propagation Sow seeds in pots as soon as ripe. Divide in spring just before growth begins.

Pests and diseases Red spider mites may be a problem.

Crocosmia 'Lucifer'

Upward-facing, bright red flowers, 5cm (2in) long, are borne on tall, strong, slightly arching stems.

Origins Of garden origin.
Flowering height 1m (39in).
Flowering time Late summer.
Hardiness Frost hardy.

crocus iridaceae

The crocus is one of our best-known late winter and early spring flowers. The name is derived from the Greek *krokos*, saffron crocus, and the genus includes the species *Crocus sativus*, which is cultivated for the spice saffron, which is obtained from its stigmas. The genus embraces more than 80 species of dwarf corms found in a wide variety of locations, from central and southern Europe, northern Africa, the Middle East, central Asia and western China. Hundreds of cultivars have been produced.

Site Grow in full sun.

Cultivation Plant corms 7.5cm (3in) deep in borders or containers in autumn for late winter- to spring-flowering crocuses and in late summer for the autumn-flowering ones.

Propagation Many crocuses self-seed naturally. Remove baby corms during dormancy.

Pests and diseases Squirrels, mice and voles eat the corms, and birds will pick off the flowers.

Crocus chrysanthus 'Blue Pearl'

The flowers have a soft blue outer colour, with white inner tepals and yellow throats. The delicate colouring is superb.

Origins Of garden origin.
Flowering height 7.5cm (3in).
Flowering time Late winter to early spring.
Hardiness Fully hardy.

Crocus chrysanthus 'Zwanenburg Bronze'

The pale yellow flowers are bronze coloured on the exterior. Plant them near purple violets or surround with a mulch of coloured gravel.

Origins Of garden origin.
Flowering height 7.5cm (3in).
Flowering time Early spring.
Hardiness Fully hardy.

Crocus × *luteus* 'Golden Yellow'

This cultivar is sometimes sold as *C.* 'Dutch Yellow'. The sterile flowers are a rich golden yellow and associate well with dwarf daffodils, *Anemone blanda* and violas. This cultivar also looks effective planted in grass. Increase by dividing the clumps.

Origins Of garden origin.
Flowering height 7.5cm (3in).
Flowering time Early spring.
Hardiness Fully hardy.

Crocus sieberi subsp. *sublimis* 'Tricolor'

Each petal has 3 bands of colour: yellow at the centre, then white, then blue-purple. The colouring is exquisite.

Origins Of garden origin.
Flowering height 5–7.5cm (2–3in).
Flowering time Late winter to early spring.
Hardiness Fully hardy.

crocus tommasinianus

cyclamen coum

cyclamen persicum

Crocus tommasinianus

The flowers vary from pale silvery lilac to reddish-purple. On dull days the slender flowers are rather modest, but in sun they open up to create a wonderful display.
Origins Woods and shady hillsides in southern Hungary, the former Yugoslavia and north-western Bulgaria.
Flowering height 7.5–10cm (3–4in).
Flowering time Late winter to early spring.
Hardiness Fully hardy.

Crocus tommasinianus 'Ruby Giant'

The slightly rounded, deep violet-blue flowers, which are sterile, associate well with white *Anemone blanda* and early primroses.
Origins Of garden origin.
Flowering height 7.5cm (3in).
Flowering time Late winter to early spring.
Hardiness Fully hardy.

cyclamen primulaceae

The name of the genus comes from the Greek *kyklos*, "circle", probably in reference to the fact that in some species the seed stalks have the curious habit of twisting after flowering. The fruiting capsule is drawn down to soil level. The genus includes 19 species of tuberous perennials, found in a wide variety of habitats from the eastern Mediterranean to Iran and south to Somalia, where there is winter rainfall and a dryish summer dormancy period. The rounded to heart-shaped leaves often have attractive silver markings.
Site Grow in sun or partial shade.
Cultivation In autumn, plant tubers 3–5cm (1¼–2in) deep in border soil. They do best in partial shade beneath trees and shrubs where the soil does not dry out.
Propagation *C. hederifolium* will self-seed naturally. Sow seed as soon as ripe, in darkness, at 6–12°C (43–54°F) or, for *C. persicum*, at 12–15°C (54–59°F). Soak seed for 10 hours before sowing and then rinse.
Pests and diseases Squirrels, mice and voles eat the tubers. Cyclamen are also prone to vine weevil, red spider mites, cyclamen mite and, under glass, grey mould.

Crocus tournefortii

The flowers are pale lilac-blue with an orange stigma and white anthers.
Origins South Greece and Crete.
Flowering height 5–7.5cm (2–3in).
Flowering time Autumn to winter.
Hardiness Fully hardy (borderline).

Crocus vernus 'Pickwick'

The white flowers are streaked with lilac-purple. Plant beneath dwarf daffodils and early species tulips.
Origins Of garden origin.
Flowering height 7.5cm (3in).
Flowering time Early spring.
Hardiness Fully hardy.

Crocus 'Zephyr'

The pale silver-blue flowers, veined with dark blue, have yellow throats and white anthers.
Origins Of garden origin.
Flowering height 10–12cm (4–5in).
Flowering time Autumn.
Hardiness Fully hardy.

Cyclamen coum

The nodding, pale purple flowers have darker staining towards the mouth. The attractive rounded leaves often have silver markings. This cyclamen associates well with snowdrops.
Origins Bulgaria, the Caucasus, Turkey and Lebanon.
Flowering height 5–7.5cm (2–3in).
Flowering time Late winter.
Hardiness Fully hardy.

Cyclamen hederifolium

This species was formerly known as *C. neapolitanum*. The pink flowers have a darker red stain towards the mouth. The attractive ivy- or heart-shaped leaves are often patterned.
Origins Italy to Turkey.
Flowering height 10cm (4in).
Flowering time Autumn.
Hardiness Fully hardy.

Cyclamen mirabile

The pale pink flowers have delicately serrated petals, with purple-stained mouths. The leaves are heart-shaped and patterned with silver blotches.
Origins Bulgaria, the Caucasus, Turkey and Lebanon.
Flowering height 10cm (4in).
Flowering time Autumn.
Hardiness Fully hardy.

Cyclamem persicum

The pink, red or white flowers have darker staining towards the mouth, and the heart-shaped leaves are often patterned. Many cultivars have been bred, and there are various shades and sizes to choose from, but look for those with a sweet scent and attractively marked foliage. Among the many florist's cyclamens are the scented, miniature Miracle Series, which are only about 15cm (6in) high, and the much larger ruffled-petalled, white-flowered 'Victoria', which is 30cm (12in) high. They are tolerant of low temperatures outdoors in early autumn. They are normally grown as pot plants and are ideal for cool conservatory planting schemes or the windowsill of a north-facing house.
Origins The species comes from the south-eastern Mediterranean to northern Africa.
Flowering height 10–20cm (4–8in).
Flowering time Early winter to early spring.
Hardiness Frost tender.

dahlia 'Bishop of Llandaff'

dahlia 'Brilliant Eye'

dahlia 'Claire de Lune'

dahlia 'Purple Gem'

dahlia asteraceae

The dahlia is one of the showiest flowers in the summer border. The genus was named in honour of the Swedish botanist Dr Anders Dahl (1751–89), who was a pupil of Linnaeus. It includes about 30 species and some 2,000 cultivars of bushy, tuberous-rooted perennials from mountainous areas of Mexico and Central America. Dahlias are available in a wide range of colours, including both strident and pastel shades of yellow, orange, red, lavender, deep purple and pink as well as white. They vary in flower size from about 5cm (2in) across, as with the Pompon dahlias, to enormous dinner-plate-sized flowers, almost 30cm (12in) across. They are also available as dwarf patio cultivars and large exhibition dahlias. Nearly all the medium to tall plants will need staking.
Site Grow in full sun.
Cultivation Start tubers into growth under glass in early spring but do not plant out until all risk of frosts has passed in early summer. Cut off top growth and remove tubers in autumn and store them in dry, frost-free conditions. Most dahlias will need staking or providing with strong supports.
Propagation Start tubers into growth in early spring and either take basal shoot cuttings or divide tubers into smaller sections, making sure each has a shoot.
Pests and diseases Caterpillars, earwigs and slugs may cause problems outdoors; stored tubers may rot.

Dahlia 'Arabian Night'
This is a small Decorative flower-head type. The velvet red petals are long, broad and gently rounded. It can be grown in borders, but also looks effective in large half-barrels.
Origins Of garden origin.
Flowering height 1m (39in).
Flowering time Summer to autumn.
Hardiness Half hardy.

Dahlia 'Bishop of Llandaff'
This popular Miscellaneous Group dahlia has deep red, semi-double flowers, with yellow anthers, and black-red leaves. Its warm hues make a valuable contribution to late summer to autumn borders.
Origins Of garden origin.
Flowering height 1m (39in).
Flowering time Summer to autumn.
Hardiness Half hardy.

Dahlia 'Brilliant Eye'
This is a Pompon flowerhead type. The bright red, rolled petals make neat flowers, which are only 5cm (2in) in diameter. It looks lovely in association with blue caryopteris or *Aster* (Michaelmas daisies).
Origins Of garden origin.
Flowering height 90cm (36in).
Flowering time Summer to autumn.
Hardiness Half hardy.

Dahlia 'Clair de Lune'
A Collerette flowerhead type where the flowers are formed by an inner ring of cream petals surrounded by an outer ring of clear yellow petals. It can be grown in borders or medium to large pots, and it looks especially lovely against bronze or pale green foliage.

Origins Of garden origin.
Flowering height 1.1m (3ft 6in).
Flowering time Summer to autumn.
Hardiness Half hardy.

Dahlia 'David Howard'
A Decorative flowerhead type, this dahlia is blessed with bronze foliage, which provides the perfect backdrop for the golden orange flowers.
Origins Of garden origin.
Flowering height 75cm (30in).
Flowering time Summer to autumn.
Hardiness Half hardy.

Dahlia 'Geerlings Indian Summer'
A small-flowered Semi-cactus flowerhead type whose pointed,

rolled petals are red. This dahlia is ideal for growing in containers, such as large half-barrels, as well as at the front of borders.
Origins Of garden origin.
Flowering height 1.2m (4ft).
Flowering time Summer to autumn.
Hardiness Half hardy.

Dahlia 'Purple Gem'
A Cactus flowerhead type with long, narrow, pointed, recurved petals that are rich purple. It is good in borders and ideal for cutting.
Flowering height 1m (39in).
Origins Of garden origin.
Flowering time Summer to autumn.
Hardiness Half hardy.

eranthis ranunculaceae

This is a small genus of about 7 species of small, hard, knobbly tubers from woodlands and shady habitats of Europe and Asia. They prefer an alkaline or neutral soil to one that is acidic.
Site Grow in full sun or light shade.
Cultivation Plant the small, pea-like tubers 5cm (2in) deep. They can be difficult to establish if too dry, so plant as soon as they are available in autumn, soaking them overnight before planting; alternatively, buy aconites growing "in the green" in spring. They are ideal for a cultivated "eye" beneath a tree, where they will flower at the same time as snowdrops. They soon form large clumps and naturalize quickly in ideal conditions, especially in alkaline soils.
Propagation Sow seed in a cold frame when ripe in late spring. Dig up and separate tubers in spring after flowering.
Pests and diseases Prone to smuts.

Eranthis hyemalis
Commonly known as winter aconite, this is one of the first flowers to emerge after midwinter has passed. The golden petals are surrounded by a collar of deeply dissected green leaves. If you can remember where they have become established in the garden, try digging up a few tubers

in mid- to late autumn and pop them into a small pot, where they will flower from mid- to late winter. They can always be replanted in garden soil after flowering.
Origins Southern France to Bulgaria.
Flowering height 5–7.5cm (2–3in).
Flowering time Winter.
Hardiness Fully hardy.

eranthis hyemalis

eremurus 'Oase'

erythronium dens-canis

erythronium 'Pagoda'

eremurus asphodelaceae

The genus name is very descriptive: *eremos* is a Greek word meaning "solitary", while *oura* means "tail". This is a reference to the tall flower spike that emerges far above the foliage. The plant is commonly known as the foxtail lily or desert candle. This is a genus of 40 to 50 species of clump-forming, fleshy-rooted perennials, which splay out from a central crown. They originate in dry areas of western and central Asia.

Site Grow in full sun in a sheltered spot.

Cultivation Choose a sunny, well-drained spot in the border, and plant the crowns in autumn just below the soil surface; take care not to disturb the roots thereafter. Protect young growth, which is susceptible to frost, with a dry mulch in spring. Offer supports in exposed sites.

Propagation Sow seed in a cold frame in autumn or divide established clumps after flowering.

Pests and diseases Prone to slug damage.

Eremurus × isabellinus
Ruiter hybrids

A group of tall perennials with long, narrow leaves and long racemes of mixed orange, copper and pink flowers. Well-established plants will form a striking picture in the garden.

Origins Of garden origin.

Flowering height Up to 1.5m (5ft).

Flowering time Early and midsummer.

Hardiness Fully hardy.

Eremurus 'Oase'

This is a shorter version of its towering cousins, but still with long narrow leaves and impressive racemes of yellow flowers which fade to orange-brown.

Origins Of garden origin.

Flowering height 90–120cm (3–4ft).

Flowering time Early and midsummer.

Hardiness Fully hardy.

Eremurus robustus

This is an especially tall species with long narrow leaves and massive racemes of pale pink flowers. These are enhanced with golden yellow stamens.

Origins Central Asia.

Flowering height 2.2m (7ft).

Flowering time Early and midsummer.

Hardiness Fully hardy.

Eremurus stenophyllus
subsp. *stenophyllus*

This is a tall perennial with long, narrow leaves and long racemes of clear yellow flowers which fade to orange-brown.

Origins Central Asia, Iran and western Pakistan.

Flowering height 1.5m (5ft).

Flowering time Early and midsummer.

Hardiness Fully hardy.

erythronium lilaceae

The genus contains about 22 species of bulbous perennials from Europe, Asia and North America. The bulbs are unusually long, whitish in colour and rather pointed, hence the common name of dog's tooth violet. The other common names, trout lily and fawn lily, refer to the attractive mottling on the leaves.

Site Grow in partial shade.

Cultivation Plant bulbs 10cm (4in). deep. They can be difficult to establish if they are too dry, so look for bulbs packaged in moist peat. Leave undisturbed so that they can form a large clump.

Propagation Divide established clumps in spring after flowering. Replant at once.

Pests and diseases Prone to slug damage.

Erythronium californicum
'White Beauty'

The delicately mottled leaves act as a beautiful cushion for the white flowers, each of which has a dark orange ring at the centre.

Origins California, USA.

Flowering height 20–30cm (8–12in).

Flowering time Spring.

Hardiness Fully hardy.

Erythronium dens-canis

This is one of the prettiest of spring flowers, with dainty, swept-back petals, which may be white, pink or lilac, and prominent anthers. The leaves have attractive blue and green markings. Plant in borders or among short fine grasses.

Origins Europe and Asia.

Flowering height 10–15cm (4–6in).

Flowering time Spring.

Hardiness Fully hardy.

Erythronium 'Pagoda'

One of the most vigorous cultivars, this is derived from a hardy Californian species, *E. tuolumnense*. It has yellow, swept-back petals and prominent, deep yellow anthers, with 2 or more flowers per stem. The glossy leaves are a plain deep green. A well-established clump could be displayed to advantage against dark green foliage.

Origins Of garden origin.

Flowering height 15–35cm (6–14in).

Flowering time Spring.

Hardiness Fully hardy.

Erythronium revolutum

The pale to dark pink flowers of the American trout lily, as it is popularly called, are pendent and have reflexed petals. They look striking above the green leaves, which are mottled with brown.

Origins North California, USA.

Flowering height 20–30cm (8–12in).

Flowering time Mid-spring.

Hardiness Fully hardy.

eucomis bicolor 'White Dwarf'

freesia 'Wintergold'

fritillaria imperialis

eucomis hyacinthaceae

This is a genus of about 15 species of bulbs found in southern Africa. The name is derived from the Greek words *eu-*, "beautiful", and *kome*, "head", which refer to the tuft of small leaves growing out of the top of the flower. Its common name, the pineapple lily, is even more descriptive.

Site Grow indoors, or in warm, sheltered areas beneath a sunny wall.

Cultivation Plant the large, rounded bulbs 15cm (6in) deep in medium-sized pots, using a soil-based compost (potting mix), with added grit, and place in full light. Keep dry and frost free in winter, and start into growth in spring. Apply a liquid feed at regular intervals throughout summer. Re-pot every year. Alternatively, in warm, sheltered districts where risk of frost is negligible, plant outdoors in a warm, sunny spot beneath a wall; mulch in severe winters.

Propagation Remove offsets in spring after flowering, at the time of re-potting, or sow seed at 16°C (61°F) in autumn or spring.

Pests and diseases None.

Eucomis autumnalis

The small, pale green or white flowers are star-shaped and carried on a dense spike. The flower spike is topped with the familiar crown of bracts.
Origins South Africa.
Flowering height 20–30cm (8–12in).
Flowering time Late summer to autumn.
Hardiness Fully hardy.

Eucomis bicolor 'White Dwarf'

Tall stems bear racemes of pale green flowers topped with a crown of pineapple-type bracts. The lower leaves are attractively wavy.
Origins Of garden origin.
Flowering height 40cm (16in).
Flowering time Late summer.
Hardiness Fully to borderline hardy.

Eucomis comosa

A popular eucomis, this plant, with its star-shaped, pinkish white flowers, also lures butterflies to the garden. The stem is spotted with purple, while the leaves, with their wavy margins, are enhanced by purple spots on the undersides.
Origins South Africa.
Flowering height 70cm (28in).
Flowering time Late summer.
Hardiness Fully hardy.

Eucomis pallidiflora

Tall and dramatic, this summer-flowering bulb is commonly known as the giant pineapple flower or the giant pineapple lily. The spikes of star-shaped, greenish white flowers, with their crown of bracts, can look especially exotic in herbaceous borders.
Origins South Africa.
Flowering height 45–75cm (18–30in).
Flowering time Summer.
Hardiness Frost hardy.

freesia iridaceae

This is one of the best-loved cut flowers, renowned for its perfume and beautiful array of colours. The genus was named by the German plant collector, C.E. Echlon, who died in South Africa in 1868, in honour of his student Friedrich Heinrich Theodor Freese (d.1876). It includes 6 or more species of corms from rocky upland sites to lowland sandy parts of South Africa. The first species to be sent to England in 1816 had white flowers, and it was not until 1898 that a yellow-coloured species was introduced, whereupon selective hybridization could begin.

Site Grow indoors or use outdoors as a summer bedding plant.

Cultivation Indoors, the corms may be planted in early spring, 7.5cm (3in) deep and 5–7.5cm (2–3in) apart. Choose medium to large pots and use a soil-based compost (potting mix), with added grit. Shade from sun and keep moist until established. Position in full light, and water freely. Keep temperatures below 13°C (55°F). Apply a liquid feed at regular intervals throughout summer once flower buds appear. Gradually reduce watering after flowering until the compost is dry. Leave dormant until re-potting in autumn. Alternatively, plant outside in late spring to a depth of 7.5cm (3in) in a warm, sheltered border for flowering in late summer. Keep well watered through their growing period. Either discard corms at the end of the season and start again with treated corms the following season or dry them off and overwinter in a frost-free environment.

Propagation Remove offsets in autumn or sow seed at 13–18°C (55–64°F) in autumn or winter.

Pests and diseases Red spider mite, aphids, dry rot and fusarium wilt.

Freesia 'Everett'

The familiar funnel-shaped flowers are pinkish red in colour. They are also fragrant.
Origins Of garden origin.
Flowering height 30cm (12in).
Flowering time Treated corms planted in pots in early spring will flower in midsummer. Those planted out in the borders from mid- to late spring will flower in late summer.
Hardiness Half hardy.

Freesia 'Wintergold'

The fragrant, funnel-shaped flowers are yellow.
Origins Of garden origin.
Flowering height 25cm (10in).
Flowering time Treated corms planted in pots in early spring will flower in midsummer. Those planted out in the borders from mid- to late spring will flower in late summer.
Hardiness Half hardy.

fritillaria meleagris

galanthus nivalis

galanthus nivalis 'Flore Pleno'

galanthus 'S. Arnott'

fritillaria lilaceae

This is a genus of about 100 species of bulbs offering a wide range of flowering types, from giant, showy crown imperials to the small but much-loved snake's head fritillaries. They are found throughout the temperate regions of the northern hemisphere, from the Mediterranean through south-western Asia and also western areas of North America.

Site Grow in full sun.

Cultivation In autumn, plant the large bulbs of *F. imperialis* and *F. persica* 20cm (8in) deep in garden soil where they will not be disturbed, or in large containers in compost (potting mix). *F. meleagris* has much smaller bulbs and so should be planted 10cm (4in) deep. Fritillaries benefit from a layer of grit beneath the bulb at the time of planting and extra lime, unless the soil is alkaline. They like a hot, dry summer after flowering. They may be grown as a clump or spaced 90cm (3ft) apart so that each plant can be fully appreciated.

Propagation Divide offsets in late summer.

Pests and diseases Slugs and lily beetle.

Fritillaria imperialis

Known as the crown imperial, the bulb produces a stout stem topped by impressive umbels of 3 to 6 pendent bells, which may be orange, yellow or, more often, red, out of which a crown of glossy, leaf-like bracts emerges. Both the bulbs and flowers have a distinctive foxy smell. Introduced into Europe before 1592, this has long been a favourite bulb, both of the grand, formal garden and the cottage garden.
Origins Southern Turkey to Kashmir.
Flowering height 70cm (28in).
Flowering time Late spring.
Hardiness Fully hardy.

Fritillaria meleagris

Commonly known as the snake's head fritillary, the tiny bulb produces a wiry stem with 1 to 2 broad, bell-shaped flowers, in pink, purple or white, each with strong checker-board markings. The patterning may have given rise to the common name; alternatively, the name may derive from the snake's head appearance of its seedhead soon after the petals have dropped. Grown in grassland, they look perfect beside cowslips and ladysmock. In a container, they look dramatic beneath white *Narcissus* 'Thalia'.
Origins England to western Russia.
Flowering height 20cm (8in).
Flowering time Late spring.
Hardiness Fully hardy.

Fritillaria persica

Commonly known as the Persian lily, the bulb produces a stout stem along which up to 30 dark purple, bell-shaped flowers emerge, each covered with a waxy bloom, giving them an exotic appearance. They like a dry summer after flowering. They look exquisite beside the bright red *Tulipa* 'Apeldoorn' and the later dark purple *T.* 'Queen of Night'.
Origins Southern Turkey to Iran.
Flowering height 80cm (32in).
Flowering time Late spring.
Hardiness Fully hardy.

galanthus amaryllidaceae

The genus name is derived from Greek *gala*, "milk", and *anthos*, "flower", a simple description for one of our most familiar bulbs, which is better known today as the snowdrop. This is one of the first bulbs to flower after midwinter has passed, growing taller as the days lengthen. The genus includes 19 species of bulbs from Europe to western Asia, mostly in upland wooded sites. Snowdrops associate well with *Eranthis hyemalis* (winter aconite), winter-flowering heathers and dwarf Reticulata irises.

Site Grow in sun or partial shade in moist soil that does not dry out in summer.

Cultivation Plant the bulbs 5cm (2in) deep in garden soil or short grass as soon as they are available in early autumn. They can be difficult to establish, although once they have settled down they will form good clumps and may self-seed. Alternatively, buy snowdrops "in the green" – that is, those that have already flowered but still have their green leaves. Plant as soon as purchased. They should establish well. Plant groups of single and double snowdrops together in a border or in grassland. They will always establish more quickly in border soil than grassland but, given time, they will certainly form large groups in either.

Propagation Lift and divide clumps of bulbs after flowering. They will self-seed.

Pests and diseases Narcissus bulb fly and grey mould.

Galanthus nivalis

The common snowdrop bears small, pure white, single flowers, 1–2cm (½–¾in) long, which fall like little drops of snow. The 3 outer petals open to reveal 3 shorter inner petals, each with an inverted, V-shaped, green mark at the tip. They have a honey scent.
Origins Pyrenees to Ukraine. Possibly native to Great Britain.
Flowering height 10cm (4in).
Flowering time Late winter.
Hardiness Fully hardy.

Galanthus nivalis 'Flore Pleno'

The double form of the common snowdrop bears small, double, pure white flowers, 1–2cm (½–¾in) long, which hang from the stems, showing irregular outer petals and heavily marked, green and white smaller petals inside. They are sterile but will multiply from offsets. Snowdrops such as this look beautiful with a curtain of dark green ivy to set them off.
Origins Pyrenees to Ukraine. Possibly native to Great Britain.
Flowering height 10cm (4in).
Flowering time Late winter.
Hardiness Fully hardy.

Galanthus 'S. Arnott'

Virgin white flowers, 2–4cm (¾–1½in) long, fall like rounded drops of snow from a slender stem. The 3 outer petals open to reveal 3 shorter inner petals, each with green markings at the base and apex. They have a strong honey scent.
Origins Of garden origin.
Flowering height 20cm (8in).
Flowering time Late winter.
Hardiness Fully hardy.

gladiolus 'Charming Beauty'

gladiolus 'Seraphin'

galtonia candicans

gladiolus iridaceae

The genus name is derived from the Latin word *gladius,* "sword", a reference to the shape of the leaves. This is a genus of about 180 species of corms with more than 10,000 hybrids and cultivars. The species are found principally in South Africa, but they also occur in Mediterranean countries, north-western and eastern Africa, Madagascar and western Asia. *G.* 'Break of Dawn' and *G.* 'Seraphin' are both medium-sized Grandiflorus hybrids which are described as Butterfly gladioli on account of their ruffled flowers.

Site Grow in full sun in moist soil that does not dry out in summer.
Cultivation In spring, plant the corms 7.5–10cm (3–4in) deep in garden soil. Lift and dry off in autumn. Divide the new corms from the old ones, discarding the latter, and replant the new ones the following spring.
Propagation Remove cormlets when dormant. Alternatively, sow seeds of hardy species in a cold frame in spring; sow seeds of half hardy to tender plants at 15°C (59°F) in spring.
Pests and diseases Grey mould, thrips, aphids and slugs.

Gladiolus 'Break of Dawn'
Funnel-shaped, white, ruffled flowers, up to 5cm (2in) across, are borne on upright stems. They look good against dark bronze foliage.
Origins Of garden origin.
Flowering height 70cm (28in).
Flowering time Summer.
Hardiness Half hardy.

Gladiolus 'Charming Beauty'
Derived from *G. nanus,* this hybrid has rose-coloured, funnel-shaped flowers, up to 5cm (2in) across, which are blotched with creamy white. They are borne in succession on slender flower spikes, starting at the bottom. It can survive relatively mild winters in a border, if well mulched.
Origins Of garden origin.
Flowering height 60cm (24in).
Flowering time Summer.
Hardiness Fully hardy.

Gladiolus communis subsp. *byzantinus*
Up to 20 funnel-shaped, magenta-pink flowers, each up to 5cm (2in) across, are borne in succession on tall flower spikes, starting at the base.
Origins Spain, north-western Africa, Sicily.
Flowering height 90cm (3ft).
Flowering time Early summer.
Hardiness Fully hardy, but it is advisable to mulch ground where frost occurs, and in areas where the ground freezes solid it is best to lift the bulbs during winter.

Gladiolus 'Seraphin'
The pretty, pink, ruffled flowers, up to 5cm (2in) across, each have a white throat and are borne in succession on tall flower spikes. It should be grown in a border and looks lovely near lime-green foliage.
Origins Of garden origin.
Flowering height 70cm (28in).
Flowering time Summer.
Hardiness Half hardy.

galtonia hyacinthaceae

The genus is named after Sir Francis Galton (1822–1911), a British scientist who travelled widely in South Africa where the 3 species of bulbs originate. They grow mainly in moist grasslands in their native home, but only one species is commonly grown in gardens.

Site Grow in full sun in moist soil that does not dry out in summer.
Cultivation In early spring, plant the bulbs 13cm (5in) deep in well-drained garden soil among shrubs or in a herbaceous border where they will be sheltered in summer. Add grit to heavy soils. They resent disturbance.
Propagation Remove offsets in early spring, or sow seeds in spring (keep seedlings frost free for the first 3 years).
Pests and diseases None.

Galtonia candicans
The Cape hyacinth or summer hyacinth, as *G. candicans* is commonly known, bears up to 30 pendent, creamy white flowers, each up to 5cm (2in) long, on tall, sturdy stems in succession over several weeks in late summer. They are best planted in bold groups and show up well against plants with dark green foliage or against a wall.

Origins South Africa (Orange Free State, Eastern Cape, Natal and Lesotho).
Flowering height 1.1m (3ft 6in).
Flowering time Late summer.
Hardiness Fully hardy, but it is advisable to mulch ground where frost occurs, and in areas where the ground freezes solid it is best to lift the bulbs during winter.

gloriosa superba 'Rothschildiana'

hippeastrum 'Christmas Star'

hippeastrum 'Mary Lou'

gloriosa colchicaceae

This is a genus of only one species, and it is unusual because it is one of the few climbing tuberous perennials. It is native to tropical Africa and India. All parts of the plant are poisonous.

Site Grow indoors in full sun.

Cultivation In early spring, plant the tubers 7.5–10cm (3–4in) deep in a large pot, using a soil-based compost (potting mix), with added grit. Place in full light. Water well when growth begins and apply a liquid feed every 2 weeks. Offer support for the plant to climb up. Keep tubers dry in winter.

Propagation Separate the tubers in spring; alternatively, sow seed at 19–24°C (66–75°F) in spring.

Pests and diseases Aphids.

Gloriosa superba 'Rothschildiana'
The graceful flowers, 7.5–10cm (3–4in) across, have bright red petals edged with yellow which are borne from the upper leaf axils. The bright green leaves are glossy. This plant is excellent for growing in a conservatory. Handling the tubers may irritate the skin.
Origins Tropical Africa and India.
Flowering height 1.8m (6ft).
Flowering time Summer to autumn.
Hardiness Frost tender.

hippeastrum amaryllidaceae

This genus of about 80 species of bulbs, found in Central and South America, is associated with many large-flowered colourful hybrids which are often, incorrectly, known as amaryllis.

Site Grow indoors in pots, as houseplants or in a conservatory.

Cultivation From autumn to winter, plant the bulbs so that the neck and shoulders are above the surface of the compost. Use a tall, heavy pot and a soil-based compost (potting mix), with added grit. Keep in a warm spot until the first signs of a new bud appear at the top of the bulb. Bring into full light and keep soil moist, applying a liquid fertilizer every 2 weeks. Provide support if necessary. After flowering is finished, allow the leaves to complete their lifecycle and then keep the compost dry while bulbs are dormant. Bring bulbs into growth again the following autumn. They resent root disturbance, so it is best to pot on every 3 to 5 years at the end of the dormancy period. Often, the later the bulbs are started into growth, the quicker they will come into flower. Try growing them on pebbles and water in late winter (but discard the bulbs after flowering), or leave them until spring and place the pot outside in sun or light shade in early summer.

Propagation Remove offsets in autumn, or sow seeds at 16–18°C (61–64°F) as soon as ripe and keep seedlings growing without a dormant period until they eventually come into flower.

Pests and diseases Aphids.

Hippeastrum 'Christmas Star'
Between 4 and 6 umbels of glorious, funnel-shaped flowers, about 25cm (10in) across, are produced. The rich red petals have white centres. The flowers are borne on stout, leafless stems. Often 2 to 3 flowerheads are produced in succession on new stems. The leaves tend to follow later. Note that all parts are mildly toxic if ingested.
Origins Of garden origin.
Flowering height 50cm (20in).
Flowering time Summer to autumn.
Hardiness Frost tender.

Hippeastrum 'Mary Lou'
Between 4 and 6 umbels of glorious, double, white, funnel-shaped flowers are produced. Each petal is edged with pink. The total width of all the flowers is about 25cm (10in). They are borne on stout, leafless stems. Often 2 to 3 flowerheads are produced in succession on new stems. The leaves tend to follow later. Note that all parts are mildly toxic if ingested.

Origins Of garden origin.
Flowering height 50cm (20in).
Flowering time Summer to autumn.
Hardiness Frost tender.

Hippeastrum 'Red Lion'
The individual scarlet flowers can reach 15cm (6in) in diameter, with a total width of 25cm (10in). They appear with a welcome burst of colour in winter. Note that all parts are mildly toxic if ingested.
Origins Of garden origin.
Flowering height 30–50cm (12–20in).
Flowering time Winter.
Hardiness Frost tender.

hyacinthoides hispanica

hyacinthoides non-scripta 'Alba'

hyacinthus orientalis 'Amethyst'

hyacinthus orientalis 'Blue Jacket'

hyacinthoides hyacinthaceae

Commonly known as the bluebell, this is a much-loved genus of 3 to 4 species of bulbs from deciduous woods and moist meadows of western Europe and northern Africa. There is nothing more enchanting in mid- to late spring than the sight of a mass of bluebells on a grassy bank or creating a sea of blue in the dappled shade of a wood. It is best to avoid planting them in a border because they are invasive and will soon take over.

Site Grow in partial shade under shrubs or trees in border soil or short grass.

Cultivation In autumn, plant bulbs 7.5cm (3in) deep. They will soon form large clumps. Allow to self-seed, or deadhead flowers to prevent this from happening. Can be planted in borders, grass or containers.

Propagation Sow seed in containers in a cold frame as soon as ripe. Remove offsets from mature bulbs while dormant in summer. They will self-seed. The English bluebell and the Spanish bluebell will often hybridize naturally in the garden if planted close to each other, resulting in a wide array of pink, blue and mauve shades.

Pests and diseases None.

Hyacinthoides hispanica

The Spanish bluebell, as it is commonly known, bears single blue, mauve or pink flowers on racemes of up to 15 bell-shaped, unscented flowers all the way around the stem. Plant them among rhododendrons and azaleas for good colour associations, or plant with small silver foliage plants in a container. There is also a white form, 'Album'.

Origins Portugal, Spain and northern Africa.

Flowering height 40cm (16in).

Flowering time Spring.

Hardiness Fully hardy.

Hyacinthoides non-scripta

The English bluebell bears single blue, sometimes white, flowers in graceful racemes, which bend over at the tip. Up to 12 pendent, narrow, bell-shaped, scented flowers are borne on one side only. Ideal for naturalizing beneath orchard trees, where they enjoy the light, dappled shade in spring and heavier shade in the heat of summer. The white form is known as *H. non-scripta* 'Alba'.

Origins Portugal, Spain and northern Africa.

Flowering height 20–40cm (8–16in).

Flowering time Spring.

Hardiness Fully hardy.

hyacinthus hyacinthaceae

Commonly known as the hyacinth, this is one of the most fragrant of all spring-flowering bulbs. It is a genus of 3 species of bulbs from limestone slopes and cliffs in western and central Asia. All cultivars are bred from *Hyacinthus orientalis*, which grows in central and southern Turkey, north-western Syria and Lebanon. It is an excellent bulb for indoor and outdoor use, but be wary of frost damage when planting in outdoor containers where the soil is allowed to get excessively wet. Good drainage is a priority, so use a soil-based compost (potting mix) with extra grit. They are fully hardy in beds and borders, combining beautifully with white or blue *Anemone blanda*, as well as with primroses, polyanthus and violas. Note that touching the bulbs can cause skin irritation to some people, so wear gloves when handling.

Site Grow in sun or partial shade.

Cultivation Outdoor bedding hyacinths such as *H. orientalis* 'Amethyst', 'Blue Jacket', 'Hollyhock' and 'Woodstock' will flower in spring borders or outdoor containers. In autumn, plant the bulbs at a depth of 10cm (4in). Use soil-based compost (potting mix) in containers, with extra grit to ensure good drainage.

For indoor use, purchase "prepared" hyacinths, such as 'City of Haarlem' and 'Pink Pearl', and plant in early autumn so that the flowers will appear for early winter. Where the bowl or pot has no drainage holes, use a special bulb compost (planting medium). Alternatively, place the bulb on top of water in a special hyacinth glass where the neck narrows in order to support the bulb. Either way, keep the bulbs in a dark, cool place at about 10°C (50°F) for about 8 weeks, allowing the roots time to develop. Bring into a light but not sunny spot until the flower bud is visible. Thereafter, take into a warm room and allow to flower. After flowering, discard bulbs which have been grown on water. All other container-grown hyacinths can be transferred to the garden, where they will flower for many years. Both 'City of Haarlem' and 'Pink Pearl' can also be bought as bedding hyacinths.

Propagation Remove offsets from mature bulbs while dormant in summer.

Pests and diseases None.

Hyacinthus orientalis 'Amethyst'

Racemes of up to 40 single, lilac-amethyst, waxy, tubular, bell-shaped flowers, which are richly scented, are borne on stout, leafless stems.

Origins Of garden origin.

Flowering height 20cm (8in).

Flowering time Spring outdoors (bedding bulbs).

Hardiness Fully hardy.

Hyacinthus orientalis 'Ben Nevis'

The dense racemes of double, white, tubular, bell-shaped flowers are delightfully scented. Plant with white violas for a stunning all-white effect.

Origins Of garden origin.

Flowering height 20cm (8in).

Flowering time Spring outdoors (bedding bulbs).

Hardiness Fully hardy.

hyacinthus orientalis 'City of Haarlem'

hyacinthus orientalis 'Woodstock'

Hyacinthus orientalis 'Blue Jacket'

The scented racemes of up to 40 single, dark blue, waxy, tubular, bell-shaped flowers make an exciting display.
Origins Of garden origin.
Flowering height 20cm (8in).
Flowering time Spring outdoors (bedding bulbs).
Hardiness Fully hardy.

Hyacinthus orientalis 'Carnegie'

The racemes bear up to 40 waxy, single, pure white, tubular, bell-shaped flowers, which are richly scented and borne on stout, leafless stems. They combine beautifully with Double Early tulips.
Origins Of garden origin.
Flowering height 20cm (8in).
Flowering time Spring outdoors (bedding bulbs).
Hardiness Fully hardy.

Hyacinthus orientalis 'City of Haarlem'

The beautiful, single, pale lemon-yellow flowers are wonderfully scented and look charming with pale blue or white *Anemone blanda* or violas.
Origins Of garden origin.
Flowering height 20cm (8in).
Flowering time Winter indoors (prepared bulbs); spring outdoors (bedding bulbs).
Hardiness Fully hardy.

Hyacinthus orientalis 'Delft Blue'

Racemes of up to 40 single, soft blue, tubular, bell-shaped flowers, which are richly scented, are borne on stout, leafless stems. This is a popular cultivar and looks very pretty with little violas.
Origins Of garden origin.
Flowering height 20cm (8in).
Flowering time Winter indoors (prepared bulbs); spring outdoors (bedding bulbs).
Hardiness Fully hardy.

Hyacinthus orientalis 'Gypsy Queen'

The delightful, salmon-pink flowers of this hyacinth are richly scented and look striking planted in old terracotta pots.
Origins Of garden origin.
Flowering height 20cm (8in).
Flowering time Spring outdoors (bedding bulbs).
Hardiness Fully hardy.

Hyacinthus orientalis 'Hollyhock'

The double, crimson-red, tubular, bell-shaped flowers are richly scented and are borne on stout, leafless stems. 'Hollyhock' will combine beautifully with blue polyanthus or perhaps with *Tanacetum parthenium* 'Aureum' (golden feverfew).
Origins Of garden origin.
Flowering height 20cm (8in).
Flowering time Spring outdoors (bedding bulbs).
Hardiness Fully hardy.

Hyacinthus orientalis 'Jan Bos'

The racemes have up to 40 single, cerise-red, tubular, bell-shaped flowers, which are scented and excellent with violas or primroses.
Origins Of garden origin.
Flowering height 20cm (8in).
Flowering time Spring outdoors (bedding bulbs).
Hardiness Fully hardy.

Hyacinthus orientalis 'L'Innocence'

The racemes bear up to 40 single, white, tubular, bell-shaped flowers, which are richly scented. This, too, is an old favourite.
Origins Of garden origin.
Flowering height 20cm (8in).
Flowering time Winter indoors (prepared bulbs); spring outdoors (bedding bulbs).
Hardiness Fully hardy

Hyacinthus orientalis 'Pink Pearl'

Racemes of up to 40 waxy, single, rose-pink, tubular, bell-shaped flowers, which are richly scented, are borne on stout, leafless stems. This is another of the old favourites.
Origins Of garden origin.
Flowering height 20cm (8in).
Flowering time Winter indoors (prepared bulbs); spring outdoors (bedding bulbs).
Hardiness Fully hardy.

Hyacinthus orientalis 'Woodstock'

The unusual, single, deep burgundy flowers combine well with grey foliage plants or pink primroses.
Origins Of garden origin.
Flowering height 20cm (8in).
Flowering time Spring outdoors (bedding bulbs).
Hardiness Fully hardy.

iris 'George'

iris 'Purple Sensation'

leucojum aestivum

iris iridaceae

This is a large genus of more than 300 species of winter-, spring- and summer-flowering bulbs, rhizomes and fleshy rooted perennials, found in a wide range of locations in the northern hemisphere. The name means a rainbow, an apt description given the many colours, primrose to indigo, of the flowers.

Site Grow in full sun.

Cultivation In autumn, plant bulbs 5cm (2in) deep in the border or containers. *I.* 'Purple Sensation' may also be planted in spring.

Propagation Separate rhizomes and bulb offsets from midsummer to early autumn.

Pests and diseases Slugs and snails are the main problems.

Iris 'Annabel Jane'

This is a vigorous, rhizomatous, tall bearded iris which has gorgeous lilac-blue flowers.

Origins Of garden origin.
Flowering height 1.2m (4ft).
Flowering time Late spring to early summer.
Hardiness Fully hardy.

Iris danfordiae

A Reticulata iris with scented, lemon-yellow flowers, 5cm (2in) across which have green markings. They look effective with winter-flowering heathers and in small pots.

Origins Turkey.
Flowering height 10cm (4in).
Flowering time Late winter.
Hardiness Fully hardy.

Iris 'George'

A Reticulata iris with a fragrant, rich purple flower, 4–6cm (1½–2½in) across, which has a yellow stripe down the centre of the fall petal.

Origins Of garden origin.
Flowering height 12cm (5in).
Flowering time Late winter.
Hardiness Fully hardy.

Iris 'Pauline'

This Reticulata iris has sweetly scented, dark purple flowers, 5cm (2in) across, with white crests on the falls. They look really wonderful in a container with *Viburnum tinus* (laurustinus) and *Euphorbia myrsinites*.

Origins Of garden origin.
Flowering height 10–15cm (4–6in).
Flowering time Late winter.
Hardiness Fully hardy.

Iris 'Purple Sensation'

The purple-blue and bronze-yellow flowers of this Dutch iris are 7.5–10cm (3–4in) across. They associate well under an arch of laburnum or wisteria and make excellent cut flowers.

Origins Of garden origin; derived from the bulbous *I. xiphium* (Spanish iris).
Flowering height 45cm (18in).
Flowering time Late spring to early summer.
Hardiness Fully hardy.

leucojum amaryllidaceae

The name is derived from the Greek words *leukos*, "white", a clue to the white colouring of the flowers, and *ion*, "violet", a reference to their delicate fragrance. They are commonly referred to as snowflakes. The genus includes about 10 species of bulbs found in a wide variety of habitats, from western Europe to the Middle East and northern Africa, but the species grown most often in gardens are the spring and summer snowflakes. They look quite similar to snowdrops, but the petals are of equal length, whereas the snowdrop always has 3 long and 3 short petals.

Site Grow in sun or partial shade in moist soil. *L. roseum* prefers a sunny, well-drained site.

Cultivation In autumn, plant bulbs 7.5cm (3in) deep in the border where they can form a good-sized clump. They naturalize well in damp grass or woodland. *L. roseum* needs protection in winter from prolonged frost and dampness.

Propagation Separate bulb offsets from midsummer to early autumn.

Pests and diseases Slugs and narcissus bulb fly.

Leucojum aestivum 'Gravetye Giant'

This is commonly known as the summer snowflake. From 2 to 8 white, bell-shaped flowers, with a distinctive green tip at the end of each petal, are borne on each stem. They look lovely near water, where their reflection can be fully enjoyed.

Origins Of garden origin; the species comes from north-western, central and eastern Europe and the Middle East.
Flowering height 90cm (36in); the species grows to 45–60cm (18–24in).
Flowering time Spring; the common name is misleading.
Hardiness Fully hardy.

Leucojum roseum

The solitary, pale pink flowers, which are 1cm (½in) long, make a splash in early autumn. They look lovely with autumn crocus or colchicums. The narrow leaves appear with, or a short while after, the flowers.

Origins Corsica, Sardinia.
Flowering height 10cm (4in).
Flowering time Early autumn.
Hardiness Frost hardy.

Leucojum vernum

Commonly known as the spring snowflake, this has white, bell-shaped flowers with a distinctive green tip at the end of each petal, borne 1, occasionally 2, to a stem. They will naturalize in damp grass and look wonderful as a large display beneath deciduous trees.

Origins Southern and eastern Europe.
Flowering height 20–30cm (8–12in).
Flowering time Late winter to early spring.
Hardiness Fully hardy.

lilium 'Enchantment'

lilium martagon

lilium regale

lilium lilaceae

The genus name *Lilium* is an old Latin name, akin to *leirion*, which was used by Theophrastus to refer to *Lilium candidum* (Madonna lily), one of the oldest established plants in gardens. The Greeks admired it for its beauty and food value, and it was used on many ceremonial occasions. The Romans took it with them as they conquered their neighbouring lands. In the Christian era it became a symbol of Christ's mother and was grown in monastic gardens throughout Europe. Although historically this one species has been of major importance, there are more than 100 species of bulbs in the genus, which come mainly from scrub and wooded areas of Europe, Asia and North America. From these, an extensive number of garden hybrids has developed.
Site Most prefer acid to neutral soil, but some, such as *L. martagon*, like alkaline soils. They require shade at their base and sun at the top, although a few enjoy partial shade. None thrive in full shade.
Cultivation In early autumn, plant bulbs 15cm (6in) deep on a bed of sand or grit to facilitate good drainage if ground is heavy. Grow in a border where they can be left undisturbed for many years and form a good-sized clump.
Propagation Sow seed as soon as it is ripe in containers in a cold frame. Remove scales and offsets or bulblets from dormant bulbs as soon as the foliage dies down. Detach stem bulbils, where produced, in late summer.
Pests and diseases Lily beetle, slugs and aphids. Grey mould can be a problem in a cool, wet spring.

Lilium candidum

The Madonna lily has 5 or more white, faintly scented, trumpet-shaped flowers, 5–7.5cm (2–3in) long, with bright yellow anthers. They have a sweet scent and are the only lilies to produce over-wintering basal leaves. They require neutral to alkaline soil.
Origins South-eastern Europe to eastern Mediterranean.
Flowering height 90cm (3ft).
Flowering time Summer.
Hardiness Fully hardy.

Lilium 'Enchantment'

The showy, vivid orange, cup-shaped, unscented flowers, which are marked with dark purple spots, are 12cm (6in) across. The dark spotting on the petals combines well with deep bronze foliage plants. This is a stem-rooting, clump-forming lily, which prefers a sunny border and produces dark purple bulbils in the axils from which new bulbs can be propagated. It is excellent for the border or deep containers, where it can stay for two or three years.
Origins Of garden origin.
Flowering height 60–90cm (2–3ft).
Flowering time Summer.
Hardiness Fully hardy.

Lilium 'Golden Splendour Group'

The impressive, funnel-shaped flowers are a rich golden yellow. The back of each petal is beautifully marked with maroon stripes.
Origins Of garden origin.
Flowering height 1.5–1.8m (5–6ft).
Flowering time Mid- to late summer.
Hardiness Fully hardy.

Lilium lancifolium

The confident appearance of the tiger lily is a true reflection of its fiery common name, having up to 40, but more usually 5 to 10, pinkish- or reddish-orange, purple-speckled flowers.
Origins East China, Korea, Japan.
Flowering height 60–150cm (2–5ft).
Flowering time Late summer to early autumn.
Hardiness Fully hardy.

Lilium martagon

The Turk's cap lily should be grown in sun or partial shade. It has glossy, nodding, unscented, pink to purplish red flowers with dark purple spots. The flowers are in the shape of a Turk's cap and are 5cm (2in) across. It is ideal growing among early summer-flowering shrubs.
Origins Europe to Mongolia.
Flowering height 90–180cm (3–6ft).
Flowering time Summer.
Hardiness Fully hardy.

Lilium regale

The regal lily, which enjoys full sun, bears large, trumpet-shaped, scented, white flowers, 13–15cm (5–6in) long, with purple streaking on the reverse. It can be grown in the border, although it needs support, and excessively alkaline soils should be avoided. It is excellent growing among deep red or white, late-flowering, old-fashioned roses. It is also suitable for large, deep pots.
Origins Western China.
Flowering height 60–180cm (2–6ft)
Flowering time Summer.
Hardiness Fully hardy.

Lilium speciosum var. rubrum

The large, scented, carmine-pink flowers, with darker crimson spots, are up to 18cm (7in) across and in the shape of a Turk's cap. This lily needs moist acid soil in partial shade as well as staking. It is excellent in deep pots.
Origins Eastern China, Japan and Taiwan.
Flowering height 90cm (3ft).
Flowering time Late summer.
Hardiness Fully hardy.

Lilium 'Star Gazer'

This bulb, with its deep rose-red flowers, edged with white, is seductive in the intensity of its colouring. Fragrance is just one of its many charms. It is also suitable for deep pots.
Origins Of garden origin.
Flowering height 90cm (3ft).
Flowering time Late summer.
Hardiness Fully hardy.

muscari armeniacum 'Blue Spike'

narcissus 'Actaea'

narcissus bulbocodium

muscari lilaceae

The name of this genus derives from the Latin word *muscus*, "musk scent", the fragrance carried by some of the species. The genus, known by the common name of grape hyacinth, embraces 30 species of bulbs from the Mediterranean to south-western Asia, the best known of which is *Muscari armeniacum*, whose cultivars are so useful in borders, grassland and all sizes of containers.

Site Full sun, although they will also tolerate partial shade in pots.

Cultivation In autumn, plant bulbs 5cm (2in) deep in small to large groups. They will multiply rapidly.

Propagation Sow seed in containers in a cold frame in autumn. Remove offsets in summer.

Pests and diseases Viruses can be a problem.

Muscari armeniacum

Dense racemes, 2–7.5cm (¾–3in) long, of beautiful blue flowers are borne in grape-like bunches at the top of the stem. This is one of the prettiest of all the blue bulbs, sumptuous as a mass planting beneath roses or along a path. It makes an excellent association with all Double Early tulips. A delightful combination is *M. armeniacum* with double pink *Tulipa* 'Peach Blossom'. The only drawback is that the foliage can grow long and untidy, but the exquisite colouring and long duration of flowering make up for any waywardness. Several cultivars are available, including double, soft blue 'Blue Spike', which, at 15cm (6in), is vigorous but slightly shorter than the species. It is good in the border or in a small pot.
Origins The species comes from south-eastern Europe to Caucasus.
Flowering height 20cm (8in).
Flowering time Early to mid-spring.
Hardiness Fully hardy.

Muscari botryoides 'Album'

Historically known as Pearls of Spain, this muscari has slender racemes, 2–5cm (¾–2in) long, of scented white flowers. These are borne in bunches at the top of the stem like tiny grapes. It is daintier than *M. armeniacum* and has much neater leaves.
Origins The species comes from France, Germany and Poland southwards in central and south-eastern Europe.
Flowering height 15–20cm (6–8in).
Flowering time Early to mid-spring.
Hardiness Fully hardy.

Muscari latifolium

The slender racemes of dark violet flowers have a crown of paler sterile flowers on top. This bulb produces one broad leaf, hence its specific name *latifolium*. This is an excellent bulb for pots if they can be kept in a sheltered spot in winter.
Origins North-western Turkey, among the open pine forests.
Flowering height 20cm (8in).
Flowering time Mid- to late spring.
Hardiness Frost hardy.

narcissus amaryllidaceae

Often known as the daffodil, this is one of the best loved of all bulbs, and the genus includes about 50 species that grow in a wide variety of habitats in Europe and northern Africa. It is found in meadows and woodlands and even in rock crevices. Many thousands of cultivars have been grown over the years.

Site Grow in full sun or partial shade in borders, grass or containers. Some narcissi, such as *N. papyraceus* (syn. *N.* 'Paper White'), are ideal for growing indoors in bowls for winter display purposes, responding well to winter warmth inside the home and flowering in a matter of weeks, without the need for a cool winter period to make root growth. Their native home is southern France and Spain and northern Africa, where they enjoy the warm climate.

Cultivation See individual entries.

Propagation Seed can take up to 7 years to produce a flowering bulb. Remove offsets as leaves fade in summer or in early autumn.

Pests and diseases Narcissus bulb fly, narcissus eel worm, slugs, fungal infections and viruses may be a problem.

Narcissus 'Actaea'

The pure white flowers have a brilliant scarlet eye. This is a delightful narcissus for borders or grassland and is an exceptionally good naturalizer.
Origins Of garden origin.
Flowering height 45cm (18in) (medium).
Flowering time Mid-spring.
Hardiness Fully hardy.
Cultivation In autumn, plant bulbs 15cm (6in) deep.

Narcissus bulbocodium

The hoop-petticoat daffodil, as this species is known, looks different from other narcissi. As its name suggests, the yellow, funnel-shaped cup, which is 4cm (1½in) wide, has the appearance of an old-fashioned hoop-petticoat. It should be allowed to naturalize on damp grassy slopes that dry out in summer, where it will provide a carpet of yellow.
Origins Southern and western France, Portugal, Spain and northern Africa.
Flowering height 10–15cm (4–6in) (dwarf).
Flowering time Mid-spring.
Hardiness Fully hardy.
Cultivation In autumn, plant bulbs 5cm (2in) deep.

Narcissus 'Carlton'

This is a soft yellow daffodil with a large cup, which is frilly at the mouth. An excellent naturalizer, it is a delightful daffodil for borders or grassland.
Origins Of garden origin.
Flowering height 45cm (18in) (medium).
Flowering time Mid-spring.
Hardiness Fully hardy.
Cultivation In autumn, plant bulbs 15cm (6in) deep.

narcissus 'Carlton'

narcissus cyclamineus

narcissus 'February Gold'

narcissus 'Jetfire'

Narcissus cyclamineus

The golden flower has a distinctive shape with its exaggerated swept-back petals and long, narrow cup, reminiscent of a cyclamen (hence its name). It is a parent of many dwarf hybrids, such as 'February Gold', 'Peeping Tom' and 'Jetfire'. It will naturalize well in grass, particularly where it is damp, and will succeed in partially shaded positions.
Origins North-western Portugal and north-western Spain.
Flowering height 15–20cm (6–8in) (dwarf).
Flowering time Early spring.
Hardiness Fully hardy.
Cultivation In autumn, plant bulbs 10cm (4in) deep.

Narcissus 'Eggs and Bacon'

Formerly known as *N.* 'Orange Phoenix', this is a sumptuous double daffodil, which combines rich yellow and a deep gold. A small group would make a dramatic centrepiece in the spring borders.
Origins Of garden origin.
Flowering height 35cm (14in) (medium).
Flowering time Mid-spring.
Hardiness Fully hardy.
Cultivation In autumn, plant bulbs 15cm (6in) deep.

Narcissus 'February Gold'

The petals have an elegant swept-back appearance, less pronounced but still similar to its parent, *N. cyclamineus*. This is one of the best of all the early dwarf daffodils, elegant, long in flower, sturdy, short and useful in so many different parts of the garden.

It looks lovely in the border with primroses, *Tanacetum parthenium* 'Aureum' (golden feverfew), violas, and is excellent in window boxes and pots, where it can be underplanted with large Dutch crocus hybrids or *Anemone blanda*.
Origins Of garden origin.
Flowering height 25cm (10in) (dwarf).
Flowering time Early spring.
Hardiness Fully hardy.
Cultivation In autumn, plant bulbs 10cm (4in) deep.

Narcissus 'Hawera'

This has up to 5 dainty, canary-yellow, hanging flowers with slim, swept-back petals and wide, short cups. Derived from *N. triandrus*, it comes from mountain meadows as well as pastures and hedgerows of northern and central Spain and Portugal and south-western France. This is a valuable daffodil in borders and is particularly good in small to medium containers, where the blooms seem to last for many weeks, spanning the season between mid- and late spring. It is ideal for a mid- to late spring hanging basket, and is also excellent for indoor use, where it will bloom for a long time.
Origins Of garden origin.
Flowering height 25cm (10in) (dwarf).
Flowering time Mid- to late spring.
Hardiness Fully hardy.
Cultivation In autumn, plant bulbs 10cm (4in) deep.

Narcissus 'Ice Follies'

This is a delicate 2-toned daffodil with white petals and lemon-yellow crown, which fades to creamy white. It makes an ideal candidate for borders or grassland, where it will create a perfect carpet beneath spring-flowering, white cherry trees, for example.
Origins Of garden origin.
Flowering height 35cm (14in) (medium).
Flowering time Early to mid-spring.
Hardiness Fully hardy.
Cultivation In autumn, plant bulbs 15cm (6in) deep.

Narcissus 'Jack Snipe'

A distinctive 2-toned dwarf daffodil with its lemon-yellow cup and swept-back white petals. It is derived from *N. cyclamineus* which comes from north-western Portugal and north-western Spain. Sturdy and long lasting, this daffodil is ideal in borders or containers, and associates well with all spring flowers, including hyacinths and primroses.
Origins Of garden origin.
Flowering height 25cm (10in) (dwarf).
Flowering time Early to mid-spring.
Hardiness Fully hardy.
Cultivation In autumn, plant bulbs 10cm (4in) deep in borders or containers.

Narcissus 'Jetfire'

A richly coloured two-toned dwarf daffodil with an orange cup and reflexed golden petals. The cup will fade in strong sunshine. It is derived from *N. cyclamineus* which comes from north-western Portugal and north-western Spain. It looks striking in borders or containers, where it makes an excellent partnership with bright blue *Muscari armeniacum*.
Origins Of garden origin.
Flowering height 25cm (10in) (dwarf).
Flowering time Early spring.
Hardiness Fully hardy.
Cultivation In autumn, plant bulbs 10cm (4in) deep in borders or containers.

Narcissus 'Jumblie'

This is a dwarf yellow daffodil with narrow golden cups and slightly reflexed petals. The flowers are borne on multiple stems and each stem is capable of bearing several miniature flowers. The flowers look in different directions, hence their jumbled appearance and name. The multiple flowers and short nature make it a really excellent choice for a winter hanging basket or window box. Mix with coloured violas and starry, blue or white anemones to provide a glorious early spring display.
Origins Of garden origin.
Flowering height 20cm (8in) (dwarf).
Flowering time Early spring.
Hardiness Fully hardy.
Cultivation In autumn, plant bulbs 10cm (4in) deep in borders or containers.

narcissus papyraceus

narcissus 'Peeping Tom'

narcissus 'Pinza'

narcissus 'Pipit'

Narcissus 'King Alfred'

This is one of the most popular of all yellow daffodils with its large golden cup. It is widely grown in spring borders, although it can be inclined to flop in rain.
Origins Of garden origin.
Flowering height 35cm (14in) (medium).
Flowering time Mid-spring.
Hardiness Fully hardy.
Cultivation In autumn, plant bulbs 15cm (6in) deep.

Narcissus 'Little Witch'

This dwarf golden daffodil has a long cup and swept-back petals. It is bred from *N. cyclamimeus*, a native of north-western Portugal and north-western Spain. Sturdy and long lasting, this daffodil is ideal for both borders or containers, associating well with all spring flowers, such as hyacinths and primroses.
Origins Of garden origin.
Flowering height 20cm (8in) (dwarf).
Flowering time Early to mid-spring.
Hardiness Fully hardy.
Cultivation In autumn, plant bulbs 10cm (4in) deep in borders or containers.

Narcissus 'Minnow'

This delicately coloured, two-toned dwarf daffodil has a short primrose-yellow cup and rounded, creamy white petals. It is a sweet little daffodil with as many as 3 to 5 flowers on each stem. Derived from *N. tazetta*, it comes from a wide region around the Mediterranean. This is a dainty

addition to borders or containers, where it might make a lasting partnership with white *Muscari botryoides* 'Album'.
Origins Of garden origin.
Flowering height 15cm (6in) (dwarf).
Flowering time Early spring.
Hardiness Fully hardy.
Cultivation In autumn, plant bulbs 10cm (4in) deep in borders or containers.

Narcissus papyraceus

Formerly known as *N.* 'Paper White', this daffodil bears bunches of 5 to 10 fragrant, glistening white flowers, 1cm (½in) across. *N.* 'Ziva' is similar but slightly shorter; *N.* 'Omri' is also shorter and has creamy yellow flowers.
Origins Southern France, southern Spain and northern Africa.
Flowering height 40cm (16in) (medium).
Flowering time Winter indoors.
Hardiness Frost hardy.
Cultivation Use special bulb fibre in indoor bowls. Plant bulbs on the surface of moistened compost (soil mix). No cold period is required. Grow in full light and warmth. They will flower within 6 to 8 weeks, so choose the time of planting according to when you want them to flower. They might benefit from the support of twigs or short canes. They can also be grown on pebbles and water.

Narcissus 'Peeping Tom'

This is a rather bold, dwarf, yellow daffodil with a long, golden cup and long, swept-back petals, like ears listening to a conversation. It is derived from *N. cyclamineus* which comes from north-western Portugal and north-western Spain. This is an excellent choice for the border with primroses and polyanthus or large Dutch crocuses.
Origins Of garden origin.
Flowering height 25cm (10in) (dwarf).
Flowering time Early spring.
Hardiness Fully hardy.
Cultivation In autumn, plant bulbs 10cm (4in) deep in borders or larger containers.

Narcissus 'Pinza'

This is a striking daffodil, with its rich yellow petals and deep red cup. Place against a dark green background or with rich blue *Muscari*.
Origins Of garden origin.
Flowering height 35cm (14in) (medium).
Flowering time Mid-spring.
Hardiness Fully hardy.
Cultivation In autumn, plant bulbs 15cm (6in) deep.

Narcissus 'Pipit'

Perhaps 2 to 3 exquisite two-toned flowers, each with a white cup and lemon-yellow petals, are borne on each stem. The colour fades with age, but this is still one of the prettiest of all daffodils. The flowers are sweetly scented and last for a long time. It is derived from sweetly scented *N. jonquilla* which is widely naturalized in meadows and damp places in southern

Europe and northern Africa. It is excellent in borders and beautiful in medium to large containers, where it associates well with all mid-spring flowers.
Origins Of garden origin.
Flowering height 30cm (12in) (dwarf).
Flowering time Mid- to late spring outdoors.
Hardiness Fully hardy.
Cultivation In autumn, plant bulbs 10cm (4in) deep.

Narcissus poeticus var. recurvus

Sometimes known as pheasant's eye or old pheasant's eye, this is one of the all-time favourite daffodils. It produces stunning flowers with tiny, red-edged, yellow cups surrounded by recurved, glistening white petals. It is one of the last daffodils to flower, is fragrant and will naturalize well in grass. It is an excellent daffodil for borders among shrubs or in grassland with camassias and buttercups for company.
Origins Widely naturalized in southern Europe.
Flowering height 35cm (14in) (medium).
Flowering time Late spring.
Hardiness Fully hardy.
Cultivation In autumn, plant bulbs 20cm (8in) deep.

narcissus 'Quail'

narcissus 'Rip van Winkle'

narcissus 'Silver Chimes'

narcissus 'Suzy'

Narcissus 'Quail'

This short, multi-headed golden daffodil may produce 2 to 3 scented flowers on each stem. It is derived from *N. jonquilla* which comes from damp places in southern Europe and northern Africa. A dainty daffodil in borders or containers, it makes a lasting partnership with white *Muscari botryoides* 'Album'.
Origins Of garden origin.
Flowering height 25cm (10in) (dwarf).
Flowering time Mid-spring.
Hardiness Fully hardy.
Cultivation In autumn, plant bulbs 10cm (4in) deep in borders or containers.

Narcissus 'Quince'

This is a short, multi-headed daffodil with a frilly yellow cup and pale yellow, slightly reflexed petals. Like *N.* 'Jumblie' and 'Tête-à-tête', only later flowering, this daffodil may produce 2 to 3 flowers on each stem, and each bulb produces more than one flowering stem.
Origins Of garden origin.
Flowering height 15cm (6in) (dwarf).
Flowering time Early to mid-spring.
Hardiness Fully hardy.
Cultivation In autumn, plant bulbs 10cm (4in) deep in borders or containers.

Narcissus 'Rainbow'

This is a beautiful daffodil: the delicate white petals, surrounding a pale pink cup, have a coppery pink rim. This is an unusual late-season daffodil for borders or in grassland, and it looks wonderful against the bright green foliage of the mock orange *Philadelphus coronarius* 'Aureus'.
Origins Of garden origin.
Flowering height 40cm (16in) (medium).
Flowering time Late spring.
Hardiness Fully hardy.
Cultivation In autumn, plant bulbs 15cm (6in) deep.

Narcissus 'Rip van Winkle'

Formerly known as *N. minor* var. *pumilus* 'Plenus', this daffodil has rather lax stems for the weight of the spiky, double yellow flowers that are produced. It is an unusual but good choice for growing in short grass, at the front of borders or in small containers.
Origins Of garden origin.
Flowering height 20cm (8in) (dwarf).
Flowering time Early spring.
Hardiness Fully hardy.
Cultivation In autumn, plant bulbs 10cm (4in) deep.

Narcissus 'Rose Caprice'

The beautiful two-toned flowers have salmon-pink cups and white petals. This daffodil is excellent in borders among lime-green or bronze foliage plants, such as *Heuchera* 'Pewter Moon' or *H. micrantha* var. *diversifolia* 'Palace Purple' and in medium to large containers.
Origins Of garden origin.
Flowering height 35cm (14in) (medium).
Flowering time Mid-spring.
Hardiness Fully hardy.
Cultivation In autumn, plant bulbs 13cm (5in) deep.

Narcissus 'Saint Patrick's Day'

This delicate, 2-toned daffodil has creamy white petals and lime-green crown. This is a delightful daffodil for borders or grassland.
Origins Of garden origin.
Flowering height 35cm (14in) (medium).
Flowering time Mid-spring.
Hardiness Fully hardy.
Cultivation In autumn, plant bulbs 15cm (6in) deep.

Narcissus 'Silver Chimes'

This pretty white daffodil, derived from *N. tazetta*, has a short cup and a sweet scent. It may produce 3 to 5 flowers on each stem. It looks good with *Fritillaria meleagris* (snake's head fritillary).
Origins Of garden origin.
Flowering height 30cm (12in) (dwarf).
Flowering time Mid- to late spring.
Hardiness Fully hardy.
Cultivation In autumn, plant bulbs 10cm (4in) deep in borders or containers.

Narcissus 'Sir Winston Churchill'

Clusters of scented white flowers with tiny orange and yellow petals in the centre are borne on each stem. Sturdy in growth, it is excellent in borders or in grassland, where it will follow on from *N.* 'White Lion'. It is sometimes grown as a pot plant.
Origins Of garden origin.
Flowering height 38cm (15in) (medium).
Flowering time Late spring.
Hardiness Fully hardy.
Cultivation In autumn, plant bulbs 15cm (6in) deep.

Narcissus 'Suzy'

Clusters of 1 to 4 yellow flowers with flattened orange cups are borne on each stem. It is bred from fragrant *N. jonquilla* and inherits its strong perfume. This is an excellent daffodil in borders, although it is also sometimes grown in containers.
Origins Of garden origin.
Flowering height 40cm (16in) (medium).
Flowering time Mid-spring.
Hardiness Fully hardy.
Cultivation In autumn, plant bulbs 15cm (6in) deep.

Narcissus 'Tête-à-tête'

This is perhaps the best known of all the dwarf yellow daffodils. There may be 2 to 3 flowers, which have short golden cups and only slightly reflexed rounded petals, on each stem. Each bulb produces more than one flowering stem. The multiple flowers and short nature make it a good choice for a winter hanging basket or window box. Mix with late Dutch crocuses, primroses or violas. This is one of the commonest bulbs forced commercially and it is sold in little pots in late winter. Combine with other spring foliage such as *Viburnum tinus* (laurustinus) and forsythia to create a pretty indoor arrangement.
Origins Of garden origin.
Flowering height 15cm (6in) (dwarf).
Flowering time Late winter indoors; early spring outdoors.
Hardiness Fully hardy.
Cultivation In autumn, plant bulbs 10cm (4in) deep in borders or pots.

narcissus 'Thalia'

narcissus 'Topolino'

nerine bowdenii

nerine undulata

Narcissus 'Thalia'

One of the taller dwarf daffodils, this has wonderful white flowers, often 2 to a stem. The petals are pointed and slightly twisted, giving the flower a distinctive appearance. Its parentage includes *N. triandrus*, which comes from mountain meadows, and pastures and hedgerows of northern and central Spain, Portugal and southwestern France. This is a useful daffodil for borders or containers, especially near blue *Muscari armeniacum* or, more unusually, with *Fritillaria meleagris* (snake's head fritillary).
Origins Of garden origin.
Flowering height 30cm (12in) (dwarf).
Flowering time Mid-spring.
Hardiness Fully hardy.
Cultivation In autumn, plant bulbs 10cm (4in) deep in borders or medium to large pots.

Narcissus 'Topolino'

This miniature Trumpet daffodil has a long, primrose-yellow cup and creamy white petals. It looks charming among a carpet of white violets, against a patch of blue or white *Anemone blanda* or in a wicker basket with pale violas.
Origins Of garden origin.
Flowering height 25cm (10in) (dwarf).
Flowering time Early spring.
Hardiness Fully hardy.
Cultivation In autumn, plant bulbs 10cm (4in) deep in borders or containers.

Narcissus 'Tuesday's Child'

This elegant daffodil, derived from *N. triandrus*, has white, swept-back petals and primrose crowns, usually 2 to 3 flowers per stem.
Origins Of garden origin.
Flowering height 35cm (14in) (medium).
Flowering time Mid-spring.
Hardiness Fully hardy.
Cultivation In autumn, plant bulbs 15cm (6in) deep.

Narcissus 'White Lion'

This is a good Double narcissus, with white petals and pale lemon segments. It is a good midseason choice for borders or in grassland. Plant en masse in grassland to follow early daffodils and to be succeeded by 'Winston Churchill'.
Origins Of garden origin.
Flowering height 40cm (16in) (medium).
Flowering time Mid-spring.
Hardiness Fully hardy.
Cultivation In autumn, plant 15cm (6in) deep.

Narcissus 'Yellow Cheerfulness'

The 3 to 4 rounded, double, primrose-yellow flowers are sweetly scented and last for a long time. This is a sport of the popular white *N.* 'Cheerfulness' and is derived from *N. tazetta*. A strong grower, it is excellent in association with shrubs and herbaceous plants.
Origins Of garden origin.
Flowering height 40cm (16in) (medium).
Flowering time Mid-spring.
Hardiness Fully hardy.
Cultivation In autumn, plant bulbs 13cm (5in) deep.

nerine amaryllidaceae

This is a genus of about 30 species of bulbs found on well-drained sites on cliffs, rocky ledges and mountain screes in southern Africa. Although all species in the genus are often referred to as the Guernsey lily, this common name is properly applied to *N. sarniensis*. In 1659, a ship of the East India Company, bound for the Netherlands, was shipwrecked in the English Channel off the Island of Guernsey. Boxes of bulbs, among them *N. sarniensis*, were washed ashore, and the islanders noted that the bulbs had taken root in the sand and began to cultivate them. Because the ship had come from the Far East, they thought the bulbs had originated from Japan. The real origin was not established for more than a hundred years when they were recognized as those growing on Table Mountain in South Africa. Note that all parts of the plant may cause mild stomach ache if ingested.
Site Full sun, well drained.
Cultivation Plant bulbs outdoors in early spring. Plant them so that the noses are just above soil level and the shoulders well below. Indoors, bulbs should be planted in autumn or early spring in pots in soil-based compost (potting mix), again with the noses just above soil level. The flowers appear in autumn, followed by the leaves in late winter, and the plant goes dormant in summer, when it likes a dry, warm period. They flower best when congested. After flowering, apply a low-nitrogen liquid fertilizer.
Propagation Sow seed at 10–13°C (50–55°F) as soon as ripe. Divide clumps after flowering.
Pests and diseases Slugs.

Nerine bowdenii

Umbels of up to 7 or more funnel-shaped, slightly scented, pink flowers, each to 7.5cm (3in) across, with wavy edged, recurved petals, are borne on stout stems. The flowers appear in autumn, followed by the leaves in late winter. The plant goes dormant in summer, when it likes a dry, warm period. It soon forms large clumps. It must have a well-drained site and is a good choice for the foot of a sunny, south-facing wall where the pink flowers look striking. In cold areas, provide a dry mulch in winter.
Origins South Africa in eastern Cape Province, Orange Free State and northern Natal.
Flowering height 45cm (18in).
Flowering time Autumn outdoors.
Hardiness Fully hardy.

Nerine undulata

Formerly known as *N. crispa*, this nerine produces umbels of 8 to 12 funnel-shaped, mid-pink flowers, up to 5cm (2in) across, with the characteristic narrow, crinkled petals.
Origins South Africa in eastern Cape Province and the Orange Free State at low altitudes.
Flowering height 45cm (18in).
Flowering time Autumn indoors.
Hardiness Frost hardy (down to -5°C/23°F).

ornithogalum thyrsoides

oxalis adenophylla 'Silver Shamrock'

ornithogalum hyacinthaceae

This genus contains 80 species of bulbs from a wide variety of locations, ranging from dry and rocky areas to meadows and woodlands in central and southern Europe, the Mediterranean, the former USSR, western and south-western Asia, tropical Africa and South Africa. Note that all parts may cause severe stomach ache if ingested and the sap may irritate the skin.

Site Full sun and well-drained soil.

Cultivation In spring, plant the bulbs of *O. arabicum* and *O. thyrsoides* 15cm (6in) and 10cm (4in) deep respectively in borders outdoors and lift after flowering. Keep dry and frost free in winter, or plant in pots in autumn in soil-based compost (potting mix). Keep in a cool, frost-free place and move outside during the summer months. In autumn, plant the bulbs of *O. umbellatum* and *O. nutans* 7.5cm (3in) and 5cm (2in) deep respectively in borders outdoors or in grassland where they should naturalize.

Propagation Sow seed in a cold frame in autumn or spring. When dormant, remove offsets.

Pests and diseases None.

Ornithogalum arabicum

Corymb-like racemes, usually of 6 to 12, scented, cup-shaped, cream or white flowers are produced, each with a black ovary.

Origins Mediterranean.
Flowering height 30–75cm (12–30in).
Flowering time Summer outdoors.
Hardiness Half hardy.

Ornithogalum nutans

Racemes of up to 20 semi-pendent, funnel-shaped, white flowers are produced, with recurved tips to the petals. Each flower has a green stripe on the outside so that the whole effect is of a pretty grey-green rather than pure white. They like a sunny spot but will tolerate partial shade.

Origins Europe and south-western Asia.
Flowering height 20cm (8in).
Flowering time Spring outdoors.
Hardiness Fully hardy.

Ornithogalum thyrsoides

The chincherinchee produces dense racemes packed with cup-shaped, white flowers, cream or green at the base, which open in long succession.

Origins Western Cape in South Africa.
Flowering height 30–40cm (12–16in).
Flowering time Summer outdoors.
Hardiness Half hardy.

Ornithogalum umbellatum

The star of Bethlehem produces corymb-like racemes of 6 to 20 star-shaped, white flowers on long stalks. Each flower has a green stripe down the outside. The long leaves wither as the flowers open. Although they like a sunny spot, they will tolerate partial shade, but the flowers need sunshine to open out.

Origins Europe, Turkey, Syria, Lebanon, Israel and northern Africa.
Flowering height 15cm (6in).
Flowering time Late spring to early summer outdoors.
Hardiness Fully hardy.

oxalis oxalidaceae

This genus contains about 500 species of bulbs, tubers, rhizomes or fibrous-rooted annuals or perennials, widely distributed in woodlands or open areas from South America to southern Africa. The name *Oxalis* is derived from the Greek *oxys*, "sharp", and *als*, "salt". This is a direct reference to the plant sap, which is acidic. The plants have clover-shaped leaves, often twisting and closing at night or on hot days.

Site Mainly sunny, but some species will tolerate shade.

Cultivation See individual entries.

Propagation Sow seed at 13–18°C (55–64°F) in late winter or early spring. Divide in spring.

Pests and diseases Prone to rust, slugs and snails.

Oxalis adenophylla

The solitary purplish-pink flowers with darker veining, 2.5cm (1in) across, look attractive against the deeply lobed, grey-green foliage. With *O. adenophylla* 'Silver Shamrock', the colouring is particularly pleasing.

Origins Andes, Chile and Argentina.
Flowering height 15cm (6in).
Flowering time Spring.
Hardiness Fully hardy.
Cultivation In autumn, plant the fibrous coated bulbs 5cm (2in) deep in sunny borders outdoors where they will soon form large compact clumps.

Oxalis tetraphylla

Formerly known as *O. deppei* and commonly known as the good luck plant or lucky clover, this produces loose, umbel-like cymes of reddish-purple flowers, 2.5cm (1in) across, which appear above the 4 deeply lobed, clover-like leaflets. These have purple bands at the bases.

Origins Mexico.
Flowering height 15cm (6in).
Flowering time Early summer.
Hardiness Frost hardy.
Cultivation In autumn or spring, plant the bulbs 5cm (2in) deep in well-drained soil.

Oxalis triangularis

Commonly known as the love clover, this produces loose sprays of light pink flowers, 2.5cm (1in) across, above strongly contrasting triangular, reddish-brown leaves.

Origins Brazil.
Flowering height 15cm (6in).
Flowering time Summer.
Hardiness Frost hardy.
Cultivation In spring, plant the bulbs 5cm (2in) deep in pots indoors. Keep in a relatively dry, cool state until leaves appear. Then increase moisture and light. Alternatively, plant outside in well-drained soil and use as ground cover, for edging rock gardens or at the base of steps. It will naturalize quickly in a sunny spot if left undisturbed.

pleione formosana 'Alba'

puschkinia scilloides

ranunculus asiaticus

pleione orchidaceae

This is a genus of about 20 species of small, terrestrial, deciduous orchids from high wet forest or woodlands from northern India to southern China and Taiwan. Each pseudobulb will produce a solitary flower and one folded leaf.

Site Grow indoors as a houseplant in a semi-shaded position or outdoors on a patio or balcony in containers in a very sheltered, partially shaded site, only after all risk of frost has passed.

Cultivation In late winter or early spring, plant the pseudobulbs 5cm (2in) deep and 5cm (2in) apart in small containers or window boxes, using a peat-based compost (soil-less mix). When in full growth, feed with a weak fertilizer. Deadhead after flowering and eventually bring outdoor pots inside to store in frost-free conditions until spring.

Propagation Divide annually when re-potting, discarding old pseudobulbs.

Pests and diseases Aphids, red spider mites, slugs and mealybugs.

Pleione formosana
The elegant rose-lilac flowers have a central white lip, which has red or brown markings and a fringed edge. It is commonly known as the windowsill orchid.
Origins Eastern China and Taiwan.
Flowering height 12cm (5in).
Flowering time Spring indoors.
Hardiness Borderline between half hardy and frost hardy.

Pleione formosana 'Alba'
The glorious white flowers have a central white lip, which has striking red or brown markings and a fringed edge.
Origins Eastern China and Taiwan.
Flowering height 12cm (5in).
Flowering time Spring indoors.
Hardiness Borderline between half hardy and frost hardy.

puschkinia hyacinthaceae

This little bulb was named after a Russian botanist, Count Apollos Mussin-Puschkin, who died in 1805. He collected plants in the Caucasus region, where this bulb originates. It is a genus of only one species and originates in mountainous areas of the Middle East, including Turkey, Syria, Lebanon, Iraq and Iran, as well as the Caucasus. It flowers in damp meadows and scrub where the snows have just melted.

Site Full sun or light shade.

Cultivation In autumn, plant the bulbs 5cm (2in) deep at the front of a border or in a stone trough. It is dainty in growth and is good among other small spring bulbs and plants. They form large groups in nature.

Propagation Sow seed in containers in a cold frame in summer or autumn. Remove offsets in summer as leaves die down.

Pests and diseases Viruses can cause damage.

Puschkinia scilloides
Compact racemes bear 4 to 10 pale blue flowers, 1cm (½in) across. Each petal has a darker blue stripe down the centre and a central white cup.
Origins Mountainous areas of the Middle East.
Flowering height 20cm (8in).
Flowering time Spring.
Hardiness Fully hardy.

ranunculus ranunculaceae

This is a widely distributed genus of about 400 species of mainly deciduous, sometimes evergreen, tuberous, fibrous-rooted or rhizomatous perennials, annuals and biennials. The name is derived from the Latin word *rana*, "frog", due to the many species that grow in damp places.

Site Full sun or light shade.

Cultivation In late winter indoors or spring outdoors, plant the rhizomes 5cm (2in) deep and 7.5cm (3in) apart (claws facing downwards) in borders or pots. They like plenty of moisture while in growth, although too much will cause the leaves to yellow. Make sure the compost (soil mix) or soil is fast draining.

Propagation Divide tuberous species in spring or autumn. Sow seed of *R. asiaticus* in autumn for flowering in late spring.

Pests and diseases Slugs, snails, aphids and mildew.

Ranunculus asiaticus
The Persian buttercup produces brilliantly coloured, double, peony-type flowers, 5cm (2in) across, in a variety of colours, including white, red, pink, orange and yellow.
Origins Eastern Mediterranean, north-eastern Africa and south-western Asia.
Flowering height 25cm (10in).
Flowering time Late spring indoors or summer outdoors.
Hardiness Half hardy.

schizostylis coccinea 'Sunrise'   *scilla siberica*   *sinningia 'Etoile de Feu'*   *sinningia 'Hollywood'*

schizostylis iridaceae

The genus, commonly known as Kaffir lily, takes its name from the Greek *schizo*, "to cut", "to divide", and *stilis*, "style", because the style is divided into 3 distinct branches. It is a genus of only one species of virtually evergreen rhizomes, which lives in damp places in southern Africa. The flowers are like small gladioli, with 6 to 10 flowers on each stem, and 2 flowers open at a time. They make excellent cut flowers.

Site Full sun.

Cultivation In spring, plant the rhizomes, at least 3 to a group, 7.5cm (3in) deep and 15–20cm (6–8in) apart, in a sunny, sheltered border where the soil will remain moist throughout the growing period. Apply a mulch in winter. Leave undisturbed. It makes a lovely association with small coloured grasses such as *Festuca glauca* (blue fescue) or *Uncinia rubra*. It can also be grown in containers.

Propagation Divide rhizomes in spring.

Pests and diseases None.

Schizostylis coccinea 'Sunrise'
Spikes of beautiful, cup-shaped, salmon-pink flowers are borne on slender stems. These are a truly welcome sight in the autumn.

Origins Of garden origin.
Flowering height 60cm (24in).
Flowering time Autumn.
Hardiness Borderline between frost hardy and fully hardy.

scilla hyacinthaceae

This is a genus of about 90 species of bulbs found in a variety of locations in Europe, Asia and southern Africa. The common name is squill, and the genus is closely related to the genera *Chionodoxa* and *Puschkinia*.

Site Full sun or partial shade.

Cultivation In early autumn, plant the bulbs 5cm (2in) deep in borders, grass or containers.

Propagation Divide clumps of established bulbs when dormant in summer.

Pests and diseases Viruses.

Scilla bithynica
Spikes of 6 to 12 star-shaped, powdery blue flowers, 2cm (¾in) across, are borne above strap-like leaves. Plant among shrubs in borders or in partially shaded grassy areas among small trees and shrubs. They will self-seed and naturalize quickly.

Origins North-western Turkey and Bulgaria in damp meadows, woods and scrub.
Flowering height 10–15cm (4–6in).
Flowering time Mid-spring.
Hardiness Fully hardy.

Scilla siberica
The Siberian squill, as this is commonly known, produces spikes of 4 to 5 bell-shaped, nodding, bright blue flowers, about 1cm (¼in) across. They should be planted at the front of a sunny border or with other bulbs in containers. They also look lovely grown informally in grass, establishing quickly to form large clumps.

Origins Russia and Turkey, among rocks, scrub and woods.
Flowering time Early to mid-spring.
Flowering height 15cm (6in).
Hardiness Fully hardy.

sinningia gesneriaceae

The genus was named in honour of Wilhelm Sinning (1794–1874), who was head gardener at the University of Bonn. It embraces about 40 species of tuberous perennials and low-growing shrubs from Central and South America. The best known plant in the genus is the florist gloxinia. It is thought that the name gloxinia was given by a Belgian nurseryman, Louis Van Houtte, who named a special new cultivar with bright carmine, white-edged, drooping petals after his wife, Gloxinia Mina. Another theory is that it was named after Benjamin Peter Gloxin. Modern cultivars are mainly from *S. speciosa* and *S. guttata*.

Site Light or partial shade indoors.

Cultivation In spring, plant the tubers on the surface of the compost (soil mix) and keep barely moist until growth is noticed. Plant one tuber in a 13cm (5in) diameter pot. Never expose the plants to direct sunlight. Apply a dilute liquid feed during the growing and flowering season. As the foliage dies down, reduce watering and keep tubers dry throughout winter.

Propagation Sow seed in fine compost in late winter. Take cuttings from young shoots.

Pests and diseases Leafhoppers and western flower thrips.

Sinningia 'Etoile de Feu'
Often referred to as *Gloxinia* 'Etoile de Feu', this sinningia produces wide, trumpet-shaped, carmine-pink flowers with wavy paler margins all summer long.

Origins Of garden origin.
Flowering height 25cm (10in).
Flowering time Summer indoors.
Hardiness Frost tender.

Sinningia 'Hollywood'
Often referred to as *Gloxinia* 'Hollywood', this sinningia produces sumptuous, violet, trumpet-shaped flowers, which are sometimes edged with silver. It makes a wonderful houseplant.

Origins Of garden origin.
Flowering height 25cm (10in).
Flowering time Summer indoors.
Hardiness Frost tender.

Sinningia 'Mont Blanc'
The pure white, trumpet-shaped flowers appear above velvety leaves.

Origins Of garden origin.
Flowering height 25cm (10in).
Flowering time Summer indoors.
Hardiness Frost tender.

sternbergia lutea

tigridia pavonia

trillium grandiflorum 'Roseum'

sternbergia amaryllidaceae

This genus of 8 species of dwarf bulb was named after the Austrian botanist Count Kaspar von Sternberg (1761–1838). Found on stony hillsides, scrub and pine forests in southern Europe, Turkey and central Asia, they are similar to crocuses but have 6, not 3, stamens and grow from bulbs rather than from corms. Like the crocus, some species are autumn flowering, and some flower in spring. All parts are poisonous.

Site Full sun.

Cultivation As soon as they are available in late summer (so that they do not dry out too much), plant the bulbs 15cm (6in) deep near the front of a sunny border beneath a wall. They establish best in alkaline soils. They will increase by bulb division, but do not disturb until the clump fails to flower.

Propagation Separate offsets when dormant in late summer.

Pests and diseases Prone to narcissus viruses, narcissus bulb flies and eelworms.

Sternbergia lutea
Yellow, goblet-shaped flowers, 4cm (1½in) across, appear at the same time as the dark green, strap-like leaves.

Origins Russia and Turkey, among rocks, scrub and woods.
Flowering height 15cm (6in).
Flowering time Autumn.
Hardiness Frost hardy.

tigridia iridaceae

Often known as the tiger flower, this genus includes 23 species of bulbs from seasonally dry lands in Mexico and Guatemala. The genus is named after the Latin word *tigris*, "tiger", a reference to the local jaguars with their spotted coats, like the central marking on the flowers. Its brilliant colouring and distinctive markings have made it a favourite plant for hybridizing.

Site Full sun.

Cultivation In spring, plant the bulbs 10cm (4in) deep in a sunny sheltered border. They need lifting before winter frosts. Overwinter in dry sand, at a temperature of 10°C (50°F), and replant in spring. They make good outdoor container plants, when planted in a soil-based compost (potting mix). They associate well with bronze foliage plants.

Propagation By offsets when dormant. Sow seed at 13–16°C (55–61°F) in spring.

Pests and diseases Prone to viruses.

Tigridia pavonia
The peacock flower, as it is known, produces a succession of orange, yellow, white, pink or red flowers, each 10–15cm (4–6in) across, with contrasting central markings.

Origins Mexico.
Flowering height 1.5m (5ft), although more often 50cm (20in) in cultivation in Europe.
Flowering time Summer.
Hardiness Frost tender.

trillium trilliaceae

This genus, which is known as trinity flower or wood lily, includes about 30 rhizomes, mainly from woodland in North America. They have a distinctive whorl of 3 broad leaves, out of which grows a flower consisting of 3 green sepals and 3 beautiful petals, hence the genus name based on the Latin *tri*-, "three".

Site Deep or partial shade and moist, deep soil, preferably neutral to acid.

Cultivation In autumn or early spring, plant the rhizomes 10cm (4in) deep in cool, dappled shade. They spoil if allowed to dry out before planting, so obtain stock transported in moist peat. They are a clump-forming perennial which should be left undisturbed to create a bold group.

Propagation Can be grown from seed but plants take 7 years to reach flowering size. Divide rhizomes in autumn or early spring, making sure that each new section has at least one growing point.

Pests and diseases Slugs and snails may damage the leaves.

Trillium grandiflorum 'Roseum'
This trillium bears pale pink, cup-shaped flowers on top of the dark green leaves. The flowers open wide and have large, slightly wavy petals, 7.5cm (3in) wide, which grow darker as they age. This trillium looks lovely beside the unfurling fronds of young ferns.
Origins Eastern North America.
Flowering height 40cm (16in).
Flowering time Late spring.
Hardiness Fully hardy.

Trillium luteum
Sweetly fragrant, golden or bronze-green flowers are borne erect on top of mid-green leaves, heavily marked with paler green. The narrow flower petals are about 9cm (3½in) long. Bluebells and lily-of-the-valley make perfect planting partners.
Origins South-eastern North America.
Flowering height 40cm (16in).
Flowering time Spring.
Hardiness Fully hardy.

Trillium undulatum
Commonly known as the painted trillium or painted wood lily, this rhizomatous perennial has funnel-shaped flowers composed of three, wavy, white or pink petals surrounded by a frill of red-edged, green sepals. The petals have a bright red stripe at the base. The single flowers are carried above oval, blue-green leaves.
Origins Eastern North America.
Flowering height 10–20cm (4–8in).
Flowering time Spring.
Hardiness Fully hardy.

triteleia laxa 'Koningin Fabiola' *tritonia crocata* *tulipa* 'Apeldoorn' *tulipa* 'Attila'

triteleia alliaceae

This genus, often known as Californian hyacinth, is composed of about 15 species of corms. Closely related to *Brodiaea*, it is mainly found in grass and woodland of western USA. It makes a good cut flower and can be dried.
Site Light sandy fertile soil in full sun.
Cultivation In autumn, plant the corms 7.5cm (3in) deep in a sunny herbaceous border, where they would enjoy the same conditions as autumn-flowering nerines. Alternatively, plant them in containers in a soil-based compost (potting mix) and stand them on a sunny sheltered patio, mixing them with white, pink or yellow lilies in a large container. Keep dry and sheltered in winter.
Propagation Sow seed at 13–16°C (55–61°F) as soon as ripe or in early spring. Separate corms when dormant.
Pests and diseases None.

Triteleia laxa 'Koningin Fabiola'
Strong stems bear loose umbels, 13cm (5in) across, of up to 25 purple-blue flowers, each 5cm (2in) long.

Origins Western North America.
Flowering height 25cm (10in).
Flowering time Midsummer.
Hardiness Frost hardy.

tritonia iridaceae

The name derives from the Greek word *triton*, "weathercock", a clue to the strange habit of the stamens in some of the species, which change directions. It is a genus of 28 species of corms, closely related to *Crocosmia*, and mainly located on grassy or stony hillsides of South Africa and Swaziland.
Site Light sandy soil, sheltered and in full sun.
Cultivation In autumn plant the corms 7.5cm (3in) deep in a sunny, well-drained border. Provide a winter mulch. Alternatively, plant them in pots in a soil-based compost (potting mix) and stand on a sunny sheltered patio. Keep dry and frost free in winter.
Propagation Sow seed at 13–16°C (55–61°F) as soon as ripe. Separate corms when dormant.
Pests and diseases None.

Tritonia crocata
Up to 10 cup-shaped, orange or pink flowers with transparent margins are borne on spikes.
Origins South Africa.
Flowering height 15–35cm (6–14in).
Flowering time Summer.
Hardiness Half hardy.

Tritonia laxifolia
This smaller tritonia has up to 10 to 12 cup-shaped, orange flowers borne on spikes.
Origins Cape Province, South Africa.
Flowering height 20cm (8in).
Flowering time Summer.
Hardiness Frost hardy.

tulipa lilaceae

One of the best known of all bulb groups, the tulip, with all its range of flamboyant colours, comes from a genus of about 100 species of bulbs found on hot, dry hillsides of temperate Europe, the Middle East and, particularly, central Asia, often growing on alkaline soils. Over the last 400 years, thousands of cultivars have been raised. The name comes from the Turkish word *tulbend*, meaning "turban", perhaps reflecting the shape and colour range of the flowers. In 1554, Ghislain de Busbecq (1522–91), then ambassador of the Holy Roman Empire to Süleyman the Magnificent, confused the name with the word *tulipam*, hence the name of the *Tulipa* genus today. Note that all parts may cause mild stomach ache if ingested, and contact with any part may aggravate skin allergies.
Site Full sun.
Cultivation Can be lifted for the summer dormancy period or left in the ground where the Darwin, Kaufmanniana, Greigii and Triumph hybrids in particular will form good clumps if left alone. Deadhead after flowering. Pull off the old stems and leaves once they have withered. Lift if required and ripen in a greenhouse. Store in a dry shed out of direct sunlight for planting again in autumn. Choose only the biggest bulbs to replant in the borders. The smaller ones can be grown on in a nursery bed. An annual potash-rich fertilizer or sulphate of potash is beneficial and should be applied in late winter before the first shoots appear. Container-grown tulips are not as successful in a second year. See individual entries for specific planting advice.
Propagation Separate offsets of species and cultivars after lifting in summer and grow on. Seed sown from the species takes 4 to 7 years for flowers to be produced. Sow seed in autumn in containers in a cold frame or cold greenhouse.
Pests and diseases Slugs, stem and bulb eelworms, tulip fire, bulb rots and viruses.

Tulipa 'Angelique'
This Double Late tulip bears large, rose-pink flowers. It looks striking planted in borders with forget-me-nots, arabis or aubrieta, while in containers, it might be under-planted with lavender-blue pansies.
Origins Of garden origin.
Flowering height 45cm (18in).
Flowering time Mid- to late spring.
Hardiness Fully hardy.
Cultivation In autumn, plant the bulbs 10–15cm (4–6in) deep in borders, or in large containers in soil-based compost (potting mix).

Tulipa 'Apeldoorn'
A Darwin hybrid, the large scarlet flowers retain their petals for a long period of time. This tulip looks beautiful with lime-green foliage.
Origins Of garden origin.
Flowering height 55cm (22in).
Flowering time Mid- to late spring.
Hardiness Fully hardy.
Cultivation In autumn, plant the bulbs 10–15cm (4–6in) deep in borders. They will survive well left in border soil and multiply to form good clumps. Alternatively, plant in large containers in soil-based compost (potting mix).

tulipa 'Chopin'

tulipa 'Ballerina'

Tulipa 'Apricot Beauty'

A Single Early, this is one of the best of all tulips for its soft apricot, tangerine-flushed colouring. It looks excellent planted with pink-cupped daffodils, such as *N.* 'Rainbow' or 'Salome', carpeted with *Tanacetum parthenium* 'Aureum' (golden feverfew) and backed by the vivid light green colouring of *Philadelphus coronarius* 'Aureus'. It is stunning planted in a container with an underplanting of white pansies.
Origins Of garden origin.
Flowering height 45cm (18in).
Flowering time Mid-spring.
Hardiness Fully hardy.
Cultivation In autumn, plant the bulbs 10–15cm (4–6in) deep in borders, or in a large container using soil-based compost (potting mix).

Tulipa 'Attila'

This Triumph tulip bears light purple flowers. It looks good among pale dwarf wallflowers, either in the ground or in large pots.
Origins Of garden origin.
Flowering height 50cm (20in).
Flowering time Mid-spring.
Hardiness Fully hardy.
Cultivation In autumn, plant the bulbs 10–15cm (4–6in) deep in borders, or in a large container in soil-based compost (potting mix). The bulbs can be left in the ground all year, and will continue to flower well in future seasons.

Tulipa 'Ballerina'

A Lily-flowered hybrid, this is one of the most striking of all tulips, with its scented, vibrant orange flowers. It is excellent planted with other orange flowers or plants with bronze foliage, or in containers underplanted with deep blue pansies.
Origins Of garden origin.
Flowering height 55cm (22in).
Flowering time Mid-spring.
Hardiness Fully hardy.
Cultivation In autumn, plant the bulbs 10–15cm (4–6in) deep in borders, or in large containers, using soil-based compost (potting mix).

Tulipa 'Blue Heron'

This Fringed tulip bears large, violet-purple flowers with lilac-fringed petals. It is a strong-growing tulip which lasts a long time in flower. In borders, it can be underplanted with grey-leaved plants or, for a more exciting combination, place them close to *Tanacetum parthenium* 'Aureum' (golden feverfew), which will really make it come alive. Its perfect partners in a container are white and mauve pansies.
Origins Of garden origin.
Flowering height 60cm (24in).
Flowering time Late spring.
Hardiness Fully hardy.
Cultivation In autumn, plant the bulbs 10–15cm (4–6in) deep in borders, or in large containers in soil-based compost (potting mix). Deadhead after flowering. The bulbs can be left in the ground all year and will continue to flower well in future seasons.

Tulipa 'Blue Parrot'

A Parrot tulip, with single, large, lilac-blue flowers, and irregular crimping along the edge of the petals. It is exciting when in bud and when the flowers first begin to unfurl. In borders, it can be planted with pink or blue forget-me-nots, while in containers, pink, lavender or violet-blue pansies are perfect.
Origins Of garden origin.
Flowering height 60cm (24in).
Flowering time Late spring.
Hardiness Fully hardy.
Cultivation In autumn, plant the bulbs 10–15cm (4–6in) deep in borders, or in large containers, using soil-based compost (potting mix).

Tulipa 'Cape Cod'

A Greigii hybrid, this is a sturdy tulip with large, orange-edged, yellow flowers and interesting purple-striped foliage.
Origins Of garden origin.
Flowering height 30cm (12in).
Flowering time Spring.
Hardiness Fully hardy.
Cultivation In autumn, plant the bulbs 10–15cm (4–6in) deep in borders, where they can be planted besides primroses and dwarf daffodils. Alternatively, plant in containers in a soil-based compost (potting mix) with violas. Deadhead after flowering. The bulbs can be left in the ground all year and will continue to flower well in future seasons.

Tulipa 'Chopin'

The large, single flowers are typical of the Kaufmanniana hybrids. The yellow flowers are streaked with red, while the leaves have attractive mottled markings. This tulip looks beautiful associated with primroses and dwarf daffodils. They are also perfect for pots, underplanted with rich blue violas.
Origins Of garden origin.
Flowering height 25cm (10in).
Flowering time Early spring.
Hardiness Fully hardy.
Cultivation In autumn, plant the bulbs 10cm (4in) deep in borders, or in large containers using soil-based compost (potting mix). Deadhead after flowering. The bulbs can be left in the ground all year and will continue to flower well in future seasons.

tulipa 'Esther'

tulipa 'Fantasy'

tulipa 'Golden Melody'

tulipa 'Mona Lisa'

Tulipa clusiana

The slim, white flowers have a distinctive dark pink stripe on the outside, with purple markings inside, and purple stamens. Plant near the front of a border with aubrieta or arabis for partners.
Origins Iran to the western Himalayas.
Flowering height 30cm (12in).
Flowering time Early to mid-spring.
Hardiness Fully hardy.
Cultivation In autumn, plant the bulbs 7.5cm (3in) deep in a warm, sunny border, where the bulbs will flower happily for years if left undisturbed. Alternatively, plant in medium-sized containers using soil-based compost (potting mix).

Tulipa 'Esther'

A Single Late hybrid, this is one of the prettiest of the all-pink tulips. It is excellent planted with blue forget-me-nots, blue pansies or try it with the slightly later flowering T. 'Queen of Night'.
Origins Of garden origin.
Flowering height 50cm (20in).
Flowering time Mid- to late spring.
Hardiness Fully hardy.
Cultivation In autumn plant the bulbs 10–15cm (4–6in) deep in borders, or in containers using soil-based compost (potting mix). They will survive well if left in the soil all year round.

Tulipa 'Fantasy'

A Parrot group hybrid, this tulip has large, pink flowers, which are crested with green, and irregular crimpling along the edge of the petals. It is sensuous in bud, especially when the petals start to unfurl. This tulip looks particularly exciting planted behind dark-leaved heucheras.
Origins Of garden origin.
Flowering height 55cm (22in).
Flowering time Late spring.
Hardiness Fully hardy.
Cultivation In autumn, plant the bulbs 10–15cm (4–6in) deep in borders, or in containers using soil-based compost (potting mix).

Tulipa 'Golden Melody'

One of the Triumph hybrids, this has large golden-yellow flowers which hold their petals for a long time. In borders, they might be planted beside grey-leaved plants such as *Senecio cineraria*.
Origins Of garden origin.
Flowering height 55cm (22in).
Flowering time Mid-spring.
Hardiness Fully hardy.
Cultivation In autumn, plant the bulbs 10–15cm (4–6in) deep in borders, or in containers using soil-based compost (potting mix). They will survive well if left in the soil all year round.

Tulipa 'Gordon Cooper'

This Darwin hybrid is strong growing and bears pink flowers. It associates well with rose-coloured wallflowers or blue polyanthus.
Origins Of garden origin.
Flowering height 60cm (24in).
Flowering time Mid-spring.
Hardiness Fully hardy.
Cultivation In autumn, plant the bulbs 10–15cm (4–6in) deep in borders, or in containers using soil-based compost (potting mix). They will survive well if left in the soil all year round.

Tulipa 'Heart's Delight'

Like many of the Kaufmanniana hybrids, this has irregularly striped leaves. It is a small tulip, and the white edges to the dark pink petals create a pretty feathering effect. It is excellent planted beside blue primulas, violas or dwarf daffodils.
Origins Of garden origin.
Flowering height 25cm (10in).
Flowering time Early spring.
Hardiness Fully hardy.
Cultivation In autumn, plant the bulbs 10cm (4in) deep in borders, or in containers in soil-based compost (potting mix). Deadhead after flowering. The bulbs can be left in the ground all year and will continue to flower well in future seasons.

Tulipa humilis Violacea Group

Although it is one of the shortest tulips, the violet-pink flowers, with the blue-black basal markings, certainly make a strong statement, particularly near the front of the border with aubrieta or violas.
Origins Turkey and Iran.
Flowering height 7.5cm (3in).
Flowering time Early spring.
Hardiness Fully hardy.
Cultivation In autumn plant the bulbs 7.5cm (3in) deep in borders, or in small pots using soil-based compost (potting mix). They will survive well if left in the soil all year round.

Tulipa 'Little Princess'

The orange-red flowers open wide to reveal black centres. It looks striking in a painted wire basket or other small container, under-planted with black violas.

Origins Of garden origin.
Flowering height 10cm (4in).
Flowering time Mid- to late spring.
Hardiness Fully hardy.
Cultivation In autumn, plant the bulbs 7.5cm (3in) deep near the front of the border, or in containers in soil-based compost (potting mix).

Tulipa 'Lustige Witwe'

Also known as T. 'Merry Widow', this Triumph hybrid bears large, single, cherry-pink flowers, edged in white. It is a strong-growing tulip, which lasts a long time in flower. It can be planted to good effect with *Lunaria annua* (honesty), a flowering rosemary bush or other grey-leaved plants.
Origins Of garden origin.
Flowering height 35cm (14in).
Flowering time Late spring.
Hardiness Fully hardy.
Cultivation In autumn, plant the bulbs 10–15cm (4–6in) deep in borders, or in large containers in soil-based compost (potting mix).

Tulipa 'Mona Lisa'

The yellow flowers of this large, Lily-flowered hybrid are streaked with a reddish raspberry-pink. This is a dramatic tulip for a sheltered spot. It is perfect beside bronze-coloured foliage or underplanted with yellow wallflowers or pansies.
Origins Of garden origin.
Flowering height 55cm (22in).
Flowering time Mid- to late spring.
Hardiness Fully hardy.
Cultivation In autumn plant the bulbs 10–15cm (4–6in) deep in borders, or in large containers in soil-based compost (potting mix).

tulipa 'Prinses Irene'

tulipa 'Queen of Night'

tulipa 'Shakespeare'

tulipa 'Spring Green'

Tulipa 'Peach Blossom'

A Double Early hybrid, this short, sturdy tulip bears large rose-pink flowers. Plant in a border with violas and bellis daisies. It is sensational underplanted with *Muscari* (grape hyacinth).
Origins Of garden origin.
Flowering height 25cm (10in).
Flowering time Early to mid-spring.
Hardiness Fully hardy.
Cultivation In autumn, plant the bulbs 10–15cm (4–6in) deep in borders, or in containers in soil-based compost (potting mix).

Tulipa 'Prinses Irene'

This Triumph hybrid has unusual orange flowers which are streaked with purple. It looks especially effective planted among dwarf, orange wallflowers in beds and borders. It also associates well with black violas or pansies.
Origins Of garden origin.
Flowering height 35cm (14in).
Flowering time Mid-spring.
Hardiness Fully hardy.
Cultivation In autumn, plant the bulbs 10–15cm (4–6in) deep in borders, or in large containers in soil-based compost (potting mix).

Tulipa 'Queen of Night'

A Single Early hybrid, this is a stunning dark purple tulip, which lasts for many weeks. It looks beautiful beneath an arch of yellow laburnum flowers or against a wall of pale blue wisteria. An underplanting of forget-me-nots is ideal either for a border display or in a container.
Origins Of garden origin.
Flowering height 60cm (24in).

Flowering time Late spring.
Hardiness Fully hardy.
Cultivation In autumn, plant the bulbs 10–15cm (4–6in) deep in borders, or in a large wooden half-barrel in soil-based compost (potting mix).

Tulipa 'Red Riding Hood'

This Greigii hybrid is one of the best-known tulips, with its large scarlet flowers and outstanding purple-striped foliage. Suitable planting partners include primroses and dwarf daffodils, while a carpet of snow-white *Anemone blanda* would provide the perfect contrast in a container.
Origins Of garden origin.
Flowering height 30cm (12in).
Flowering time Spring.
Hardiness Fully hardy.
Cultivation In autumn, plant the bulbs 10cm (4in) deep in borders, or in containers in soil-based compost (potting mix). Deadhead after flowering. The bulbs can be left in the ground all year and will continue to flower well in future seasons.

Tulipa saxatilis Bakeri Group 'Lilac Wonder'

For a late-flowering tulip, this is unusually short. The delicate lilac-pink petals have a strongly contrasting yellow centre. It is excellent planted with *Tanacetum parthenium* 'Aureum' (golden feverfew) and dark purple or black violas.
Origins Of garden origin.
Flowering height 15cm (6in).
Flowering time Late spring.
Hardiness Fully hardy.
Cultivation In autumn, plant the

bulbs 7.5cm (3in) deep in borders, or in a small container using soil-based compost (potting mix).

Tulipa 'Shakespeare'

A Kaufmanniana hybrid, this small but elegant tulip has comparatively long flowers, which are salmon-pink, flushed with orange and yellow. In a border, they can be planted beside primroses and dwarf daffodils, while *Muscari* (grape hyacinths) or *Anemone blanda* are perfect partners in a container.
Origins Of garden origin.
Flowering height 25cm (10in).
Flowering time Early spring.
Hardiness Fully hardy.
Cultivation In autumn, plant the bulbs 10cm (4in) deep in borders, or in containers in soil-based compost (potting mix). Deadhead after flowering. The bulbs can be left in the ground all year and will continue to flower well in future seasons.

Tulipa 'Shirley'

The flowers of this Triumph hybrid are an unusual combination of white with a mauve-purple edge, which becomes more defined with age. It is excellent planted with tall *Fritillaria persica* or *T.* 'Queen of Night', with which it shares a similar colouring on the edges of the petals.
Origins Of garden origin.
Flowering height 50cm (20in).
Flowering time Mid- to late spring.
Hardiness Fully hardy.
Cultivation In autumn, plant the bulbs 10–15cm (4–6in) deep in borders, or in a large container in soil-based compost (potting mix). Deadhead after flowering. The

bulbs can be left in the ground all year and will continue to flower well in future seasons.

Tulipa 'Spring Green'

The flowers of this Viridiflora hybrid are an unusual creamy white with broad green stripes on the petals. It looks delightful against bright green foliage in the border, or in a pot with pansies.
Origins Of garden origin.
Flowering height 50cm (20in).
Flowering time Late spring.
Hardiness Fully hardy.
Cultivation In autumn, plant the bulbs 10–15cm (4–6in) deep, or in large containers, using soil-based compost (potting mix).

Tulipa 'Stresa'

This small but showy Kaufmanniana hybrid has red flowers with broad yellow edges to the petals. Like many tulips, it creates a stunning display in borders, planted with primroses and dwarf daffodils, for example.
Origins Of garden origin.
Flowering height 25cm (10in).
Flowering time Early spring.
Hardiness Fully hardy.
Cultivation In autumn, plant the bulbs 10cm (4in) deep, or in containers in soil-based compost (potting mix). Deadhead after flowering. The bulbs can be left in the ground all year and will continue to flower well in future seasons.

tulipa 'Striped Bellona'

tulipa 'West Point'

watsonia angusta

zantedeschia aethiopica 'Crowborough'

Tulipa 'Striped Bellona'

This is a Triumph hybrid with utterly stunning striped red and yellow flowers.

Origins Of garden origin.
Flowering height 50cm (20in).
Flowering time Mid-spring.
Hardiness Fully hardy.
Cultivation In autumn, plant the bulbs 10–15cm (4–6in) deep in borders, or in containers using soil-based compost (potting mix).

Tulipa tarda

A short, late-flowering tulip with floppy white and yellow flowers. Each bulb might produce more than one flowering stem.

Origins Central Asia.
Flowering height 10cm (4in).
Flowering time Mid- to late spring.

Hardiness Fully hardy.
Cultivation In autumn, plant the bulbs 7.5cm (3in) deep in the border, or in a hanging basket in soil-based compost (potting mix).

Tulipa 'West Point'

This striking Lily-flowered hybrid has distinctive primrose-yellow flowers, which look especially charming underplanted with blue forget-me-nots. The contrast of colours is breathtaking.

Origins Of garden origin.
Flowering height 50cm (20in).
Flowering time Late spring.
Hardiness Fully hardy.
Cultivation In autumn, plant the bulbs 10–15cm (4–6in) deep in the border, or in containers using soil-based compost (potting mix).

watsonia iridaceae

The genus is named in honour of Sir William Watson (1715–87), an English apothecary, physician and naturalist who is known for his research into electricity. This is a genus of about 60 species of corms, usually found on grassy slopes and plateaux of South Africa and Madagascar, and quite similar to gladioli.

Site Light sandy soil, sheltered, in full sun.
Cultivation In autumn or spring, plant the corms 15cm (6in) deep in a sheltered sunny border where the protection of a winter mulch is important. They enjoy the same conditions as autumn-flowering nerines. Alternatively, plant them in soil-based compost (potting mix) in a large, deep container on a sunny sheltered patio, or plunge the pot in the open border during the summer months. Overwinter in a frost-free environment.
Propagation Sow seed at 13–18°C (55–64°F) in autumn. Separate corms when dormant.
Pests and diseases None

Watsonia angusta

The long flower spikes bear up to 20 graceful pale orange flowers, each about 4cm (1½in) long.

Origins South Africa.
Flowering height 1–1.5m (3–5ft).
Flowering time Summer.
Hardiness Half hardy.

zantedeschia araceae

This genus, which is named in honour of Giovanni Zantedeschi (1773–1846), an Italian botanist and physician, includes about 6 species of rhizomes, usually found on moist soil around lakes or swamps in southern and eastern Africa. They are evergreen in warmer climates, but deciduous in cooler areas. All the species are commonly called arum lily or calla lily.

Site Damp soil, sheltered and in full sun.
Cultivation In spring, plant the tubers 15cm (6in) deep in soil-based compost (potting mix) in deep containers, 30–45cm (12–18in) apart, or in a sunny, sheltered border where the protection of a winter mulch is important. Alternatively, plant one tuber to a pot, and plunge in the open border or beside water for the summer months. It is vital that the tubers are kept moist during the growing period. Bring pots under shelter in winter and then re-pot in spring. *Z. aethiopica* 'Crowborough' can also be grown as an aquatic plant in a planting basket, 25–30cm (10–12in) across, in heavy loam soil and placed in water to 30cm (12in) deep. Retrieve for winter months, and keep sheltered and frost free.
Propagation Divide in spring.
Pests and diseases Fungi and aphids.

Zantedeschia aethiopica 'Crowborough'

Large, white, funnel-shaped spathes are carried above the glossy leaves.

Origins Of garden origin.
Flowering height 90cm (3ft).
Flowering time Early to midsummer.
Hardiness Fully hardy to borderline frost hardy.

Zantedeschia aethiopica 'Green Goddess'

A succession of green spathes, with a central white area splashed with green, appear in summer above deep green, arrow-shaped leaves. This is a curious flower which will appeal to anyone with a keen eye for design or floristry.

Origins Of garden origin.
Flowering height 45–100cm (18–39in).
Flowering time Summer.
Hardiness Fully hardy to borderline frost hardy.

Zantedeschia rehmannii

The flower stem of this pink arum carries a yellow spadix surrounded by a reddish pink spathe which reaches 7.5cm (3in) in length.

Origins South Africa.
Flowering height 40cm (16in).
Flowering time Summer.
Hardiness Frost tender.

Zantedeschia 'Solfatare'

The large, funnel-shaped spathes are a rich yellow, and make an impressive contribution to the early or midsummer garden.

Origins Of garden origin.
Flowering height 60cm (24in).
Flowering time Early to midsummer.
Hardiness Frost hardy.

index

allium rosenbachianum

muscari (grape hyacinth)

naturalized daffodils

tulipa 'Jewel of Spring'

white zantedeschias and blue iris

acknowledgements

author's acknowledgements

I wish to thank John D. Taylor C.B.E., John D. Taylor II and John Walker of O. A. Taylor and Sons Ltd. of Holbeach for their wonderful support and technical advice. I would also like to give special thanks to Michelle Garrett for her unfailing patience in taking so many stunning photographs in my Bedfordshire garden and to Jonathan Buckley for all the glorious scenes he captured elsewhere. I would especially like to show gratitude to my editor Caroline Davison whose enthusiasm and guidance has been so evident throughout the making of this book. As always, very many thanks to my family, including Simon, Jonathan and Suzanna who each helped in a multitude of ways.

publisher's acknowledgements

The publishers would like to thank the following for allowing their gardens to be photographed for this book:

Chenies Manor, Hertfordshire; Upper Mill Cottage, Kent; Beth Chatto Gardens, Essex; Great Dixter, East Sussex; The Coppice, Surrey; The Savill Garden, Surrey; Kew Gardens, London; and West Dean Gardens, West Sussex.

The publishers would also like to thank the following photographers and picture agencies for kindly allowing their photographs to be reproduced:

KEY
t = top   b = bottom   c = centre   r= right   l = left

A–Z Botanical Collection Ltd. for the pictures on pages 50tr; 127tl.
Jonathan Buckley for the pictures on pages 18tl; 47br; 47b; 92 (all); 93 (all); 94–95 (all); 96–97 (all).
The Garden Picture Library for the pictures on pages 59cr (Neil Holmes); 125tr (John Glover); 127cr (Howard Rice); 127tr (Howard Rice); 129tl (John Glover); 129tr (John Glover); 137tl (JS Sira); 146cr (Didier Willery); 146 tr (Philippe Bonduel); 147tl (Chris Burrows); 147tr (John Glover); 148tc (Marijke Heuff); 148tr (John Glover); 149tl (John Glover); 149cl (Neil Holmes); 150tl (Howard Rice); 150tc (Eric Crichton); 151tl (JS Sira); 151cl (John Glover).
Peter McHoy for the pictures on pages 38 (all); 39 tl; 39tr; 39cr; 39br.

The publishers would also like to thank the following institutions for kindly allowing their works of art to be reproduced for the purposes of this book:

The Bridgeman Art Library for the 'Portrait of William and Mary Wordsworth, 1839' on page 10.

Curtis Botanical magazine (copyright, the Board of Trustees of the Royal Botanic Gardens, Kew) for the print of *Nerine sarniensis* on page 11.

Massachusetts Horticultural Society for the picture of 'Chinese Wilson' on page 12.

University Library, Erlangen, Germany for 'Councillor Herwart's Tulip' on page 9.

a host of tulips

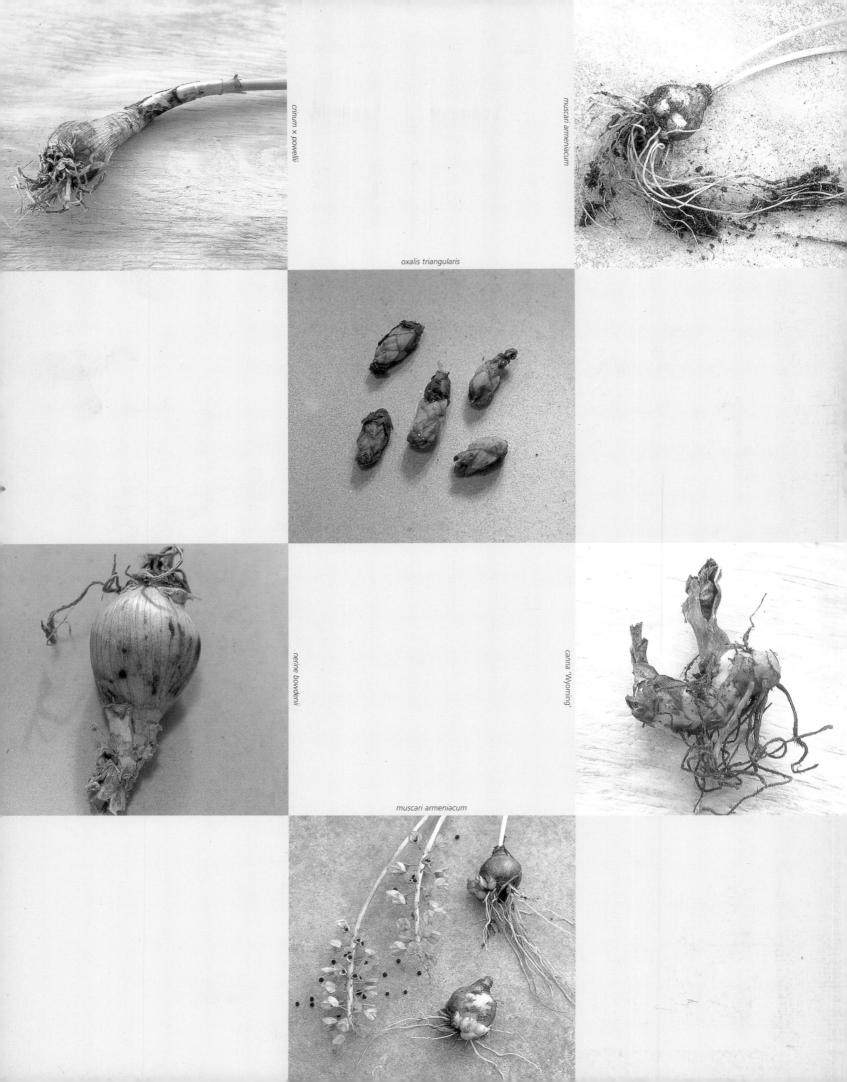

crinum x powellii

oxalis triangularis

muscari armeniacum

nerine bowdenii

canna 'Wyoming'

muscari armeniacum